D0443812

SECRETS
OF THE
INVESTMENT
ALL-STARS

SECRETS
OF THE
INVESTMENT
ALL-STARS

Kenneth A. Stern

AMACOM
American Management Association
New York • Atlanta • Boston • Chicago • Kansas City • San Francisco • Washington, D.C.
Brussels • Mexico City • Tokyo • Toronto

This publication is designed to provide accurate and authori-
tative information in regard to the subject matter covered. It is
sold with the understanding that the publisher is not engaged
in rendering legal, accounting, or other professional service. If
legal advice or other expert assistance is required, the services
of a competent professional person should be sought.

Library of Congress Cataloging-in-Publication Data

Stern, Ken
    Secrets of the investment all-stars / Kenneth A. Stern.
      p. cm.
    Includes index.
    ISBN 0-8144-0456-1
     1. Investments—United States.   2. Stocks—United States.
    3. Capitalists and financiers—United States—Interviews.
    4. Investment analysis.   5. Wall Street.   I. Title.
    HG4910.S66   1999
    332.6′0973—dc21   99–17567
                                                      CIP

Printing number

10   9   8   7   6   5   4   3   2   1

For
Susan
and
Rachael

Contents

Part Two: Presenting the All-Stars

Acknowledgments

A project of this magnitude could not be completed without the help of many wonderful and dedicated people. Many thanks to:

My agent, Jeff Herman, for believing in the project; my publisher, AMACOM, and Ray O'Connell, for all their support and encouragement.

Everyone at Asset Planning Solutions for running the business during my sabbatical. Asset Planning Solutions has helped so many people accomplish their goals that this book is simply an extension of their work.

My friend, critic, and incredibly talented editor at large, Mark Johnson. Mark, thanks for your expertise in writing and composition, research abilities, and computers. At least now I know how to use a Zip drive. You are truly a jack-of-all-trades, and an expert of all.

Without the time and help from all the all-stars, the book would not be the resource it has come to be. These all-stars generously gave of their time and expertise, and for that we are all thankful.

And, finally, my biggest thanks goes to you, the reader, for your insatiable appetite for constant improvement. Your quest for knowledge is the reason why I keep writing.

SECRETS
OF THE
INVESTMENT
ALL-STARS

Introduction

Failure cannot cope with persistence.
If you want to achieve success, follow through by
Being a good finisher of everything you begin.
Don't give up at the first sign of defeat!
—Napolean Hill,
Motivational writer
and speaker

Are you ready for some stunning news? The Standard & Poor's 500 stock index has averaged an annualized return of roughly 17% since the beginning of 1984 through the end of 1997. Sounds great, doesn't it? However, according to many sources the average equity fund investor has averaged less than 7% for the same time period! That's only a 7% return in one of the best times to invest. Imagine what happens during bad investment periods. It's no longer enough to simply invest. You have to learn the strategies and secrets to investing, to invest smart.

Everywhere you turn people are hocking investment advice. We can classify those pushing investment advice into two categories. In the first category we have those who know nothing (except perhaps marketing) but are getting rich teaching you about stocks. You must wonder why, if they are so successful as investors, do they need to sell you their system?

The second category of investment adviser have proved, beyond any doubt, that they are the real thing—teachers who back their theories with a substantial, hugely successful investment histories. These are the investment all-stars, and, quite frankly, they don't need to sell to you. They are very wealthy

1

and have created their wealth through investing. They all have a specific, definable strategy to investing.

Investing is fun, and exciting. It could also be tremendously profitable. It involves more skill than the average poker game. But it's going to take work. By reading about the investment all-stars, you can gain valuable lessons about life, success, and how to become a better investor.

What This Book Can Do for You

This book profiles people who have made millions investing—Wall Street's all-stars. These all-stars don't claim that you can be as successful as they are. They don't say you can get rich quick, and they don't argue that their investment styles are the only ways to build wealth. In fact, these individuals often ask for advice from one another. These individuals are so successful that they are beyond trying to get you to buy in to their concept. However, they welcome you to try their investment styles. The all-stars are not shy about sharing their secrets.

Why are they willing to share the information? After getting to know these investment mavens, I'm convinced that they have mastered their craft and now what is important to them is leaving a record of their tremendous presence. This book may be that mark.

By reading *Secrets of the Investment All-Stars,* you'll be able to:

* Get to know the personalities of the all-stars shaping the money world.
* Identify investment models that will guide and stabilize your approach to building wealth.
* Understand how being successful in life will help you become a successful investor.
* Develop a basic understanding of stocks, indices, and indicators.

* Find and interpret critical investment information.
* Understand Wall Street lingo.
* Become a much more confident mutual fund investor.
* Screen stocks that meet your fundamental criteria.
* Read and analyze a stock graph, monitoring trends and price movements.

Although *Secrets* began simply as an investigation of the investing strategies of the all-stars, the hours I spent with them taught me that their personalities and worldviews are essential to their own financial success. Their styles of investing are manifested by their own lives. While this observation is an abstract notion, I think that by meeting the all-stars, you will glean, and perhaps even adopt, some of the worldviews that ground their investment philosophies. Not only did I learn about investing, but I also learned about living life, running a company, dealing with setbacks. So, to a lesser extent, you will get to know the all-stars and their personalities, and how making money has as much to do with humanity as with crunching numbers and analyzing charts. What I learned, and you will too, is that to become a successful investor, you need to look beyond investing. Successful investing is about being successful in life.

Meet the All-Stars

If you had already made your millions, what would you do? Work on your tan? Hop on a cruise ship and never come back? What would inspire and motivate you?

It takes more than just money to continue motivating the world's best investors; it takes the desire to be the best. This inherent need to excel is a trait that's common to all the all-stars—it has to be, for none of them needs to go to work in order to bring home enough cash to pay the mortgage. Their wealth eclipses the mundane concerns that weigh upon the rest of us. The will to push their talents, knowledge, and investment skills that the all-stars share is infectious. I'm excited to help you to get to know these special people.

The Investment All-Stars

* **John Bogle,** Chairman and founder of Vanguard, created the first index fund. In less than 30 years the Vanguard Group has become the second-largest mutual fund institution on the planet.
* **Marty Zweig,** Chairman of the Zweig group of funds, a regular on Louis Rukeyser's PBS-TV show *Wall Street Week,* is commonly praised as one of the world's best market forecasters.
* **Don Phillips,** Chief Executive Officer of Morningstar, is credited by investors with providing investors the best and easiest way to research mutual funds.
* **Louis Navellier** is owner of Navellier and Associates and editor of the *MPT Review,* one of the longest running, best performing newsletters.
* **Harry Markowitz** won a Nobel Prize for modern portfolio theory, which is considered the standard of how to diversify a portfolio for maximizing return based on risk.
* **William J. O'Neil** is famous both for founding *Investor's Business Daily* and for his reputation as Wall Street's unparalleled resource for information and research.
* **Mario Gabelli,** Chairman of the Gabelli Asset Management Co. (GAMCO) and manager of the Gabelli funds, is often hailed as the world's best value investor. In 1997 he won Portfolio Manager of the Year for The Gabelli Value Fund.
* **Foster Friess** is one of Wall Street's best-kept secrets. Foster's Brandywine fund is consistently ranked among the best and longest-lasting no-load mutual funds.

> ★ **Ron Elijah,** Portfolio Manager and Vice President at Robertson Stephens, is responsible for devising "theme investing," a clever way to look at the market backwards.

Chapters 3 through 11 each profile a different all-star. By reading each of these chapters, you will be filled with a wide array of information. Not only will you learn investment tips and strategies that have allowed these investors to make millions of dollars, but you will learn about their thoughts on life, success, and investing in general.

You will find that each all-star has very distinct and different views from that of their peers. This is revealing in many ways. Most importantly, it confirms to an investor that there is more than one way to skin a cat, and more than one way to make money at investing. It also provides a whole array of different styles and disciplines for you to greedily absorb. By studying so many different styles, you will have a distinct advantage for investing and in life. You don't just get one all-star life and investment road map, you get nine.

Prior to the interviews, the first two chapters focus on providing you an investment understanding sufficient to fully appreciate the information provided by the all-stars. Learning about balance sheets, ratios, charts, and graphs are the answers to the investment riddles. Those that can interpret the answers have a greater chance of solving the investment riddle. Those that solve the riddle, as the all-stars have, have enjoyed many profitable years of investing.

The last two chapters put everything you have learned into practical case studies. You will use all of the tools and information provided by the all-stars to try and determine what stocks should be bought and sold. Be sure to check out the 20-point checklist for picking stocks. I think you will find it tremendously helpful as a reference tool when you begin researching stocks. Each all-star is included in this book for a different reason; each has a very unique approach, both on investing and life. They are all leaders. Many are responsible for significantly changing the investment world.

These all-stars have been in the business for years. They've ridden potent bull markets and survived crushing bears. All are self-made. They created wealth by building investment empires. Luckily for us, they all have a definable approach to investing, and all were willing to share some of the keys to their financial and personal successes.

Similarities and Differences

Prior to interviewing the all-stars, I thought they would all have similar views regarding investing. Nothing could be further from the truth. One all-star might insist on never buying a stock with a price/earnings ratio higher than 20 times earnings. Another would insist it doesn't matter. One money manager might tell you it is critical to gauge the direction of the market to be a successful investor. Another all-star might tell you if you spend 10 minutes trying to forecast the market, you'll have spent 9 minutes too long. The bottom line is that all of the all-stars are brilliant investors with sometimes startlingly different theories about the best way to earn money on Wall Street.

As I researched this book, other surprising facts surfaced. I thought all of the all-stars would live at the market's ground zero, New York. In fact, of all interviewed, Marty Zweig is the only one headquartered in Manhattan, and his offices aren't even on Wall Street. At the time of the interviews, only two actually lived in New York, Marty Zweig and Mario Gabelli. The rest were scattered from California to Nevada to Wyoming to Pennsylvania. The all-stars' diverse home states is encouraging—you can invest successfully regardless of where you live.

Although all of the all-stars here are men, this is not by

design. The three women investment all-stars I wanted to profile in this book declined to be part of the project.

Most of the all-stars interviewed have small research staffs. Many of the all-stars still attend research meetings, do their own research, and make many of their own investment decisions. All of the advisers are inveterate readers. Their thirst for knowledge is huge, and to quench it they reach to books, newspapers, magazines, and the Web. Much of the information they obtain is accessible to you. This fact reinforces my strong conviction that individuals can be successful investors even if they aren't finance majors or MBAs. Indeed, you may be surprised to discover the large number of philosophy, history, and English majors in our constellation of investment all-stars. And seeing that you're reading this book, I sense that you already share the all-stars' desire to constantly educate oneself by reading as much as possible.

Heroes, Yes . . . Regular People? That Too

The investment success stories in this book are not only about inspirational financial figures. These are also colorful strands in the fabric of America's rich cultural history. The all-stars are sources of knowledge, insight, and hope on those days when the markets just don't want to go your way. These individuals have risen to become the best of the best—the Babe Ruths, Michael Jordans, and Muhammad Alis of investing. And not only can they play the game, I think that you'll find that they can coach as well. All of the information they share will help make you a successful investor.

On meeting the all-stars, I found that they were ordinary people who made a choice to excel in a business that made them rich. Marty Zweig was suffering from knee surgery and had just spilled salad dressing on his floor. Mario Gabelli was deciding how to pick up his daughter after work. Louis Navellier had to pick his mother-in-law up from the airport after our interview. Ron Elijah's wife wanted to know what time he would be home for dinner. In many ways, these individuals are no different than you and me.

You Can Be an Investor

Why Even Deal With Investing?

Why do your stocks and mutual funds always go down? Frustrating isn't it? Especially when all your friends are telling you investing is the easiest thing in the world—yeah right!

Are you simply scared to invest? Does it make you feel small and intimidated? Good for you! Those are some of the traits a successful investor needs: humility and the sense that you can always learn more. Combine those personality traits with a framework, a model to work within to help you invest, and you find investing can be enjoyable *as well as* profitable.

As scary as investing might be, the thought of not investing is much scarier. We are living longer than ever. Pension plans have been reduced, it's questionable how long Social Security will survive, and health-care costs are increasingly the consumer's responsibility. As expenses rise and our life span increases, it's clear that to sustain our standard of living investing is essential.

What about just trusting a broker? That's not a bad idea. However, do you want to trust a single person with your entire financial future? This is your money, your hard-earned savings, and your retirement. Even if you use a broker or a money manager, a little knowledge as to the details of the broker's business can't hurt.

Let's assume you agree you need to invest. You now need to know how. Taking tips from friends or a magazine is dangerous. Recently stocks have been performing so well that everybody thinks he or she is an "all-star" investor. Many of us will be lured into thinking investing is a "sure thing." Those individuals will ultimately feel the wrath of a bear market—an extended period of time when the stock market doesn't gain value at a strong, steady clip.

This book provides a framework to make you more confident in creating your own investment style. This knowledge will help you in several ways: You will make better investments on your own regardless of whether the investments are in mutual funds or in stocks directly. You'll be able to ask your broker astute questions. And you'll be better equipped to make informed decisions. You will be a more knowledgeable investor.

Think of it like this. How long did you plan your last vacation? How hard did you work for your savings? If you put that much effort into making your money, put at least half that effort into understanding how to make your money work for you. Because ultimately the way to make big money is not by working, but by allowing your money to work for you.

Stop Gambling and Start Investing!

Very few people who actually own stocks, bonds, and mutual funds are investors. They gamble; to wit:

investor: One who uses skill, research, and discipline to reduce risk through prudent speculation to appreciate assets.

gambler: One who throws caution to the wind and hopes that gut instinct and blind luck will increase his or her holdings.

Did you ever buy a mutual fund as a result of a clever ad or because a friend recommended it? Did you ever buy a stock after reading a positive article on the company? If you don't know your goal with that investment, what the potential return is, and the risk associated with it, you are gambling. The investment all-stars have a lot to say about how to become a sophisticated investor rather than a blind gambler. Want to gamble? Go to Las Vegas. At least in Vegas you will get a free cocktail. Want to invest? Heed the voices of the investment all-stars.

Becoming an All-Star Investor

> There is nothing I do, that a
> 10 year-old child can not do,
> with 15 years of practice.
> —Harry Blackstone, Jr., magician

How bad do you want to make money at investing? The fact is, if you want it bad enough, not only is it possible to consistently make money while investing, it is rather probable. So why is it then that so many people actually lose money when investing? People lose money for three main reasons:

1. Not following the rules of investing or sticking to a chosen discipline

2. Gambling with their money instead of truly investing

3. Not practicing

I am convinced that certain investment strategies are more successful than others are. It's not an accident that certain investors are more successful than others. Ordinary people can become successful investors. I am also convinced that there is more than one road map to wealth. You will learn several disciplines from the all-stars profiled in this book—all of them proved wildly successful in their own unique way. You may choose one or more of these disciplines to follow. The key is to decide on a discipline and stick to it. Haphazardly switching from one investment strategy to the next can undermine the long-term results that are built into a given discipline. Most important, discipline and knowledge are the keys to successful investing.

Can you be an all-star? I don't see why not. Before meeting the all-stars, I envisioned people with secrets I would never know. I envisioned these all-stars as being glued all day long to a stock quote machine. I believe that only three of the all-stars even had a stock quote machine on their desk. (Ron Elijah, Marty Zweig, Mario Gabelli). As previously stated, they don't even live within spitting distance to Wall Street. What they do is stay focused, work hard, and continue to have a burning desire to be the best. Study these individuals, never quench your insatiable appetite for learning, and follow a discipline. Then you too can be an all-star.

Will it be easy to learn how to invest? It shouldn't matter. The more you work at it, the more you study, the better you will understand money.

The market must always be respected. You can learn how to become a terrific sailor and sail the seas, but you always respect the sea. The market owes you nothing. It is a vast, indifferent animal. If you want a sure thing, put your money in the bank. If you are nervous about risk, a bank account may be good for you. However, those who respect and understand market risk will be able to seek out profits that far exceed the pathetic rates paid by American bank accounts.

First, you need to learn and understand money and the markets. You need to get a feel for how money works, you need to learn basic definitions, strategies, and where to find the information. The first part of this book will help you accomplish these tasks.

After you have mastered the basics, decide what investment discipline suits you. Once you pick a discipline or disciplines, stick with it. Nothing could be worse than, for example, starting out as a value investor, find it isn't working, and then becoming a momentum investor. I'm not suggesting you should not have two disciplines, one for momentum and one for value. But if you change your stripes before giving your strategy time to mature and develop, you'll get burned.

Understand that picking a great investment isn't just crunching numbers. You can't create a van Gogh using paint by numbers. This is the beauty of investing; there is a great deal of analytical skill you can build on to make yourself a better investor. But, ultimately, the best investors combine imagination and thirst for knowledge with perseverance and patience.

Never invest until you know your objective, your time horizon, your risk tolerance, and your discipline. Follow a system and never let your emotions dictate your investments. Be honest about your risk limitations. Finally, properly diversify.

PART ONE
INTRODUCING THE BASICS

1

Becoming a Successful Investor
The Ingredients You Need

Learning the Lingo

f someone says to you, "the market went up today," what does that mean? The Dow Jones Industrial Average went up? The New York Stock Exchange went up? Or perhaps they were referring to the bond market. Or maybe the Standard & Poor's 500 stock market index.

To understand the work of the all-stars and to be able to assess the relative progress of your own investments, it's helpful to be able to distinguish between a stock market exchange, an index, and a sector. You also need to know about market capitalization, the bulls and the bears, and stock market risk and volatility.

Stock Exchanges

Where do stocks trade? If you responded, "In New York, on Wall Street," you're right, but only partially so. A **stock ex-**

change is an organized marketplace where stocks are traded. As a company you decide where you want to list your shares. You may choose the Over the Counter/National Association of Securities Dealers Automated Quotations (OTC/NASDAQ) market, you may choose the New York Stock Exchange (NYSE), or you may choose the American Stock Exchange (AMEX). Each exchange has a certain set of criteria that you will need to meet in order to list on it. Each exchange has rules.

In the past the NYSE was where the largest, most prestigious companies choose to have their shares traded. To a big extent this is still true. The NYSE is located on Wall and Broad streets in New York City.

The OTC/NASDAQ market focuses on smaller companies, new companies, and technology and biotechnology companies. Certain companies such as Microsoft and Intel have become huge, enormously prestigious companies, but they have remained on the NASDAQ market.

Though the NYSE is most well known and often perceived as the granddaddy of all stock exchanges, the NASDAQ market is much larger. It simply accounts for more stocks and more trading than the NYSE. Stocks that trade on the NASDAQ don't trade on Wall Street. In fact, NASDAQ has no physical trading location. Buy and sell trades are matched via computer. The AMEX deals generally in stocks concerning natural resources, precious metals, utilities, etc.

Indices

A stock market **index** is a statistical composite that measures changes in certain stocks. The Dow Jones Industrial Average (DJIA) is a good example of a popular index. When the Dow "is up," it doesn't mean that all the stocks that traded were up that day. Instead, the phrase means that an indicator of the general worth of a group of stocks was up. Indices were created to help an investor measure the general direction of the market or a specific part of the market without having to look at all the stocks.

Indices can be deceiving, so you need to be careful. Let's look again at the DJIA. The DJIA comprises only 30 stocks—not many stocks to be completely representative of a stock market consisting of thousands of publicly traded companies. Furthermore, the DJIA is weighted based on the size of the company: Each company is not treated as an equal 1/30 of the index. General Electric, a huge company, plays an inordinate role in the Dow index movement. If General Electric has a bad day and the stock drops considerably, there is a good chance the whole DJIA will be down, even if many of the other 30 stocks are up.

The same is true for the Standard & Poor's (S&P) Index. As I write this I am watching my stock screen. The S&P 500 index closed up on the day. However most of the stocks in the index actually were down on the day. How can this be? Also as I write, the NASDAQ Composite Index, which comprises thousands of stocks, has been up so far this year. However, most of the stocks in that index have been flat or down. Four stocks—Cisco, Dell, Microsoft, and Intel—represent roughly 25% (depending on the day) of the NASDAQ index. Four stocks account for 25%, while there are more than 5,000 stocks in the entire index. This is a gross example of how indices are often not representative of the entire market.

To illustrate my point, I went to one of the premier research firms, Ned Davis Research, and asked to see how an investor would have done if he or she had invested in the

☆ ☆

Popular Stock Indices

* Dow Jones Industrial Average
* Standard & Poor's 500
* NASDAQ Composite Index
* Russell 2000

☆ ☆

largest NASDAQ stocks, the medium-size stocks, and the smallest ones. The results shown in Figure 1-1 tell a lot about how your selection of stocks can either dramatically out- or underperform stock market indices.

For the one-year period between June 30, 1997, and June 30, 1998, if you invested in the five largest NASDAQ stocks you would have made more money than the market as a whole. The top five stocks accounted for more than 64% of the entire NASDAQ market's gains. Remember, the NASDAQ market consists of thousands of stocks. Even the top 50 stocks didn't do as well, accounting for just over 50% of the entire market's gain. Whereas the entire market (farthest bar on the right of the chart) only accounted for 31% of the gain.

Figure 1-1. NASDAQ Composite Index price changes for the period 6/30/97 through 6/30/98 showing the performance of the stocks in the NASDAQ Composite according to the companies' sizes. (It's obvious that the largest companies have enjoyed the highest run-up in stock price.)

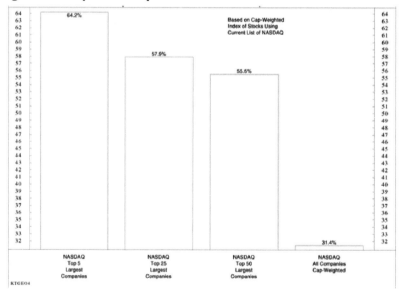

Courtesy Ned Davis Research

Sectors

A **sector** of the market is a specific grouping of stocks that are in the same, or virtually the same, business. Technology, utility, health care, and specialty retail are all examples of various sectors.

Many analysts watch the sectors first, then the individual stocks. The thought is that the best-performing sectors are where you want to invest. Once you find the best-performing sector, you then search for the best stock in that sector.

I was so intrigued by this approach that I again called upon the good folks at Ned Davis Research and asked them what would have happened if I had invested in the best sectors as compared to the worst sectors since 1980. Figure 1-2 clearly illustrates that if you invested in the top-performing sectors

Figure 1-2. The best-performing sectors compared to the worst: The best seem to keep getting better.

Courtesy Ned Davis Research

compared to the bottom, you would have been a happy investor. Let's coin a new phrase: "Buy high, sell higher."

Market Capitalization

Just like people, stocks are stereotyped, classified and put into
groupings. When investing, almost everything reverts back to
what size companies you or your mutual fund invests in. To
define company sizes on a scale from small to large, it's typical
to measure companies based on market capitalization. **Market
capitalization** is basically what the company is worth. If you
take the total number of the shares of a company and multiply
that number by the share price, that is the company's worth,
or market cap, that day.

For example, let's say you decided you wanted to one-up
Bill Gates and own *all* of Microsoft. You would have to buy all
the shares. Suppose Microsoft shares cost $100 per share on
the day you wanted to write that big check, and there were 1
million shares outstanding. The market cap—the price you
would need to pay to own the entire company—would be
1,000,000 × $100, or $100,000,000. (Can you fit that many
zeroes on your checks?)

Note the following specific terms that you'll probably encounter in connection with market capitalization:

* *Small cap* stocks are generally anything less than $1 bil-
  lion dollars.
* *Mid cap* stocks are generally $1–5 billion.
* *Large cap* stocks are generally anything over $5 billion.

About the Bulls and Bears

The terms **bull market** and **bear market** are used to describe
a type of market environment. Although there are many stories
about how the labels "bull" and "bear" became so popular,
the truth is sketchy. My gut feeling is that the use of those
terms has something to do with the fact that bulls and bears

used to wrestle one another. In addition, bears go into hibernation. So bears seem fitting for down market, bulls for up. Note the following descriptions:

* *Bull Market:* A prolonged rise in the price of stocks. The number of quarters the markets need to rise and the amount they need to go up to become a bull market is fairly nebulous. However, a bull market is usually characterized by at least four quarters of positive returns equaling roughly 10%.
* *Bear Market:* A decline of 20% or more in the price of stocks. The decline can take place in one dreadful day, or it can drag out over a long, painful series of years.

As you'll learn from the investment all-stars, bear markets and bull markets are more complex than they might first appear. Bull markets aren't always good for everyone, but a bear market is usually bad for everyone. (If you're interested in the market psychology of a down market and investment opportunities and perils of the bear market, I encourage you to read Chapter 8's profile of Marty Zweig. Zweig is the world's premier market forecaster and more scared of bear markets than anyone I know.) People often think that if the market is actually going up, everybody is making money. But look beyond the surface. The market is usually measured by various indices (the Dow, the S&P, and the NASDAQ). Sometimes one of these indices will go up possibly as a result of one or two good stocks. Since the index is up, everyone believes that all stocks are up. Reality often shows most of the stocks in the index down. This situation actually occurred during 1990 and 1994, and now in 1998. The individual stocks were down more than the overall markets.

Furthermore, advertising you read regarding mutual funds will often say that mutual funds are safer in bear markets. In actuality I believe it is very hard to diversify away from a bear market. Like a tidal wave, when it comes, nothing is spared (see Figure 1-3).

Figure 1-3. Effectiveness of diversification in a bear market.

Domestic Equity Fund Styles	8/25/87-12/4/87	7/16/90-10/11/90
Large-cap growth	-30.2%	-19.2%
Large-cap value	-25.4%	-16.0%
Mid-cap growth	-33.7%	-22.5%
Mid-cap value	-27.1%	-17.5%
Small-cap growth	-35.3%	-26.3%
Small-cap value	-32.0%	-22.0%

Zweig Mutual Funds

Source: Strategic Insight. Returns do not include sales charges. The performance data quoted represent past performance, which is no guarantee of future results.

Courtesy Zweig Mutual Funds

Stock Market Risk and Volatility

Risk is the measurable possibility of loss. When you invest money in the stock market, you encounter two basic risks: systematic and nonsystematic. **Systematic risk** is also known as diversifiable risk because if you diversify broadly, you significantly eliminate the risk of your portfolio being wiped out should one company go bankrupt. If one company did go out of business, it should have a minimal effect on a portfolio that is spread out among many companies.

It is comforting to know that the more companies you buy, the lower your systematic risk becomes. Basically, you are not putting all your eggs in one basket. However, as an investor, you are still subject to the systematic risk of the stock market. If all of your investments are in stocks, even if they are broadly diversified, it will not eliminate the risk of the stock market. If the stock market goes down, there is the chance that all of your stocks, no matter how broadly diversified you might be, will go down. In other words, there is an inherent risk in any class of investments that can't be avoided. Think of non-systematic risk as heat in the kitchen; if you want to cook (increase wealth through the stock market), you have to be able to withstand a certain amount of heat (nonsystematic risk).

As we continue, you'll learn more about risk (see the section "Modern Portfolio Theory and Risk" in Chapter 3). You'll be asked how much risk you are willing to take. However, I believe when people talk of risk, they are really talking about **volatility,** the tendency toward rapid and extreme fluctuations.

Consider Figure 1-4 that shows the performance of the Dow Jones Industrial Average over 10 years. Let's assume you invested your money in the DJIA index. If you invest for just one year—1990, for example—your possible investment gain and the investment loss has a wide deviation. Had you invested in all the stocks in the Dow on January 1, 1990, by mid-year you would have made money. A few months later you would have lost money. By New Year's eve, you'd be about

Figure 1-4. A one-decade weekly chart of the Dow Jones Industrial Average.

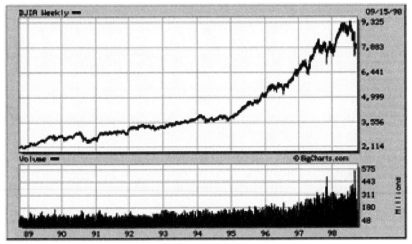

Courtesy BigCharts

where you were a year earlier. However, had you kept your money in the market for eight years, you would have made a significant amount of money. And in retrospect, the heart-stopping ups and downs of 1990 would seem like insignificant blips. Volatility diminishes over time.

What most investors do is buy at the wrong time and sell at the wrong time. Although the markets have gone up since the late 1980s, I have seen statistics that as high as 75% of investors have actually not made any money or have lost money. Why do you think this is? The answer is that because of times like 1990 or 1994, or even the second half of 1998, people sell their stocks when they get cheap, and buy them once they are expensive again.

The longer you invest the better your odds of making money. The market historically has gone up over time. If this is true for the next 10 years, then the significance of one or two bad years of market declines is greatly diminished over 10 years. In the short term, the risk you really incur is volatility risk. Long-term investors have less concern for volatility risk. Volatility risk is lessened over longer periods of time. As a result, investments that might seem bad in a short time period (and would be bad if you dumped them and lost money) can often end up being sound investments over the long term.

✫ ✫

Essentials for the Successful Investor

Being a successful investor requires skills similar to those of a successful chef. Every cookbook stresses that you need to read the entire recipe before beginning, make sure you have all the ingredients, and not deviate from the recipe until you have practiced it several times. This wonderful advice, if adhered to in investing, will virtually guarantee an improvement to your investment return.

1. *Be observant.* I respect and admire the all-stars, but I don't believe they are inherently superior people. They are

simply savvy at observing life. They are very good at looking under rocks for opportunities, trends, and cultural shifts that the rest of us don't see. Or, where we just see a rock, the all-stars see financial opportunity. These people look under more rocks than anyone else. And they know which ones of these rocks will unveil value that should make a stock rise. They are always thinking investing. When they go shopping, they look at what is being bought. When they listen to the news or read the paper they are thinking, "How will this event affect my investments?" When their kids come home and tell them they *have* to have a new pair of green canvas shoes, the all-stars instinctively begin to analyze how this new schoolyard craze might affect not just shoe manufacturers, but also the sellers of canvas, cotton, and green dye.

2. *Never think that being a successful investor is just picking stocks.* Being a successful investor requires timing, proper asset allocation, and patience.

3. *Learn basic accounting.* Much of stock analysis is based on what companies are worth. To know the worth, you need to be able to read the financial statements and then be able to interpret them. Free cash flow, return on equity, price to earnings and sales ratios should be second nature to you. In the "Fundamental Analysis" section of this book I provide a cursory overview of how to use accounting while evaluating a stock. While you don't need to take an accounting class (accounting courses often don't teach how to evaluate a company), I do recommend reading a book on accounting that focuses on how to use accounting to evaluate a company. Robert A. Cooke's *36-Hour Course in Finance for Nonfinancial Managers* (McGraw-Hill, 1993) is an excellent starting point.

4. *Learn basic charting.* Charting will help you spot trends and time your purchases.

5. *Find out where to get information.* We live in an information age. Just about anything you need to know is readily

available on the World Wide Web and at your local library. Not only do you need to know where to get the information on the Web or in your library, you also will need to become proficient at sorting out useful information from noise.

6. *Have clear investment goals.* What are you trying to accomplish? How long will this money be invested? What are the tax consequences? Never invest unless you have a plan, unless you know exactly what you are trying to accomplish. How much do you need to save? What return on your investment do you need to meet your goal and time frame? Too many people invest aggressively in a way that could lose them money, even though their plan said they didn't need huge returns. Now they jeopardize their whole plan if they lose money, whereas they would have been fine if they would have taken the low-risk approach and stuck to the plan.

7. *Truly understand your risk tolerance.* You and I have lied to ourselves about this before. You say you can stand risk, but only if you are making money, right? How will you feel if you invest $100,000 and the day after you write your investment check, your account drops 30% to $70,000? It happens fairly often. Are you really ready to weather such a market drop? Can you still follow your discipline? The bottom line is never invest without knowing the risk versus reward ratio. What are the chances of the investment going up, and by how much? What are the chances of the investment going down and by how much? Embrace risk—without it there is no profit.

8. *Forget what the stock price was a year ago.* Forget what you paid for the stock. You will learn that if you are worrying about buying a stock because it's too high, or you don't want to sell a stock because it's either not up enough, too far up, or down, you're focusing on the wrong stuff. Evaluating a stock has no bearing on what it was worth a year ago, or what you paid for it.

9. *Stick to your discipline and don't become emotional.* This is easy to write, harder to say, and even tougher to do.

However, maintaining a coolly disciplined, unemotional view of your investments will make you a better, richer investor. If you decide to be a value investor, stick with your value discipline through thick and thin. Understand, I am not recommending you chose only one discipline. Many investors use several disciplines. But what you should not do is become frustrated with the one-month or one-year return on your value investments, then switch willy-nilly to momentum investments. Time rewards your tenacity and discipline. In the words of Sir John Templeton: "Buy when the blood is in the streets, even if it is your own."

Don't invest in fads. You'll continually hear new theories. For example, buy the lowest priced Dow Jones stocks with the highest dividends. If everyone begins to do this, the anomaly that might have existed is blown. Finally, don't get emotional and don't second guess yourself. The one time you second guess is the one time you'll miss the "big one."

10. *Level with yourself.* You aren't going to pick every winning stock. You can be right and wrong, because if you invest properly, you probably need to be right only 55% of the time. I remember being shocked at first when I interviewed Foster Friess and David Katzen (of Zweig and Associates). I asked what percentage of stocks they actually lost money on. They smiled and said sometimes 40% or more. I then asked how they could still maintain such an incredible track record. Their response was because the stocks that they lose on generally go down less than the gain on the stocks that go up. I used to beat myself up if I had one losing stock. I don't anymore.

If you ever get to the point where you think you've figured out the market, cash in everything. You'll never completely figure out the market. There is no single key to the market. It is ever changing and it is rarely logical. Did you ever see a stock that just had the greatest news, but it went down? Why? You will be given hints, but remember that no hard and fast rules exist. And never forget that every time you think you bought a winning stock, someone was willing to sell you that same stock.

11. *Invest for the long term.* Attempting to guess short-term swings in individual stocks or the economy is a difficult, almost impossible, task for even the best stock pickers or economists.

12. *Remember, cash is king.* Regardless of the market you're in, cash is, and always will be, king. Even if you're earning only 4% or 5%, you need to always have some cash. The cash is necessary to buy more stock, limit losses, and be ready for a good deal. Never be 100% invested in stocks.

☆ ☆ ☆ ☆ ☆ ☆ ☆ ☆ ☆ ☆ ☆ ☆ ☆ ☆ ☆ ☆ ☆ ☆ ☆ ☆

Sources of Information

Hooray! We live in the information age. If you're diligent, you have access to the same information as Wall Street's "good old boys" network. (The good old boys don't like that at all, but their loss—privileged access to information—is your gain.)

The overabundance of available information has made stock picking easier in one respect; information is easier to obtain. However, in another respect it has made it more difficult. Too much information can be hard to interpret. You need to separate valid information from garbage. Another reason why too much information makes investing more difficult is the fact that everyone has access to the same information. This leads to more efficient markets, which makes it harder to be the first investor to turn over the rock that hides a gem.

The following sources of information are all terrific. Use as many or as few as you like. If you haven't already, get connected to the Internet. To get the best information, as quickly as possible and for the lowest cost, information that is available on the World Wide Web is second to none and a necessary trick in your bag.

Company Reports

All public companies file 10Q and 10K statements. The 10K is the annual report. The 10Q is the quarterly report. This information is useful for getting to know the company because it gives you a chance to read an independent auditor's report as well as the company president's report on the state of the company. How pretty is the annual report? Is it too pretty? Are they spending too much money on an annual report when they should be putting it back into the company? Company reports are available by calling the company, at the library, or on the company's Web site. (To find the company's Web site, go to a search engine such as www.yahoo.com or www.excite.com and search for the company by name.)

The Company

Contacting the company directly is a great exercise. You can get the phone number by calling directory assistance, looking up the company Web site, or referring to company reports such as Value Line (available at most public libraries). Or you can ask your broker to get the number for you. When you phone the company, ask to speak to shareholder services. If you have a specific question for the CFO (chief financial officer), ask for him or her (they are more accessible than you might imagine). Most companies also encourage investors to contact them through e-mail. Look for a shareholder services e-mail address on the company Web site. When contacting a company, ask to be put on its mailing list for money managers. That keeps you in the loop when there is a press release or a public announcement you'll want to know about.

When dealing with a company, a telephone call will often help you get a feel for how enthused the employees are by how they respond to you. Quality products and solid earnings potential often match a positive working environment.

Business Newspapers

To analyze stocks, you need information such as earnings reports, what sectors are moving, volume, and forthcoming earnings reports. The *Wall Street Journal, Investor's Business Daily,* and *Barron's* (weekly) are the leading newspaper sources of these types of information.

The Library

The library offers a wealth of knowledge and research materials on publicly traded companies. For individual stocks, *Value Line* and *Standard & Poor's* are excellent stock analysis resources. To graph a stock, ask the librarian for *Daily Graphs.* For mutual fund information, turn to publications by Morningstar and Lipper.

The World Wide Web

The Internet is probably the best way to obtain a great deal of information quickly, accurately, and inexpensively. Explore on your own, but try these sites:

* ★ **www.assetplanningsolutions.com** This is a superior site for general financial and estate planning knowledge. Remember, investing is only one component to being successful. Learning how to make more, keep it, and protect it are invaluable to a successful person.
* ★ **www.dailystocks.com** Plug in a company name or symbol and this site gives back a wondrous list of links to news, quotes, charts, discussions, and just about any other type of information about a stock.
* ★ **www.investools.com** This site offers many different kinds of reports from graphs to company earnings projections. While much of the site is free, it also sells research reports such as those from Standard & Poor's. You can create your own stock screens here.

* **www.quicken.com** This site offers a vast amount of free financial knowledge. Compare stocks to competitors, find out earnings projections, even look up sectors. It is extremely user friendly.
* **www.morningstar.com** This site is the unparalleled leader for subjective and objective information regarding mutual funds.
* **www.zacks.com** This research firm does the screens for you. The site offers proprietary screens, commentary, and more.
* **www.valueline.com** Value Line provides a wealth of good old-fashioned fundamental information. With Value Line, not only do you receive an unbiased commentary, but the site compiles historical information on such fundamental criteria as earnings, return on equity, and profitability. With this site, you really don't need many other sources of information.
* **www.investor.msn.com** The Microsoft Investor site is a phenomenal resource. With the fundamental research that is provided, you could track just about anything, including insiders buying and selling, profitability ratios, and earnings ratios. Some of the site is free. In-depth information requires a fee.
* **www.bigcharts.com** If it's charts you want, this is the place. From markets to indexes to companies, if it's information that can go on a chart, you'll probably find it here.
* **www.cnnfn.com** This site provides up-to-the-minute market news.
* **www.ndr.com** This is the site for Ned Davis Research, one of Wall Street's premier research and advisory firms.
* **www.firstcall.com** This site is a first-rate source for real-time, research, earnings estimates, and corporate information.
* **www.sec.gov** The U.S. Securities and Exchange Commission (SEC) enforces federal securities laws. Its task

is to protect investors from fraud, to ensure that U.S. markets operate fairly, and to ensure that publicly traded companies make available all the information that the law requires them to. Along with lots of useful investor information, the SEC site features access to EDGAR (electronic data gathering, analysis, and retrieval system), a database that maintains and tracks submissions by companies who are required by law to file forms with the SEC.

A Quick Lesson About Wall Street (or How Wall Street Works)

The term *Wall Street* is synonymous with investing. Actually it's just industry lingo. (What does Wall Street think? Wall Street doesn't like the stock. Wall Street likes the numbers.) Wall Street is the term used because the New York Stock Exchange, the auction where stocks that trade on the NYSE are bought and sold, is on Wall Street in New York City. If I say, "what worked on Wall Street," I really mean what is happening to make stocks go up. Wall Street's opinion is generally a consensus among people that are influential in determining stock prices. Usually these people are the analysts who study companies and issue recommendations as to whether a stock should be bought or sold.

What does make a stock go up? Do you think if there is a great company out there, with a great product and great earnings, the stock will automatically go up? No, of course not. Stocks often go down after positive news. Regardless of how good the *company* is doing, if more people are selling the *stock* instead of buying it, the stock will go down.

Joe's Filling Station: How the Whims of Wall Street Can Sink a Good Company

Joe had a great product. Ten years ago he created a unique restaurant called Joe's Filling Station. People were so excited to dine at Joe's that they would wait hours to eat. It had great food at great prices, in the most unique atmosphere ever introduced to restaurants.

Joe's Filling Station did so well that he opened two more, then eventually another three. Each one was every bit as good as the first. Joe figured out a turnkey system where he could easily duplicate these restaurants. His system would allow him to open ten Filling Stations per year. As good as the plan was, alas, he couldn't implement it; he didn't have the money. Sure, his restaurants were making money, but it took $1 million to open each restaurant and Joe didn't have that kind of money. So he went to a special kind of bank, an investment bank. Some of the big investment banks include Goldman Sachs, Bear Stearns, and Smith Barney. He approached several investment bankers: "I have a great concept and a great restaurant. Each of my three restaurants had gross sales last year of $10 million and our expenses were only $7 million. We pulled in a net profit of $3 million, or 30% per restaurant. Further, Joe's Filling Station is hard for an outsider to duplicate. There are high barriers of entry: We have a unique way of training our employees and our food recipes are secret. I could easily duplicate this strategy and with each new store achieve economies of scale, reduce the cost, and increase the profit margins. With ten stores we would be wildly profitable."

The analysts who worked for the investment banker analyzed everything. They saw that every year Joe's expenses per restaurant went down, yet sales went up. This activity is called **earnings growth** as well as **profit margin growth.** They analyzed the fact that he had a unique concept that would be hard for a newcomer or an outsider to duplicate. They agreed that if he did open more restaurants he could create economies of scale and his expenses would go down even further (things are cheaper when bought in bulk). Such savings would allow earnings to accelerate at an even faster rate.

The analysts figured that each restaurant would earn $2 million the first year ($20 million for all ten). Notice this amount is less than his current restaurants' $3 million earnings. Why? The investment bankers estimated that it would take each restaurant at least one or two years to build the business and earn repeat customers. In the second year, restaurants would earn $24 million, and the third year, $30 million. So the investment bankers surmised that not only was Joe's profitable, the profits and the earnings kept increasing every year.

The investment bankers told Joe, "If in the first year your restaurants reach net earnings of $20 million, your company would probably be worth at least $160 million. This is because the average restaurant chain, with growth like yours, sells for eight times earnings. Multiply the earnings of $20 million by 8 = $160 million. But we think your company is worth even more and the stock will rise because we believe your earnings next year will be $24 million. If your company still trades at eight times earnings, it will be worth $192 million ($24 million × 8) next year, and that should make the stock go up. We believe the stock will go up mostly because of your earnings growth. You grew 20% in the first year and 25% the second year. So not only is your company earning good money (strong earnings), your earnings are growing every year." This activity is called **earnings momentum,** and it is something that Wall Street analysts look closely at. So by pricing the stock at only eight times earnings when you are growing by 20% is cheap; Wall Street analysts will like the stock and it should go up.

So the investment bankers say to Joe, "Let's create 16 million shares of your company and price them at $10 per share ($160,000,000)." This offering is called the **float**—how many shares are outstanding. Understanding that this is an arbitrary number the investment bankers came up with. The bankers go on to say, "Joe, you own 20% of your company stock. Once we sell all of the shares, your 20% at $10 per share will be worth $32,000,000. We'll offer to investors 80% of the company or 12.8 million shares."

This stock was to be sold as an initial public offering (IPO).

The company symbol (all companies need a trading symbol) was JOE and it would trade on the New York Stock Exchange. Now the problem was getting people excited about the offering so they would buy the stock. So here is what the investment bankers did. First, they put together an attractive presentation package. They included accounting projections, graphs, and pie charts. They sent this package to stock analysts. Stock analysts usually work for major brokerage firms such as Prudential, Dean Witter, or Merrill Lynch. Their analysts looked over the information and sent a memo to their brokers recommending that they buy the stock for their clients. Further, the investment bankers held an analyst meeting. They flew all the analysts out to one of the restaurants in San Diego. The analysts they invited included powerful money managers of mutual funds. If these analysts liked the stock, they would have a great deal of money to invest and could buy lots of shares. As it turned out, the analysts loved the restaurant. Finally, the investment bankers did a road show where they traveled the country advertising their new stock-to-be.

On the day of trading, the NYSE gave the investment banker a trading pit. (On the NYSE, each stock has its own "pit" where traders gather to auction stock shares.) The market opened and the trader said: "I have stock of JOE. I'll start the bid at $10 per share." What happened? Pandemonium. The stock was premarketed so well that everyone was lusting for it. People thought this could possibly be the Microsoft of the restaurant world. The trader kept raising the price. Let's say you wanted to get in on this IPO of JOE. If you told your broker to buy 1,000 shares at $10, the broker gets it. But he calls you back one hour later telling you that people are willing to buy stock for $15, so you sell. Remember, there are only 12.8 million share available and everyone wants it. Buy the end of the day the stock closes at $30 per share.

What is JOE worth? We said earlier that the company was probably worth eight times earnings or $160 million. But on the initial day of trading, the company appeared to be worth

$480,000,000! That is, its market capitalization (or market cap) was 16 million shares multiplied by $30 per share. Was Joe's restaurant chain really worth $480 million? Maybe after five years. Should the stock be worth $30 per share? Probably not. But remember, Wall Street isn't about logic—hope, greed, and impatience are constantly whipping the Street into illogical, inexplicable froths.

The next quarter all of the Wall Street analysts who recommended buying JOE greedily await JOE to report its quarterly earnings. JOE's earnings increased an impressive 20%. But all of the analysts had predicted a 25% increase in growth. So although the company did well by growing by 20%, the stock tanked. Mutual fund managers didn't want to be caught with a loser stock, so they sold. There was no new demand to buy the stock, so the price headed down, fast. If you were watching the news and saw your stock JOE experiencing a big sell off, you'd call your broker. By that time the stock would be down to $5 per share. What ever happened to buy low, sell high?

This kind of tragedy is far too common on Wall Street. I tell it to you for several reasons. One is that if you are going to play stocks, you need to know the harsh realities. Even great companies that are earning money can see their stock go down. The cardinal sin is disappointing Wall Street. I also tell it to help you understand the lingo and how Wall Street works. Reviewing the story in hindsight it seems so easy to see that the stock was overvalued. But once you get caught in the frenzy, just like bidding on a house, you can let your emotions dictate your moves. Stick to your discipline.

Our all-stars, depending on their discipline, would play JOE differently. Some would have bought after the stock started gaining people's attention. They might have sold immediately when they saw others began to sell. Another all-star might be buying now that the stock is down and out, and wait for its earnings, and Wall Street investors, to get excited about the stock again.

Why Analysts Sometimes Get It Wrong

As you can see from the story of Joe's company, analysts are critical to the Wall Street equation. Besides marketing stocks to investors, their job is attempting to figure out the direction of both individual companies and entire industries. If an investment company has a "buy," "hold," or "accumulate" (or any other of a myriad of other qualitative terms) recommending that you buy or sell a stock, they usually derive this recommendation from the work of analysts.

The good news is that these analysts make their information public. An individual investor can read all of the hard work that an analyst has put into analyzing a company in one easy report. The bad news is that, unfortunately, many analysts get it wrong.

One problem is that analysts, and their recommendations, often are not completely unbiased. The analysts generally works for a firm (an investment banker or brokerage firm) that

✯ ✯ ✯ ✯ ✯ ✯ ✯ ✯ ✯ ✯ ✯ ✯ ✯ ✯ ✯ ✯ ✯

Analysts *want* the market and stocks to go up. When stocks go up, usually their bonuses go up. Whenever I read an analyst's report, I discount how optimistic they are by at least 10% or 20%. When investing, err on the side of caution.

✯ ✯ ✯ ✯ ✯ ✯ ✯ ✯ ✯ ✯ ✯ ✯ ✯ ✯ ✯ ✯ ✯

is a client of the firm they are analyzing. This situation poses a conflict of interest for the employee of an investment firm that wants to take a company public. The higher the stock price and the faster it sells, the more money the sponsoring investment bank makes. So it's not too often that you'll find analysts speaking poorly of a stock that their firm is offering. For example, assume General Electric is the client of Merrill Lynch. Merrill Lynch would receive millions of dollars every year advising General Electric about issues such as whether it should issue more stock or float a bond. Yet the analyst also works for Merrill Lynch. Is it likely that he or she would be completely unbiased?

I also believe that analysts are sometimes too optimistic regarding the companies and the economy. Analysts *want* the market and stocks to go up. When stocks go up, usually their bonuses go up. Whenever I read an analyst's report, I discount how optimistic they are by at least 10% or 20%. When investing, err on the side of caution.

To take this "too optimistic" theory a step farther, when was the last time you heard an analyst that worked for one of the big brokerage firms such as Merrill Lynch, Smith Barney, Goldman Sachs, or Dean Witter issue a "sell" recommendation? Usually when I see someone say "sell," it's too late—the company is already going bankrupt and the stock has already tanked. In fact, if I ever heard an analyst give a stock a "hold," "neutral," "unattractive," or "underperform" rating, I would get out of that investment—fast.

Conclusion

As you are beginning to see, there is less mysticism and gambling associated with investing than you probably thought. While it is true that investing is somewhat of an art, it is also a science. Chapter 2 covers the essential research tools to help you become more comfortable with the science of investing.

2

What Works on Wall Street

The Beginnings of an All-Star Investor

The market is not logical; however, *you* must still make logical decisions when investing. Presumably, over time, Wall Street will recognize your logic. In the short term, you and every other investor are at the whim of the risk and volatility of the market. That's why this book focuses on investors instead of on the market. Those who have a long-term perspective and discipline should reduce risk and increase the odds of positive investment returns. In comparison, both gamblers and people who trade stock on a daily basis (day-traders) may have a system for making money, but without skill, research, and discipline they are a far cry from being investors.

Your logical skills come in to play when it comes to reading and interpreting incredible amounts of data. Discerning what data is important to you is your counterbalance to the illogicality of the market. Reading and interpreting the data seems like it would be an easy task. However, in Part Two you'll see that if you give the same sheet of information to all of the all-stars, without fail, each one would read it differently. Reading it differently doesn't mean one is right and everyone else is wrong. It means that each has a discipline that provides clues, and that each will listen to those clues. And the all-stars don't mix different disciplines. The best of investors don't try to change their colors. Those that chase the latest trend will get crushed.

You should also be aware of the difference between being a successful *stock picker* and being a successful *investor.* Being successful at investing entails watching the economy and market movements. It means watching, and investing, in the right asset classes and the right sectors. It means investing in the best stocks. Therefore, being a successful stock picker is part and parcel of being a successful investor. So how do you become a successful stock picker? You may read about a "hot Internet stock" that doubled in value in just one day. These stocks may rise for several months. Sooner or later you may get greedy and say, "I should buy some of this stock." If you are buying it because it went up, you might be too late. But how do you know if you are too late or getting in on the ground floor of the next Microsoft? You must be able to put a price tag on the stock to justify a certain price. This is the difference between being an investor and gambling on a hot stock. You might love shopping at Home Depot and might consider it a good company. But just because Home Depot is a good company, determining if its stock will rise is a different matter. Remember Joe's Filling Station restaurants? Many great companies never see their stocks rise.

Ten years ago the stocks that went up the most were the stocks that paid dividends. Investors were in love with dividends. Dividends may be no less important today than they were 10 years ago, but I assure you that if you do a search of the companies that pay the highest dividends, you'll find that those stocks are not the best performers of late. Why not? Are dividends any less important? No, they're still important, but, for some reason, Wall Street isn't interested.

To become a successful stock picker, then, you need to find out what is important to picking a good stock today. Although dividends may be important for a company, ask yourself if dividends are important for making the stock go up. You need to constantly be asking yourself "What works on Wall Street?" because the answer constantly changes. The rest of this chapter is devoted to teaching you how to become a successful stock picker as part of the foundation of becoming an all-star investor.

Stock Analysis for Investors 101

From here on assume you've enrolled in a university class— "Stock Analysis for Investors 101." Every analyst must learn and use basic fundamental and technical analyzing skills. If you can master these all-important analyzing styles you have 80% of what you need for becoming a skilled stock picker, the other 20% being intuition and imagination. While you can learn how to analyze different styles, as for intuition and imagination, well, you're on your own. All I can say is that early on you'll make mistakes, probably as a result of an active imagination. This experience will help give you intuition. My advice is that you don't lose your imagination as you gain experience. And don't use your lunch money at the beginning of your investment journey either.

The Beginnings of an All-Star Investor

Knowing how to interpret technical and fundamental information is the primary secret as to why some investors are great and some aren't. If you notice that one of your stocks has decreasing volume, yet the stock price continues to reach new highs, does that bit of information tell you that the stock is bearish or bullish? If you see Coca-Cola is selling more cans of soda (higher sales) but at a lower profit, does that mean you should be bearish or bullish on the stock? Both dropping prices and increasing sales volume are indicators, but how do we read them? How do we interpret this data in a way that helps us make logical investment decisions?

There are two major approaches to stock market analysis: fundamental and technical. **Fundamental analysis** involves discovering what gives a company value apart from the general market by examining its balance sheet and income statement. You will study income trends, profitability ratios, investment returns, and so on. You will look at a company's competition to determine what impact it might have on the future value of the company. You will also look at management, employees, and how strong the company's goods or services are. For example, if General Electric workers decide to strike, that is fundamental knowledge that may affect the balance sheet.

All of this information is essential to fundamental analysis and all has very little to do with the stock market. Fundamental analysis does not consist of analyzing the market or the market trends. You aren't analyzing if more people are buying or selling this stock. You aren't analyzing if the stock price is rising on a day the market is falling. Tracking those indicators belongs to **technical analysis,** which is the study of the market actions and how these actions affect stocks. Pure technical analysts read charts. They don't care what the company's business is, what its earnings are, or about any of the other fundamental criteria. Technicians use their charts to gauge both the direction of the market and the direction of individual stock prices.

Some analysts believe that only fundamental analysis or only technical analysis makes sense. Others (most of the all-stars, in fact) use both approaches. Once you understand both fundamental and technical analysis, you'll be better equipped to understand the various investment strategies that the all-stars use.

Fundamental Analysis

Fundamental analysis refers to research that attempts to determine what a company is worth and what factors make that company worth more or less than what the stock is currently trading at. Once you determine the company's worth, or **valuation,** you can then determine if the stock price is trading at a discount or a premium in relation to what you believe the company to be worth. Perhaps the most important aspect of fundamental research is learning how to determine a company's worth by understanding its financial statements and analyzing its sales, income, and profit trends. You need to learn the numbers and you need to be able to locate the appropriate numbers and decide if they are good or bad. To do that you need a basic working knowledge of accounting and fundamental principals.

Suppose you would like to buy the ice cream shop down the street. To come up with a fair price, you would want answers to the following questions:

* What were the gross sales?
* What were the expenses?
* What were the net earnings after expenses?
* What were the earnings last year?
* What is the earnings estimate for next year?
* How much debt is there?
* Are there any new products?
* What is the competition up to?
* Who is on the management team?
* And, finally, what is the asking price?

These are great fundamental questions. The answers will help you decide if you want to own the shop.

You should be able to determine the fair price of the shop regardless of the asking price. Let's assume that the shop has net earnings of $100,000. Assume that all else is equal (no debt, the lease is not increasing, etc.). What is the shop worth to you? To answer this question you probably need to form a ratio. Maybe you are willing to pay five times net earnings. So you would be paying five times earnings to that of what you could buy another ice cream store for. Perhaps another shop owner is willing to sell at four times earnings.

You have just learned what is basically the price to earnings ratio (P/E Ratio), which is arguably one of the most important, if not most widely used, measures in fundamental analysis. So, if you do learn basic accounting principles and learn how to interpret what the numbers mean, the benefits to you can be truly limitless. These principles will make you a more astute investor, but you can also use them in everyday life. You'll be better able to negotiate the purchase or sale of a business, car, or real estate because you'll be able to determine what the true value is. You'll understand what drives your company, thus making you a more valuable employee. At the least, you won't be so tempted to buy a stock on a "tip" again. You will always be able to fall back on the numbers. Fundamental analysis is so important because it enables you to determine if what you are buying has value to you.

For purposes of this discussion, I introduce the following factors that are essential for conducting fundamental analysis:

* *Historical growth rate.* This information helps you determine how predictable the company is, which in turn helps you to predict future growth.
* *Earnings and profitability ratios.* Learning these ratios will help you to determine if a company is over- or undervalued based on the market and similar stocks in the same sector.
* *Financial strength.* It is important to know how solid a company is. Research in this area will reveal if the company can withstand a bad year or a recession, if it has too much debt, and the like.
* *Financial forecasting.* Mostly used by the growth investor, the goal of forecasting is to try to determine what a company will earn in the future.

Earnings and Profitability Ratios

It's one thing to know the earnings and the historical performance of a stock. It's another to figure out if the stock is cheap or expensive in relation to a company's earnings or sales. You do that by using ratios. Similar to the ice cream shop example, you need to know how much you are paying for a company's stock and what you are getting in return for that payment. Consider another tangible example such as rental real estate. If you wanted to buy an apartment building, one of the first questions you would ask is, "What are my gross rents?" You would probably, all else being equal, look for the apartment building that had the highest rents and the lowest asking price. The same is true with stocks. Most investors seek the highest earnings companies, the companies that make the most money for the cheapest price. Examining a company's earnings and profitability will help you determine a stock's valuation.

Historical Growth Rate

Knowing a company's growth history is essential to your decision making. Predictable growth—meaning that a company, regardless of recession or economic booms, grows its earnings or sales or whatever at, say, 15% per year—shows stability. These stocks tend to perform well and are rewarded for their stability. Stable stocks are often sought after on Wall Street.

Comparing a stock's historical performance is also important because it provides investors with clues as to how the stock will react during certain economic conditions. For example, suppose you are interested in Citicorp Bank and you think it is a good stock. But assume that at the time you are going to buy the stock, you read and hear on the news that our economy is beginning to see inflation and that the federal reserve might raise interest rates. An astute investor would check to see how well Citicorp's stock performed when interest rates were going up. If it went down every year interest rates were rising, that could tell you why the stock looks cheap, and that if interest rates do rise, the stock may look even cheaper.

COCA-COLA—AN HISTORICAL CASE STUDY

Coca Cola (KO) is a very predictable company. Using the Value Line data shown in Figure 2-1, study KO's sales, cash flow, and earnings. Year in and year out, this company grows. Its earnings growth rate averages out to be about 15% growth per year. Because its historical earnings and growth are so predictable, KO stock has been rewarded, growing from around $8 per share at the beginning of the 1980s, to over $80 per share in 1988. Thus, investors like to invest in and will reward a company that has historically predictable growth.

Figure 2-1. Stock data as it appears in *Value Line*.

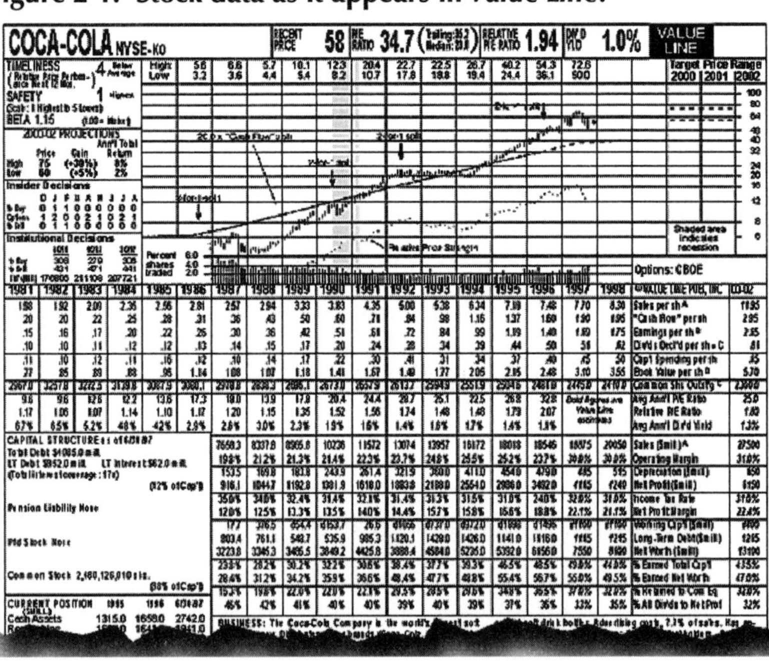

Courtesy Value Line

Price to Earnings Ratio

The **price to earnings ratio** (P/E) equals the price of a stock divided by its earnings per share. This ratio is probably one of the most well known, and, for some investors, most useful ratios of fundamental analysis. The P/E is so popular because it is a fairly reliable quick indicator. A share of stock is basically a claim on the profits, and future profits, of a company. The P/E tells investors how much they are paying for each dollar of that profit. Assume a stock you are interested in has a current price of $10 per share. Assume the earnings per share equal $1. The P/E equals 10 to 1; the stock is trading at 10 times its earnings. But is that good or bad? That's what the all-stars will tell us.

Usually an investor will look at the P/E ratio of a stock and compare it to four criteria:

1. The stock's historic growth rate (as we analyzed Coke)

2. The company's projected future growth

3. Other stocks in the same industry

4. The market as a whole, as measured by, say, the Dow Jones Industrial Average or the Standard & Poor's 500 Index

The higher the P/E ratio, the more money you are paying for the stock. Internet stocks have virtually no earnings but the stocks keep going up and up. Their P/E ratios are sometimes in the hundreds. If you have a stock that trades at $100 per share but earned only one penny per share, the P/E ratio would be 1000 to 1! The reason why some investors are willing to pay so much for a stock with a high P/E ratio is because they expect that earnings will grow rapidly in the future. These investors are trying to predict future earnings. This type of investor is traditionally known as a **growth investor.** Some investors would never buy a stock based on a projection of future earnings. Rather, these investors will only look at the stock and the current earnings to determine if the stock is expensive or cheap. Such an investor is traditionally called a **value investor.**

So imagine using the P/E ratio practically. Assume that you found a company trading at $20 per share with a P/E ratio of 10 to 1. You did further research and you found other stocks in the same industry trading at 12 to 1 (more expensive). But you also found that this company has been growing its earnings at 15% per year. This company's earnings growth is higher than what the current P/E of 10 to 1 would seem to indicate. Many value investors would find it quite attractive to have a stock's P/E be less than its earnings growth rate.

THE COKE CASE STUDY REVISITED

At the top of the *Value Line* report on KO (Figure 2-1), we see that the current price is $58. Immediately to the right of the price, the P/E is shown (34.7). How was this computed? Take the price of $58 and divide it by its approximate earnings per share for 1998 ($1.70).

Recall that KO as a company was growing at roughly 15% per year. But for some reason, investors were in love with this stock and kept it going higher and higher. Think of how high the P/E ratio was when the stock was trading in the $80 price range. Now, is KO worth $80 per share? Comparing the stock to a 15% average growth rate, a stock trading at a P/E of over double (34.7 currently) seems very high. So although the stock has come down from nosebleed levels, it still, from a valuation standpoint, seems high. How did it get so high? Irrational exuberance?

Value investors might make an argument that KO's earnings are only growing at 15% per year. KO is not the kind of company that would double its size overnight (unlike, perhaps, an Internet stock). So even at a P/E ratio of 35 you are paying a lot of money for the company. Put another way, assume you were a multibillionaire and you decided to buy every single share of KO. In essence, you want to buy KO. Remember the ice cream shop analogy. Do you believe that KO is *worth* paying 35 times its earnings?

On the other hand, a growth investor might argue that KO has the world's best brand name, it has not tapped the entire world yet, and its growth prospects are excellent. They might argue that, trading at 38 times earnings, KO is a steal.

Price to Sales Ratio

The **price to sales ratio** (P/S) is exactly like the P/E ratio but uses the sales data instead of the earnings data. The thought process is that some growing companies do not earn, or plan to have, net earnings for many years. Also, earnings can be manipulated so many different ways based on accounting methods. Some companies may want to manipulate earnings upward or downward and thus the investor doesn't get a true number to work with.

Conversely, sales numbers are harder to manipulate, thus giving the investor a more realistic number with which to determine a ratio. To find the P/S, take the price of the stock and divide it by sales. You can find annual sales numbers on Value Line reports, for example.

Price to Cash Flow

Analyze a company's **cash flow ratio** as you would a company's earnings or sales. Take the price of the stock and divide it by its cash flow. Some analysts think that a company should have lots of cash flow. Some analysts, although I don't know if a true accountant would agree, also would define cash flow as EBITDA (earnings before interest, taxes, depreciation, and amortization). Think of cash flow as gross profit prior to taxes and other such expenses. Imagine that you decide to buy a printer and wish to charge people for making copies. What amount of money do you make when you sell a copy? You would have to take the price you charge for the copy and reduce it by the cost for your paper supplies (paper cost), employee, and various other expenses. What is left is your cash flow.

A company that has cash flow could be attractive for many reasons. If you have lots of cash flow you might be in a position to buy other smaller companies. Perhaps you could acquire your competitors. However, a company that has cash flow is usually attractive to other companies and might be a target for takeover by a larger company. Regardless, I don't think lots of cash flow can be bad.

Many analysts insist that investors track cash flow to

earnings. Although companies might have good earnings, if the cash flow is being reduced it could signal disaster for a company. Accountants often argue that companies with reducing cash flow are headed for trouble. In fact, studies show that companies that had high net income but low net cash flow underperformed stocks in general.

Return on Equity

A few years ago, very few fundamental analysts paid much attention to return on equity (ROE), but recently it has become very important. It is important now because Wall Street analysts track ROE. They tend to recommend stocks with high or increasing ROE. The point is that ROE was just as important to the company 10 years ago, but it didn't affect the stock price because nobody looked at it. Now investors look at it, so it is important to have good ROE for a stock to get recommended and, hopefully, go up in price.

The **return on equity** is basically equal to the company's income before taxes. To understand it better, let's compare ROE to a bank. If you put money in the bank, your ROE is whatever the interest rate is (say 3%). The way I would compute ROE is to look at what a company makes on the same money invested. So, if I owned a printing company and invested $50,000 in it, what is my ROE (before taxes) if that $50,000 gives me 15% or $7,500? That would be the return for my investment. I then make ROE more difficult by subtracting from ROE whatever the bank would have paid me, because I would have received that if I did nothing except put money in a bank. So in this case my ROE would be 12%.

In theory, the better the ROE, the better the company is using and investing your money. Stocks with high ROE should be rewarded over time.

Profit Margin

I believe it would be hard for a company to have a great stock, over the long term, if it were not making money—if it were not showing a profit. Further, the strongest companies grow their profits. They find ways to cut costs, or sell higher profit-margin products and services. If you again refer to the Value Line illustration (Figure 2-1), you can view the net profit margin for KO. KO consistently improved its margins right into 1998 when the global recession caused the company to have lower profit margins than the previous year.

Financial Strength

When researching a stock, it's critical to know how stable a company is. If it has borrowed a great deal of money, what would happen if the company had a few bad earnings quarters and could not pay back the banks the money it borrowed? The banks could take over the company; they could bankrupt it.

If the company has less debt, the current ratio will be stronger (more equity compared to debt). The better the ratio, the better the financial strength of the company. The same is true for the book value. The higher the book value, and lower the book value ratio (the number of times a company trades compared to its book value), the more financial strength a company has. The company is stronger as it has less debt and trades closer to its book value. A company with financial strength (strong balance sheet) is considered to have less downside risk and thought of as a "safer" company.

Price to Book Value Ratio

The **book value** of the company is the actual worth of the company as reflected on the balance sheet (not the stock price). For example, if you took all the assets of Coke—its name value, real estate, inventory, equipment, and so on—and subtracted all of its liabilities, you would arrive at its book value. Let's assume the book value of XYZ company is $1 million and there are 100,000 shares outstanding. The book value of the company per share is $10 ($1 million divided by 100,000). What if the stock is trading at $20 per share? You would say the stock is trading at twice book value. Historically, stocks trading at two to two and a half times book value are considered high or expensive. This rule holds especially true among value investors. More recently, stocks have been trading at valuations much higher than two or two and a half times book. But use price to book as a measure of whether a stock is expensive or cheap.

Current Ratio

The **current ratio** is determined by dividing current assets by current liabilities. This ratio helps to determine how liquid a company is. A liquid company would have twice as many current assets as current liabilities (2 to 1). Liquidity is important if the company wants to buy another firm, real estate, or piece of equipment. The more liquid a company is, the safer it is considered. If the economy slows, the company would be in a better position to weather the storm if it has cash on hand (liquidity).

Of course, you should always compare the liquidity, as well as the book value ratio, to other companies in the industry as well as to the market as a whole.

☆   ☆   ☆   ☆

As you continue your quest for investment ideas, you will undoubtedly come across technical analysts. Many "technicians" will argue (vehemently, I might add) that to find good stocks and the direction of the market, all you need is technical analysis. Although this single approach may work for some people, I believe it is akin to seeing objects underwater without goggles. Although you may see the desired object, it's not as clear to you as it could be. Personally, I usually decide if I like a stock based on fundamental indicators and then use technical charting to give me a feel as to when is the best time to buy the stock. Technical analysis is a great way to spot trends in overall markets and individual stocks.

Technical Analysis

Tell me if this doesn't sound crazy: A technician might ask, "What is the strongest sector of the market?" From that information the technician will analyze various criteria to determine the best sector. He or she will usually analyze which sector has gone up in value (the stock prices are higher) the most, has the strongest momentum, and has the strongest volume (more people are trading this stock and bidding the price higher than other stocks). From this, he or she might conclude to buy stocks in that sector. Sounds backward doesn't it? That technician is buying a stock at a high price, has no idea what that stock does as a business, and doesn't care about the economy, or the balance sheet of the company. Though it might not seem to make much sense at first, this type of "investing by the numbers" can be very effective. Of the all-stars interviewed, I would say that William O'Neil and Marty Zweig are more technicians than anyone else. O'Neil uses charts primarily to confirm that he found a good stock, and Zweig uses them to chart the direction of the market.

What a Technician Measures

Technical analysts look for a trend in almost anything. If they think they are on to a trend, they'll try to chart and prove the trend. For example, assume that you notice that the days that a certain stock has a lot of trading activity (meaning more people are buying and sell this stock than usual), the stock tends to go up. So you come up with a theory that if the stock goes up in heavy volume it is a bullish signal. Incidentally, it is fairly easy to see if trading activity is heavy (heavy volume). Go to one of the Internet sites mentioned in Chapter 1. If you type in a symbol for the stock and ask for a full quote, many of these sites will tell you the trading volume for that day (how many shares have been traded). Further, it will usually tell you what that stock's average trading volume is. That way you can determine if the volume is heavier or lighter than what is average for a particular day.

Technicians have many more tricks up their sleeves than just volume. For example, assume you study the price of the stock. You notice that every time it breaks out of a 200-day moving average the stock tends to go up. This would be another important trend a technician would watch.

Technical analysts assess several important indicators to gauge the potential performance of a stock:

* Price movement
* Moving averages
* Trading volume
* Relative strength

Price Movement

A technician believes that much of that which is known about a stock is reflected in its price. As a result, technicians will study **price movement** and look for a pattern on a weekly or daily basis. Usually the first pattern they observe is simply a trend line. To create a trend line, technicians connect stock price tops or bottoms on a chart to see if the stock has a definitive pattern. In Figure 2-2, I drew a line on a six-month stock price chart for Compaq Computer (CPQ). The trend line shows that, over time, the price of CPQ is increasing, even when measured on the dips. In addition, the stock doesn't often drop close to or below the trend line. A technician might argue that if you see a positive trend line such as this, it might make sense to buy the stock if the price falls at or below the trend line. CPQ fell below the trend line.

An investor might also consider continuing the trend line out into the future, perhaps for six months or a year. You might use this trend line to gauge if the stock is trading cheap or expensive. Often when graphing a stock's price movement you'll see that winning stocks tend to move higher and stocks at their lows often move lower. Note that this information con-

Figure 2-2. Example of a trend line using the chart of Compaq Corporation (CPQ).

Courtesy BigCharts

tradicts the old notion of buying low and selling high. A technician generally believes you should buy high and sell higher.

Note that few technicians would use this indicator alone. They also consider volume, as shown at the bottom of the chart in Figure 2-2, and at what point the stock should be bought if in fact it does drop below its trend line to avoid catching a falling knife.

Another way that technicians analyze price movement is by using two trend lines. As shown in Figure 2-3, Intuit (INTU) had a distinct trading range over the course of a year. Notice the trend line drawn by connecting the stock's lower price. Every time the stock came close to this trend line, it bounced back up. Notice also on the high points that the stock experienced resistance in breaking out of its high end of the price range. Connecting the stock's high prices created this line, resulting in a "channel" between the two trend lines that could offer possible buy and sell signals.

Notice in August that INTU broke below its downside channel. It hovered below it for a few days. A cautious techni-

Figure 2-3. A one-year daily chart of Intuit, Inc., as of 9/29/98.

Channel Buster

Courtesy BigCharts

cian would probably wait to see if the stock begins to trend back up or down. In this case INTU trended even lower, down to about $35 per share. The stock then began trading to the upside forming some sort of a cup (a term William O'Neil likes to use). If the trading continues to the upside, it might be considered another buying signal as it gets closer to the low end of the channel.

Moving Averages

Almost all technicians use **moving averages,** or averages that are continually updated by picking up the latest figures and dropping the oldest. The purpose of the moving average is to smooth out the random fluctuations of a stock's price. If you wanted to figure the average price for a stock for the past 15 days, it wouldn't be too hard. You would just add up the price of the stock over the past 15 days and divide it by 15. To find the *moving* average over the past 15 days, you would use today's price, add it to the figures for the past 14 days, and divide by 15. The next day you would drop the earliest day, add the new price, and divide again. Moving averages are commonly stated as 50-day, 200-day, or 30-week moving averages.

Charted moving averages can be used to show trend signals. For example, look at how the stock price of a fairly new company, Peterson (PTN) breaks out of its 50-day moving average (the curved line) as shown in Figure 2-4. Notice how since the beginning of the chart in February, the stock doesn't do very much. It sort of stagnates, not moving up or down much and sticking close to its 50-day moving average. Suddenly in July it dips below its moving average, and then on high volume it begins to shoot up to brand new highs. The heavy trading volume is matched by a sharp price break beyond the moving average; for the technical analyst, this is a classic bullish signal.

Conversely, the signal turns bearish when a stock is well above its moving average and begins coming down, usually in heavy volume. Notice in Figure 2-4 how the chart illustrates the stock coming back down, but on fairly light volume. The

Figure 2-4. PTN's 50-day moving averages as of 9/11/98.

Peterson

Courtesy BigCharts

stock market as a whole began selling off hard during that time, and the stock of PTN might have just been selling off in sympathy with the markets. A technician might watch the stock as it dips below the moving average in September. If the stock begins to have heavy volume and move back up, he or she would use it as another buying signal.

Another bearish sign is when a stock begins to sell off below its moving averages. Figure 2-5, a graph of America Online (AOL), shows just such an event taking place in late August and early September. The stock price drops below the 50-day moving average and is simultaneously matched by a heavy increase in trading volume. For the technical analyst, this activity would be bearish sign for the stock.

Trading Volume

Volume illustrates how often the stock trades, that is, how many times the stock gets bought or sold on a given day. Heavy volume means a stock trades often. Knowing if the volume is

Figure 2-5. AOL's 50-day moving average as of 9/11/98.

America Online

heavy or light is quite meaningless in itself. The technician will want to know if the volume is heavy compared to what that particular's stock average volume is, not necessarily the average volume of the market. A technician would then analyze what happens when the stock does have heavy volume (is heavily traded)—does the stock usually go up or down?

Technicians often believe that expanding volume on a rising price of the stock is bullish. Conversely, less volume while the stock going up is bearish. (This interpretation, by the way, is true for either the market or an individual stock.) You might wonder, "Why is it bearish if the stock is going up?" That's a good question. The stock going up with lower volume could be bearish because you need more and more investors buying the stock to continue its rally. If volume slows, it means fewer people are investing. The stock might be reaching a peak. Or perhaps the stock is going up simply because the market as a whole is going up. When the market turns around (as it always does), the stocks that rose on light volume could very well be the ones that have little support and go down more than stocks with heavy support. ("Support" means that the stock is actively traded and has heavy volume, usually to the upside.) Recall Figure 2-2 showing a trend line for CPQ. Some chartists will sell a stock if it begins to drop close to or below the trend line when accompanied by heavy volume.

Relative Strength

This technical indicator measures if a stock is performing better or worse than the market or an index. **Relative strength** denotes the rate at which a stock rises relative to other stocks in a rising market or falls relative to other stocks in a falling market. The rationale is that if the stock is not performing as well as the market, it's bearish because, if you are a technical analyst, you generally want to own leading stocks that are outperforming the index.

Charting the Market—A Technician's Laboratory

Thus far, I have covered charting individual stocks. Actually, charting is used just as often, if not more often, to find a trend or forecast the direction for the market as a whole. For technical data on a weekly basis, turn to the *Wall Street Journal, Barron's,* and *Investor's Business Daily* to chart sectors or the market as a whole. On Fridays and Mondays both *IBD* and the *WSJ* have excellent raw economic data. On Saturdays *Barron's* publishes a section called Market Laboratory that offers more raw data than most investors need or want, including such indicators as the **market breadth**—the percentage of stocks participating in a particular market move—for the week. Most of the major business papers list the stocks that reach new highs or new lows. They will usually provide information on trading volume and market breadth. On the Web, head to bigcharts.com and the business section of yahoo.com for up-to-the-minute on-line charts that you can customize to suit your technical needs. With this information, you can begin analyzing your own technical information to determine directions in the market.

If you do decide to try to chart the course of the market, one thing you can do is look at **advance-decline** (A-D) measurements, the ratio of the number of stocks that have advanced and the number that have declined over a particular period of time. I previously discussed watching the stock indexes such as the Dow Jones Industrial Average (DJIA). Often the 30 stocks that constitute the Dow can be up, yet the other thousands of stocks can be down. The daily A-D is one of the best indicators to track the direction of the market. If more stocks were down than up, that is a negative (bearish) indicator. The indicator turns even more bearish if the market is down in heavy volume. If it's light volume, it's not as bad.

Consider Figure 2-6. This chart represents the advance-declines during 1998 until the end of August. If you recall, the

Figure 2-6. Advance-decline lines.

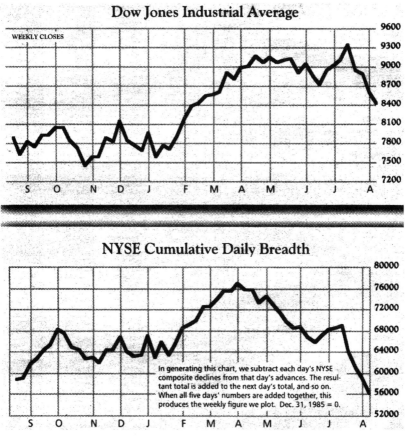

Dow Jones Industrial Average

NYSE Cumulative Daily Breadth

In generating this chart, we subtract each day's NYSE composite declines from that day's advances. The resultant total is added to the next day's total, and so on. When all five days' numbers are added together, this produces the weekly figure we plot. Dec. 31, 1985 = 0.

Courtesy *Barron's*

market cratered (went way down) in late July and August. This chart gives a hint that that was going to happen based on a negative A-D line. Look at the lower chart showing the NYSE (New York Stock Exchange) daily breadth. On the days that the line on the graph went higher, more stocks were up than down. You would refer to that as "positive advance/decline," or positive breadth. It's very interesting to note that the breadth of the NYSE started to turn negative as early as late April. Recall that the NYSE comprises hundreds and hundreds of stocks while the DJIA is made up of only 30 stocks. It's quite chilling to see how great of an indicator this turn could have been if used properly. The market as a whole began to fall apart perhaps two or three months before the DJIA stocks began to fall.

You might find that when more stocks are hitting new lows rather than new highs, it is a bearish signal and a bear market for all stocks could be close. You might find that if trading volume is high but stocks are not rising, it is a bearish signal and the markets are poised for a correction. Try many different strategies and see what works for you. See Chapter 6 for further insight on charting the market.

Financial Forecasting

The discussion of fundamental analysis began with looking at the history of a stock. History helps tell how predictable a company is and how the stock has performed during various economic conditions. The discussion continued with learning about the value and worth of a company through ratio analysis and about its solvency through the use of two key financial indicators.

As important as all of this fundamental research is, however, it is only half the story. The significance of the preceding research is greatly reduced if we can't, in some way, take an estimated guess as to how a company will perform in the future. For this, we need to forecast the future.

It is extremely important to understand how critical forecasting is. Have you ever heard the saying, "Buy on the rumor, sell on the news"? Many analysts spend all of their time researching companies and then coming out with a report as to what they think the company will show for earnings for the next quarter and the next year. Let's assume an analyst studies IBM and decides that it will grow its earnings by 25% next quarter. The stock is very likely to rise based on that forecast, which may seem kind of silly since IBM has not achieved this growth yet. So far, it's just an educated guess. Yet the stock goes up based on the rumor or the forecast.

Let's further assume one quarter goes by, and IBM does report earnings of 25%. Do you think the stock will actually go up again? Wall Street loves a company that surprises everyone and actually beats an analyst's forecast. In this case IBM hit the forecast, but didn't beat it. So a strong possibility exists that the stock will go down. The point is that the forecast is more important than the actual earnings report. Thus buy on the rumor, sell on the news.

Companies must publicly report their earnings every quarter as well as annually. These events have an important effect on stock price. As an individual investor, examine the following earnings per share (EPS) criteria to try to forecast a stock's performance.

Earnings per Share Criteria

★ *EPS Forecast.* As already stated, analysts will forecast what they think a stock will do in the next quarter and the next year. Look at what all the analysts are saying about the stock. Most sources of information provide this to you in a consensus. Good sources for EPS forecasts on the Web include Microsoft Investor, First Call, and Zack's.

In addition to just the forecast, you want to see how many analysts restated or actually changed their guesses. If many analysts are revising their estimates upward, that is bullish. If the revisions are downward, it's bearish.

★ *EPS Growth.* Stocks that tend to do the best have consistent earnings growth. If a company can regularly grow its earnings 15% or 20% a year, that is an excellent track record that will usually be rewarded in the stock price.

★ *EPS Momentum.* Stocks that tend to move up the most are stocks that not only have earnings growth, but also incrementally increase that earnings growth every year and every quarter. For example, let's assume that in the past quarter the company grew at 15%. To have momentum the company will need to grow by 17% in the same quarterly period for next quarter, and then grow perhaps 20% the next same quarterly period. Momentum is important for more than just earnings. It's important for profitability, sales, and return on equity—virtually all fundamental indicators.

Forecasting efforts can also benefit from information about the following:

* *Management Insider Trading.* Some people feel it's very important that if managers, officers, and/or insiders who own 5 percent or more of the company are buying shares of the company, the people that work for the company should be buying too. This is called insider buying. Conversely, if many insiders are selling, you would want to know about that as well.

* *Competition.* Is there too much competition in the marketplace? Will this shrink profits? Wall Street hates it when a company decelerates.

* *Life Cycle, Value, Acquisitions, Industry.* Look at the industry the company is in. Is it growing, or dying? Is there a need for it? How does it compare to social and economic trends?

* *Inventory, Book-to-Bill, Receivables.* Although the easiest and usually most accurate method of forecasting is by following the analysts that follow the stock, this is not a substitute for using your own brain. Consider, for example, if you worked for an automotive supplier. If you saw that the car companies are slowing their orders, you might know more than the analysts who are recommending that automotive stocks are the ones to buy. Smart investors keep their eyes and ears open all the time for clues that can be found in even the most mundane places.

CASE STUDY II—FORECASTING COCA-COLA

The listings shown as Figure 2-7 through 2-14 were copied directly from Microsoft Investor (investor.msn.com). The information they provided can be extremely useful in evaluating historical perform-ance and analyzing forecasts.

Figure 2-7 shows how the Coca-Cola company (KO) has grown over the last five years and in 1998, and what is projected for it in the future. It's interesting to note that the rest of the industry (beverages—soft) has grown faster than KO and is projected to con-tinue growing faster. The P/E of 39.1 is much higher than both their historical and projected growth. The projected growth rate is derived basically by polling all of the analysts following the stock for a con-sensus.

In Figure 2-8 notice that KO's income and EPS over the last quarter as compared to the same period a year ago has not grown. Rather they have declined. Historically stocks that do the best have increasingly, or at least stable, sales and earnings. In addition, as you will learn from many of the analysts, stocks that do better than had been predicted (providing a **earnings surprise** which can be either a higher or lower profit than projected) tend to do well. As shown in Figure 2-9, KO has not had a positive earnings surprise since 6/97.

Figure 2-7. Data on actual and predicted earnings growth rates for Coca-Cola and the soft-drink industry.

Earnings Growth Rates	Last 5 yrs.	FY 1998	FY 1999	Next 5 yrs.	98 P/E
Company	18.00%	-2.60%	16.50%	16.90%	39.10
Industry	23.10%	-4.70%	23.10%	17.40%	27.00
S&P 500	13.90%	5.70%	5.70%	7.40%	21.40

Zack's Industry: BEVERAGES-SOFT

Courtesy MoneyCentral.msn.com

Figure 2-8. Comparative data on income and EPS for Coca-Cola, the soft-drink industry, and the S&P 500.

Growth Rates %	Company	Industry	S&P 500
Sales (Qtr vs year ago qtr)	4.30	-6.70	8.20
Income (Qtr vs year ago qtr)	-11.00	-18.30	28.40
EPS (Qtr vs year ago qtr)	-9.90	-24.70	22.00
Sales (5-Year Avg.)	6.80	5.31	7.32
EPS (5-Year Avg.)	15.23	13.18	2.92
Dividends (5-Year Avg.)	12.33	10.15	-7.17

Data provided by Media General Financial Services.
Courtesy MoneyCentral.msn.com

Figure 2-9. Quarterly record of Coca-Cola's earnings changes.

Earnings Surprise	6/98	3/98	12/97	9/97	6/97
Estimate	$0.47	$0.34	$0.34	$0.41	$0.50
Actual	$0.47	$0.34	$0.33	$0.41	$0.53
Difference	$0.00	$0.00	$-0.01	$0.00	$0.03
% Change	0.00%	0.00%	-2.94%	0.00%	6.00%

Zack's Industry: BEVERAGES-SOFT

Data provided by Zack's Investment Research.
Courtesy MoneyCentral.msn.com

So why has KO traded up so high? One of the reasons could be that it makes a great deal of income per employee compared to the industry and the S&P 500 (see Figure 2-10). Furthermore, KO has a great deal of revenue per employee. Management is very efficient and it has historically made a great deal of money per employee. The company's profits are enviable. A net profit margin of more than 20% is almost three times the average company's profits in the S&P 500, and almost double that of the industry (see Figure 2-11). These figures largely explain why someone would be willing to buy the company.

As an investor, you need to research the answer to the question, "Will KO be able to increase its profit margin, or will it have to be reduced"? Figure 2-12 KO shows that has low debt and low debt to equity ratios. This state of affairs helps make the company a safer investment in bad years (as it appears it is currently experiencing). Nonetheless, perhaps the most important way to research a company is to review its 10-year history (see Figure 2-13). Since 1988

Figure 2-10. Management efficiency data for Coca-Cola, the soft-drink industry, and the S&P 500.

Management Efficiency	Company	Industry	S&P 500
Income/Employee	$131,000	$24,000	$19,000
Revenue/Employee	$653,000	$209,000	$257,000
Receivable Turnover	10.6	9.0	6.9
Inventory Turnover	5.2	7.8	7.1
Asset Turnover	1.1	0.9	0.4

Data provided by Media General Financial Services.
Courtesy MoneyCentral.msn.com

Figure 2-11. Profit margin percentages for Coca-Cola, the soft-drink industry, and the S&P 500.

Profit Margins %	Company	Industry	S&P 500
Gross Margin	72.6	60.8	47.1
Pre-Tax Margin	29.8	15.0	10.4
Net Profit Margin	20.1	11.4	7.4
5Yr Gross Margin (5-Year Avg.)	66.5	56.2	45.5
5Yr PreTax Margin (5-Year Avg.)	25.6	12.3	9.5
5Yr Net Profit Margin (5-Year Avg.)	17.9	8.5	6.2

Courtesy MoneyCentral.msn.com

Figure 2-12. Comparative data on the current financial condition of Coca-Cola, the soft-drink industry, and the S&P 500.

Financial Condition	Company	Industry	S&P 500
Debt/Equity Ratio	0.09	0.85	1.09
Current Ratio	0.9	0.9	1.4
Quick Ratio	0.5	0.5	0.8
Interest Coverage	22.6	6.9	2.5
Leverage Ratio	2.3	3.4	6.1
Book Value/Share	$3.24	$3.76	$12.65

Courtesy MoneyCentral.msn.com

Figure 2-13. A 10-year financial history of Coca-Cola shares.

	Avg P.E.	Price/ Sales	Price/ Book	Net Profit Margin (%)	Book Value/ Share	Debt/ Equity	Return on Equity (%)	Return on Assets (%)	Interest Coverage
12/97	37.40	8.73	22.53	21.9	$2.96	0.11	56.5	24.4	24.5
12/96	32.70	7.04	21.22	18.8	$2.48	0.18	56.7	21.6	17.1
12/95	27.60	6.16	17.27	16.6	$2.15	0.21	55.4	19.9	16.9
12/94	23.60	4.06	12.56	15.8	$2.05	0.27	48.8	18.4	19.7
12/93	24.90	4.15	12.61	15.7	$1.77	0.31	47.7	18.2	20.0
12/92	32.60	4.19	14.05	14.4	$1.49	0.29	48.4	17.0	17.0
12/91	25.90	4.61	12.01	14.0	$1.67	0.22	36.6	15.8	13.4
12/90	20.40	3.04	8.24	13.5	$1.41	0.14	36.6	14.9	9.7
12/89	14.40	2.90	8.18	13.3	$1.18	0.17	38.1	14.7	6.7
12/88	14.30	1.90	5.21	12.5	$1.07	0.25	34.3	14.0	7.9

Courtesy MoneyCentral.msn.com

KO has increased its P/E from 14 to where it is now at about 37. It is also trading at historically high P/S and price to book ratios.

Why would investors be willing to pay such high multiples? Is the brand name that strong? Is it because KO carries little debt? Could be. It could also be because of KO's net profit margin and return on equity, which are high and keep getting higher. In addition to those reasons, it's also a good idea to look at the trend of planned sales and purchases of company **insiders,** people in management or on the board of directors, or who own 5% of stock. Their actions could be a good barometer. Some of KO's insider trading activity is listed in Figure 2-14.

Is Coke overvalued? This is the ultimate question. A growth investor can argue that KO has not expanded to all the markets in all countries and that profits are high and get higher. KO has so much extra cash it will be able to buy smaller companies. Get analysts' research reports and see what they have to say.

A value investor could argue that KO's long-term growth rate is much lower than its P/E ratio; that although Coke is a great franchise and a great company, the stock needs to sell off to get closer to the intrinsic value of the company (see Mario Gabelli's interview in Chapter 5). How much of a sell-off? Perhaps the stock should be trading at a P/E closer to its long-term growth rate or perhaps closer to its book value. That is for you to determine.

When the stock was trading at $80 per share it was clearly overvalued. Since the stock has come down significantly (to about $65 per share), it seems to be priced right, if not still a little expensive. Because so many people and mutual fund managers love this stock,

Figure 2-14. A sampling of Coca-Cola insider trading.

Date	Name	Transaction	Num Shares	Price(s)	Value
07/21/98	HAAS TIMOTHY J	Sold	48,000	$39.94	$2 Mil
07/21/98	DAFT DOUGLAS N	Sold	40,000	$39.94	$2 Mil
04/20/98	CHESTNUT JAMES E	Purchase	63	$27.13	$1,709
04/20/98	ALLEN RONALD W	Purchase	4,000	$27.13	$108,500
02/24/98	DAFT DOUGLAS N	Sold	10,000	$27.13	$271,250
11/03/97	MCHENRY DONALD F	Purchase	1,000	$39.94	$39,938
10/29/97	ISDELL E NEVILLE	Purchase	400	$39.94	$15,975
10/28/97	DAFT DOUGLAS N	Purchase	86	$39.94	$3,435

Courtesy MoneyCentral.msn.com

I don't believe it will drop much further, but to be a true value it should go down enough for the P/E to be only slightly above its long-term growth rate of 15–20%. Furthermore, as long as the world markets are weak, I don't see the stock appreciating a great deal because I don't foresee any upside earnings surprises of an earnings rate greater than their historical 15–20%.

Now take all this information and think about it. KO has never traded more expensive. Its P/E and P/S have never been higher. Why is the stock trading at roughly 50 times earnings? Because of KO's predictability and safety. KO has little debt, its profits, as well as its ROE, are huge and growing. KO has a great franchise with little competition and over the long-term will probably be able to continue its 15–20% growth rate. However, if you look at many other stocks that have the same growth rate, I doubt you will see multiples so high. So while I agree that the aforementioned factors should allow KO to trade at a modest premium, 50 times earnings is not modest.

Although I am fully aware that KO may go up even further, and that investor perception is extremely important, as a *prudent investor* I am willing to miss some good stocks and err to the side of caution and safety. I believe for an investor to be willing to pay such a high price for a stock, everything has to be perfect. Today, I don't think everything is perfect. For one thing, you have a stock market that is extremely high. If it begins to sell off, chances are stocks with high multiples such as KO will sell off as well. Furthermore, much of KO sales are derived from the United States (see Value Line). Because foreign markets are in a recession, and it is more expensive to buy KO because of devaluation in currency, sales could slow and hurt profits.

In summary, the risk versus reward ratio is not great. KO is fully valued. Much of the upside is recognized, but not much of the downside. Too many more things could go wrong than right. By the time you read this, you'll be able to see how KO has fared since I wrote about it.

Conclusion

Every job has its dirty work: a chef has to clean the cooking utensils; a business person has to fire people; a homemaker has to discipline children; a salesperson has to fill out forms. And a true investor must perform fundamental and technical analysis. But don't view analysis as dirty work. Look at it as the key to becoming successful as an investor. The more research you do, the better your odds should be, over the long-term, of buying a good stock.

In the rest of this book you will read about the all-stars, those individuals who have made millions investing. Let me save you some time. If you believe these individuals simply wave a magic wand and, poof, a great stock appears, you might as well not read any further. As dynamic and incredible as all of these investors are, they all do their research and analysis.

If you can combine the research skills presented in this chapter with the personality traits of the all-stars, you'll be well on your way to becoming an all-star in your own right.

PART TWO
PRESENTING THE ALL-STARS

3

Harry Markowitz
Is Knowing How to Diversify 80% of the Battle?

Name, residence	Harry Markowitz, San Diego, California
Accomplishments	Nobel prize for founding modern portfolio theory
Hobbies	Walking on San Diego beaches, listening to music, especially J. S. Bach
Favorite reading	Winston Churchill's *History of the English-Speaking Peoples* and Leonard J. Savage's *The Foundations of Statistics*
Influential figures	The 18th-century British philosopher David Hume, for his *Treatise of Human Nature, Book 1: Of the Understanding*; Charles Darwin; and Descartes
Quotable	"Investing is all math."
Investment style	Efficient frontier, modern portfolio theory

What percentage of my assets should be in which sectors of the market? Will I have enough money to retire? Chances are you have asked yourself these questions before. If not, you should. If you ever ask a financial planner these questions—or have done research online, you've probably received a pretty pie chart with a computer printout illustrating how much money should be in which asset classes. Pensions provide the same things. If you are in a 401(K) you might have received different pie charts that tell you what is the best allocation depending on your risk level. How do the computers know what to put where? On what are they basing such decisions? All of this research is based on modern portfolio theory (MPT).

Modern portfolio theory, an investment decision-making approach based on the relationship between risk and return and the assumption of compensation for risk-taking, was created by Harry Markowitz. It encompasses two major approaches to diversification. I call the first approach the simple method, and the second, academia.

The Simple Approach to Diversification

If you are one of those brave souls who wants to truly understand why something is diversified, you need to read this entire chapter. Some of us want the short cut; here it is.

What Is Asset Allocation?

Asset allocation is the study of diversifying your investments within various asset classes to reach the highest level of return for the lowest amount of risk. Think of it this way: Which would you rather have, a 10% return or a 12% return? Probably the 12%. What if the 12% return was significantly higher in risk than the 10%, which was fairly low risk? You might then want the 10%.

But what is the acceptable level of risk if you are going for the 12% return? I don't believe most people are honest with themselves about risk. The topic is covered in more detail later in this chapter.

Is Asset Allocation Important?

If you only knew how much debating goes on among professors and money managers regarding whether or not asset allocation is a reliable way to beat the market with less risk. One thing that the experts do agree on is that asset class selection is extremely important. Figure 3-1 is from a study that attempted to figure out which investors performed the best. It clearly illustrates that those who diversified their assets properly were among the most successful of investors.

Figure 3-1. Display of study data comparing investment strategies.

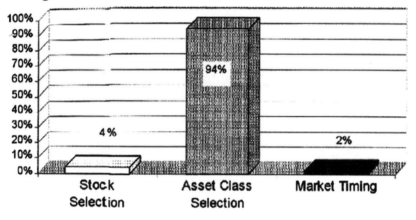

Take a real-life example. Let's look at the first six months of 1998. Indexes as a whole were up. Yet certain sectors were down: oil, emerging and international, transportation, and aerospace. These stocks were down so much that they already experienced their bear market. If you were in the wrong sectors, you would have lost money.

To achieve the highest return for the lowest risk, the first key is to own all types of asset classes, from large stocks to emerging market stocks. Further, you need to know which sectors you should have more money in and which need to be lightened up. The idea of owning many different sectors such as aggressive growth and emerging markets may sound like you are increasing risk but, in fact, you're doing just the opposite. You are probably reducing your risk and increasing your return.

The second key is to rebalance the portfolio regularly. Suppose the following is your portfolio:

15%	International stocks
15%	Cash
20%	Dow Jones Industrial Average
15%	Russell 2000 Small Cap Index
20%	Treasury bonds
15%	Corporate bonds

Assume that over the year international stocks got clobbered, yet your Dow Jones stocks doubled. What would you do? Most of you would say, "Gee this Dow Jones index is doing great, I think I should buy some more." I'm not saying this decision is wrong, but what happened to buy low, and sell high? Wouldn't you want to buy international now that it's low? "Of course not," you say, "international stocks did horribly last year." Isn't that the point—to buy low and sell high?

According to MPT, you should keep the same percentage in various asset classes depending on your tolerance for risk. If your international portfolio drops and your Dow Jones Index portfolio is way up, you would sell enough of the Dow Jones to get back to your original investment balance. You would also add enough to the international portfolio to get back to your original investment spread.

Another key to diversification is to figure out what the best mix of assets is for your risk level. To do so you will find assets that are negatively correlated, meaning that the investments move in opposite directions. So if oil is cheap and oil stocks are down, that should help airline stocks since airlines spend so much money on the price of oil.

To recap, a central tenet of MPT investing is to get in the market and then constantly rebalance your holdings in consideration of negatively correlated assets.

Academia—Asset Allocation in Detail

Imagine sitting around with your friends talking about investing. One of you asks, "How can we maximize our investments with the least amount of risk?" What a great question! The an-

swer is math, math, and more math. Imagine not only invent-
ing the math necessary to answer this question, but to have
done so before personal computers. Harry Markowitz and William Sharpe actually invented the math to determine what the
asset class should be and when to invest in it in order to
achieve maximum returns for a certain accepted risk level. Talk
to any money manager today and he or she will use simple
numbers and ratios such as the Sharpe ratio, efficient markets,
standard deviation, alpha, and betas, all thanks to Markowitz
and Sharpe, who won the Nobel prize in economics for devel-
oping MPT. So I went to see Harry Markowitz. I walked out
hours later with my head on fire.

I walked into Dr. Markowitz's unpretentious office in La
Jolla, California. A grandmotherly lady offered me a soft drink
(too late for coffee, she opined). Then Dr. Markowitz greeted
me. I truly believed he was my grandfather. Dr. Markowitz was
tall and lean, dressed in a comfortable old sweater (in the middle of summer), and carried a cane.

I looked around his office. "Where is the computer?" I
asked. He chuckled, "Where we are going you don't need a
computer." At this point I knew I was in trouble. "But how do
you do the math, calculate the standard deviations, the corre-
lations?" I asked. He gestured to the dry-erase boards on the
walls—all four walls. Blank canvases. We were ready to create
art.

"We are going to do the math today," stated Professor
Markowitz. By the end of the day, all the dry-erase boards were
filled. My head was pounding. What little hair I had left was
gone. But doggone it, I learned the math that until that day my
trusty computer gave to me!

The following is an encapsulation of my time with Harry.
To try to present this section in interview format would not do
it justice. I don't believe you need to learn the actual math in
order to use MPT. However, if you are interested in the math
behind Markowitz's theories, get his classic text, *Portfolio
Selection: Efficient Diversification of Investments*.

Modern Portfolio Theory and Risk

Modern portfolio theory tells you if you are taking too much risk for your return. Think of MPT in terms of your total portfolio. You have a choice about which investments you make. If two investments have identical returns for a given time period, you would want the one with less risk. How you build a portfolio with the least risk for the greatest return is the goal of all investors. But everyone defines risk differently. During the time I spent with Dr. Markowitz, I learned how an academic would identify and quantify risk.

The Two Types of Risk

* **Diversifiable risk** is a risk you can minimize by broadly diversifying your assets. If you invest in many different asset classes, you reduce your risk because if one stock goes down, it only affects a small part of your portfolio.
* **Nondiversifiable risk** is a risk you cannot diversify away from, such as is inherent in the stock market. The only way to avoid nondiversifiable risk is to invest in less risky asset classes such as Treasury bills.

We all know that risk is a part of investing. Risk is something that virtually everyone would want to minimize or avoid. The reason MPT is vital to investing is that it provides insight to the investor as to how to frame individual investments into an efficient portfolio in the hopes of providing the highest return with the least amount of risk for that return.

The Four Basic Premises of Modern Portfolio Theory

1. *Investors are risk adverse.* Investors should not just think of investment performance (return). You need to

focus on risk-adjusted returns to increase the probability of investment success. A basic trade-off exists: To obtain greater returns on investments, the investor must be willing to take greater risk. MPT suggests that investors prefer higher returns to lower returns. Similarly, for a given level of expected return, investors prefer less risk to more risk. In other words, you don't want to take more risk without the chance to make more money.

2. *Markets are efficient.* Modern portfolio theorists believe in the efficient market hypothesis: markets are truly efficient and individuals cannot beat the market over time. Used practically, MPT can help an investor seek optimal returns while minimizing long-term risk by working with the market instead of trying to beat it.

Note that this theory is controversial. The all-stars do not agree on it. For example, John Bogle absolutely believes in the efficient market hypothesis and therefore champions the index, or passive, approach to investing. Don Phillips, Mario Gabelli, and many others say that it's not true—you can beat the market over time.

If you think about it, the market does seem quite efficient. Take an individual stock like Exxon. Do you remember the Exxon Valdez oil spill? The stock went down that very day, even though nothing had happened to the company's earnings that day. However, throughout 1997 and 1998 the company continued to spend millions fixing the legacy of the oil disaster.

3. *Less attention should be given to individual security analysis and more to the portfolio as a whole.* In other words, Markowitz and his followers believe that investors are better off spending time tending their overall investment forest rather than obsessing over individual trees. I would not be surprised if Dr. Markowitz, William Sharpe, and other MPT followers don't own any individual stocks. Rather I would believe they simply invest in indexes, such as the Standard & Poor's

500 Index and the Russell 200 Index, and diversify based on how much they should have in each of these asset classes. The idea of owning individual assets is really a foreign concept to MPT investors who are trying to make the most money with the least amount of risk through asset allocation.

4. *For every level of risk there is an optimal combination of assets.* If you are an aggressive investor, you are someone who is comfortable with wide swings in the value of your portfolio. You aren't uncomfortable with the thought that your portfolio could drop on any given day by 20% or possibly more. You are okay with this because you believe it is a fair trade-off in trying to achieve higher returns.

You could be an aggressive investor by placing all of your asset in one stock. Then you live with the possibilities that the stock could go up 30% or it could go down 40%. But if you buy five stocks in different asset classes—one small stock, one blue-chip, one overseas stock, one technology, and one health-care stock—most people would agree you still have an aggressive portfolio. However, now you might have the probability of still being up 30%, but only being down by 30% as well. Diversification lowered your risk. Thus, of the two aggressive approaches, the second is obviously preferable since it provides the same probability of upside potential with lower downside risk.

Computing Risk

It is extremely important to know how risk is computed when analyzing individual asset classes. If you know how to calculate the risk of each asset, you should then be able to calculate the risk of a certain asset class, and ultimately the risk of your portfolio. The following are a few common ways of measuring risk.

Alpha

Alpha is the return of a specific stock or mutual fund independent of the market. The higher the alpha, the higher your return would be in a flat market. If you put $10,000 into the market and a year later pulled out all of your gains and only received $10,000 that is called a flat market. If your mutual fund or stock made money in a flat market, you would have a positive alpha.

You'll notice that many of the Web sites and research reports such as *Value Line* for stocks or Morningstar for mutual funds show the alpha and beta.

Beta

Beta is a measure of volatility. The benchmark is the Standard & Poor's 500, which has a beta coefficient of 1. If your investment (stock or mutual fund) has a beta higher than 1, it will be more volatile than the market. Thus it could move higher than the market when the market is up, but could also move lower than the market when the market is down.

Investors used to want the stocks (or mutual funds) with the highest beta. Studies have shown that the highest beta stocks tend to be extremely volatile and don't necessarily beat the market. Now the trend is to find stocks and mutual funds with high alphas and low betas. When reading Louis Navellier's chapter, you will see how alphas, betas, and standard deviations are actually wed.

Standard Deviation

Markowitz defines standard deviation as the square root of the average squared deviation. Basically, consider the market as having a deviation of 1. The more your portfolio deviates from 1, the more risk you assume. In other words, assume that you find a stock that has a well-defined trading pattern. It moves between $10 and $12 per share. Any time it moves out of that trading range, it deviates more than its standard. Therefore, the standard deviation would increase. The only reason to want an investment with a high standard deviation is if you think you will be handsomely rewarded (make more money than the market).

Studies have shown that stocks with the highest deviation tend to be the riskiest. And although they have the potential for making more money, the risk usually outweighs the reward. Therefore, MPT suggests that an investor accept no more deviation than the market.

Covariance

Covariance can be defined as cooperation. All stocks don't move up or down at the same time. Sometimes certain stocks move up, while others will move in the opposite direction. Picture a see-saw. If you put all the weight on one end, you wouldn't have balance. If you buy all of one type of stock, you have no balance and will increase your risk as a result. A classic example is stocks and bonds. Over the long, long term stocks and bonds don't move together. Take the third and fourth quarter of 1998 as an example. As stocks dropped, bonds went up. This is covariance. You also have certain stocks that tend to do well while others perform poorly. That is another example of covariance.

To reduce volatility in a portfolio you need balance. Incidentally, this will probably cause you at any given time to have a certain asset class that is underperforming or losing money. That does not mean you should sell it! There is nothing more frustrating as when an investor says something like, "Stocks are doing great, and my bonds are not. I will sell my bonds and buy more stocks." Your bonds are your insurance for when the stocks aren't doing so well.

The Importance of MPT and How to Use It

As previously mentioned, the goal of investors is to make the most return for the least amount of risk. We've all heard that diversification reduces risk. But how we choose these diverse assets is about as scientific as throwing darts, blindfolded. MPT provides a scientific approach for building the most efficient portfolio to maximize return and minimize risk. Again, the math isn't covered here. To try to do the math for an entire portfolio is a huge undertaking and actually unnecessary. Get an asset-allocation computer program based on MPT to do the math for you.

Most of us realize that if we buy the stock of a start-up company, it's risky but offers a potentially higher return than a larger, more predictable company. But if we put half of our money in the start-up and half into a proven big company (like General Electric), the trade-off will reduce our risk. Understanding the trade-off between risk and reward is only part of the whole picture. MPT states that its not the performance of the individual asset, but how all the holdings within your portfolio interact with each other that affects its overall risk and return. MPT analyzes those relationships through the notion of covariance and correlation.

Once you have computed the covariance, plot it to determine the efficient frontier. The **efficient frontier** method states that from all the possible investments available to you, somewhere lies an optimal portfolio that will provide the right combination of return and risk. See Figure 3-2 as an example. Notice that the efficient frontier line going down to up shows your possible return. The higher the alpha, the higher your return. The higher you go the better your return. However, the farther out you go, the more risk you take. So if you could be anywhere on this graph, where would you be? You would want the highest possible return with the lowest risk. That would be way up the alpha axis but with 0 standard deviation. The efficient frontier indicates that this positioning is not possible. Look at one of the plotting points (dots) below the efficient frontier. Is this a desirable asset? No—you are taking more risk and not getting enough return for the level of risk you are taking.

Now that you see what an efficient portfolio looks like, find the best asset allocation mix by deciding how much risk

Figure 3-2. Plotting of covariance to determine optimization on a portfolio-wide basis.

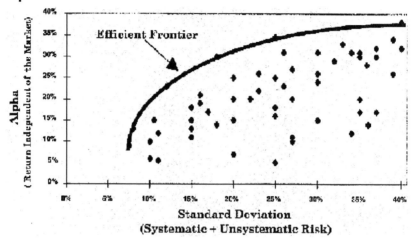

you would like to take. Let's assume you wish to be at a 25% standard deviation. Or you could work the math backwards and figure what your goals are, which will show how much return you need and at what the risk level you should be. Consider the following: Mr. and Mrs. Sample have a goal of retiring this year. They expect to live for 30 years and wish $30,000 in retirement income rising at 3% per year for inflation. Figure 3-3 represents their current portfolio, and Figure 3-4 represents a proposed portfolio. Look at the first pie chart and then look at the second. The difference is not dramatic. However, by optimizing the portfolio, the proposed portfolio actually lowered the standard deviation, which could be translated into lowering risk. Yet at the same time it actually increased the return slightly. The result is an efficient portfolio.

Commentary

How many of us have 10 different mutual funds and believe that is a diversified portfolio? Chances are the portfolio is not diversified because each of the mutual funds probably buys and sells the same stocks as the others. Diversification through

Figure 3-3. Representation of a sample current portfolio.

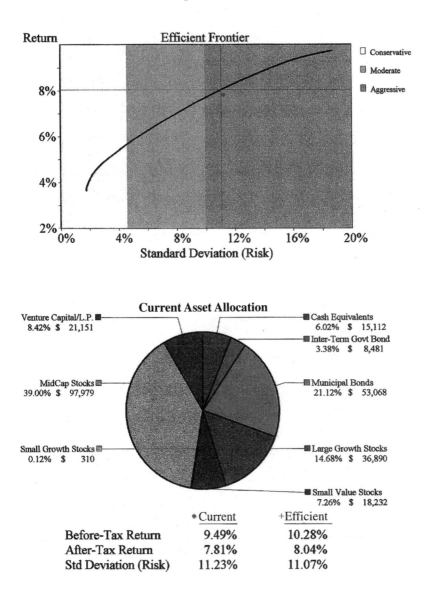

Efficient Frontier: Nonqualified Assets, Present Mix

Current Asset Allocation

	• Current	+Efficient
Before-Tax Return	9.49%	10.28%
After-Tax Return	7.81%	8.04%
Std Deviation (Risk)	11.23%	11.07%

Figure 3-4. Representation of a sample proposed portfolio.

Efficient Frontier: Nonqualified Assets, Proposed Mix

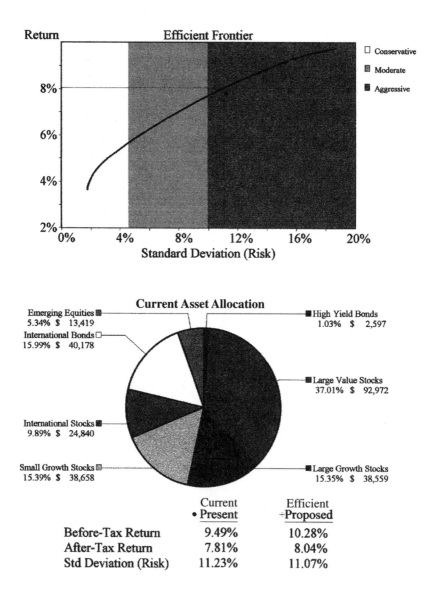

	Current • Present	Efficient +Proposed
Before-Tax Return	9.49%	10.28%
After-Tax Return	7.81%	8.04%
Std Deviation (Risk)	11.23%	11.07%

the use of MPT can significantly increase your investing success. Most good financial planners have diversification software that uses MPT. You can assess the diversification of your
portfolio with personal finance software such as Quicken.

That being said, many of the all-stars included in this book
will tell you to use diversification models cautiously. Models
are models, and to rely too heavily one can be dangerous.

4

John Bogle
Investing (and Making Money)
Without Thought—The Argument
for Passive Investing

Name, residence	John (Jack) Bogle, Valley Forge, Pennsylvania
Accomplishments	Founder of Vanguard Investment Group
Hobbies	Playing squash, sailing, reading ("I'm trying to get back into golf.")
Favorite reading	*King Lear*; Benjamin Graham's *The Intelligent Investor*; Charles MacKay and John Templeton's *Extraordinary Popular Delusions and the Madness of Crowds*; E. L. Doctorow's *Loon Lake*
Influential figures	Winston Churchill, "because of his use of the beautiful English language and his grasp of history." Walter Morgan (founder of Wellington) "because of his friendship, strong values, and for giving me my first break."
Quotable	"We have a lot of information. . . . Is it leading to knowledge? I doubt it. Is it leading to wisdom? I can't imagine it."
Investment style	Index

Background

On the evening of August 1, 1798, Lord Horatio Nelson sailed his flagship, the HMS *Vanguard* of the British fleet, into Egypt. Napoleon Bonaparte was on a campaign to conquer the world "from Egypt to India."

In a night encounter, the British fleet annihilated Napoleon Bonaparte's ships in what is still considered the most complete victory in naval history. Lord Nelson lost none of his fleet.

Vanguard was chosen as the name for the Vanguard group of investment companies not only because of the significance of the traditional meaning (leadership of a new trend), but also to incorporate the significance of this great and historic battle. It's an appropriate name for a company that has revolutionized the investment industry and has become the standard that investment companies aspire toward.

Armed with a tart tongue, blunt remarks, and tireless energy, Vanguard's founder, John Bogle, has revolutionized the mutual fund industry. To the consternation of many money managers on old boy–oriented Wall Street, he has also made a name for himself as founder, father, and champion of index investing. In fact, Bogle was part of the mutual fund industry before there really was such an industry. From an environment where mutual funds were all but unheard of, Bogle built his firm into what is today the second-largest mutual fund company in the world—$250 billion in assets strong.

Index, or passive, investing means you go out and buy the market; not the whole thing, but a representative share from all the companies that make up a particular market index. As mentioned earlier (Chapter 1), an index is simply a grouping of stocks, such as the Standard & Poor's 500 Index. If you bought a S&P 500 index fund, you would own a small piece of all 500 stocks that make up that index. There is no thought or analysis involved, and no active buying or selling. The only time a new stock is bought is if it is added to the index. For example, let's assume two companies that are part of the S&P Index merge. That means there are now only 499 stocks in the index. An independent committee chooses a new stock to add to the index. When this stock is added, your index fund will buy this stock regardless of its fundamentals and the services and products it offers.

This book is devoted to strategies on how to become a

better investor. So when I talk about indexing, I almost feel as if I'm shortchanging you. You don't have to do anything. It doesn't take any special skill, and it doesn't take much thought or time. However, when an investor begins to make investment decisions, sooner or later he or she is faced with the decision to make passive or active investments, or both.

When Bogle started the first index fund in 1976, The Vanguard Index Trust, he could only raise $11 million. It took will and determination just to keep the fund going. Critics laughed and predicted the fund would only earn mediocre returns. Today indexing is extremely popular. While Wall Street pundits predicted the imminent failure of indexing, investors voted otherwise by putting billions of dollars into index mutual funds. It took a visionary, a pioneer to bring indexing to where it is today. The man, of course, is John Bogle. His company is the Vanguard Group. His quest: to reform the mutual fund industry.

The candid interview of this all-star is intended to provide:

* Personal insights into John Bogle and his company
* A compelling argument for index investing
* The three variables you need to know to make money in mutual funds
* Truly priceless morsels of information that you as investor, and as a human being, can use right now to become both a better person and a better investor

Preinterview Info

Before meeting Jack Bogle, I knew that Vanguard was a great story and that its founder was a great man. Yet driving through the green, empty fields of Pennsylvania, I almost convinced myself that a firm the size of Vanguard couldn't be headquartered here. I couldn't even find a building taller than one story. Then I saw it: The Vanguard Campus.

The campus consists of several buildings encompassing acres and acres. The company's nautical theme is carried throughout the campus; each building is named for a ship of Lord Nelson's fleet. Employees are called crew members. The cafeteria is called The Galley. Building interiors are decorated with original paintings of great ships and battles, and nautical artifacts.

I know that Jack Bogle has a soft voice but harsh words. He lashes out at the mutual fund industry. He is its severest critic, chastising mutual fund companies for gouging investors with higher fees. Is Bogle for real? With the fervor and nearly evangelistic approach he has used to carry his message, Bogle is either a true idealist working only for good, or Jack Bogle is the greatest marketing genius ever.

I wondered what to expect as I was pondering my meeting with Bogle. I felt as if I were going to meet royalty. Chauffeured limos—the whole bit. The reality is, he rarely drives. He and his wife share a Volvo. In spite of his resplendent reputation, Bogle is not a flashy man. Furthermore, if you think the Bogle family is in the business to increase personal wealth, think again. The Bogle family has given away a great deal of its wealth to various charities and civic organizations.

I walked into the corporate headquarters. The smiling receptionist's name tag told me that her name was Marilee Stillwell. I explained to Ms. Stillwell that I was here to interview Mr. Bogle. Her eyes beamed, a smile formed. She said, "Mr. Stern, this will be an experience that will change your life." For the next ten minutes she told me of her love for Vanguard and Mr. Bogle. Ms. Stillwell went so far as to pull a personal file she was keeping. Complete with a plethora of press clippings on Vanguard and Mr. Bogle, the file included a personal poem Mr. Bogle wrote to her for having a tenure at Vanguard of over 17 years. I was awed, trying to think how much I would have to pay my associates to provide this testimonial. I'd only been in the building for 10 minutes and it was already clear to me that Vanguard wasn't just about money.

John Demming, of Vanguard's marketing and public relations department, greeted me and began expounding the Vanguard principles: the fight for lower fees, better service, and so on. He was anxiously telling me how they devised a way to lower expenses even further by offering shareholders' account statements via the computer. "Just in postage and printing we would save billions for the shareholders!" John exclaimed.

I finally made it to John Bogle's office. He walked in wearing a disarming smile and rosy cheeks. I wondered, could this cherubic fellow (who a few years before had a complete heart replacement) truly be the fierce crusader who has so radically changed the mutual fund industry?

I began by humbly stating that I knew how busy he was and told him I would try to be brief. He nodded graciously. Later, when talking about the exorbitant rates that he feels the mutual fund industry charges for mediocre results, the disarming smile turned into a sneer. His eyes sparked with fight, and I knew time was no factor.

The Interview

KS: *I am sure our readers would be very interested to hear how you began, and the impetus behind Vanguard.*

JB *[smiling]:* Well that's a story and a half.

> *[Although he is not a physically big man, I liken Mr. Bogle's voice to John Wayne's; not the Southern drawl as much as the authority. He speaks with force and conviction.]*

It's very odd how little turns in the road bring you to where you are. In 1949 I was graduating from Princeton University. It was time to write my thesis. I wanted to write on a subject that nobody else had written about—this little-known but fascinating new business called mutual funds. After writing this thesis, I knew mutual funds was the place to be.

I was hired as a clerk by Walter Morgan, who was chairman and majority shareholder at the Wellington Fund. The Wellington Fund was a balanced fund, which was odd for that day and age. You must remember that at the time most mutual funds were very aggressive, highly leveraged investments. Often only the rich used them. I saw the Wellington Fund as the future. It was balanced, which offered lower risk. It wasn't popular at first, but its popularity increased after the market crash [of 1929].

Walter Morgan was a true visionary. He is still an incredible mentor and friend. I think he will be 100 years of age this year.

In 1967 Walter Morgan gave me a tremendous opportunity. He told me to run Wellington. As an ambitious, stupid young kid, I had dramatic expansion plans. I wanted to merge with other great funds. I wanted to hire more money managers.

So we found a firm to merge with and we formed a new parent company. The merger turned out to be a mistake. They dominated the board of directors and in 1974 I was fired. It was a heartbreaking experience.

However, the shareholders of the Wellington Fund would have to also oust me from the Wellington Fund itself. I received enough votes to stay on at Wellington. I urged the board to take a drastic step—allow me to form a new company. I asked why a management company is needed—it isn't! I wanted the funds to truly mutualize. Let the shareholders own the funds and give them control, not the fund company. I wanted to go no-load. These ideas would save the shareholders millions of dollars.

The board didn't go for it. Basically I could stay running Wellington, but I couldn't market nor do investment management.

So I started out creating the new firm. A salesman

came in to my new office selling prints. His prints were of this great naval battle of Lord Nelson's. I now had a name, Vanguard.

Quietly I had been researching this idea that funds could not beat market indexes. Everybody said the idea was absolutely ludicrous. Well after much effort, we got some big firms to underwrite it and the first index fund was formed, the Vanguard 500 Index Trust. We didn't raise very much money. Our critics said the fund wouldn't last; that the returns would be mediocre in terms of return. I guess they were wrong.

KS: *It's not easy to build one of the largest companies in the world in a few decades. What is your secret?*

JB: The firm was founded on ancient principles and beliefs that one would learn in first grade. I believe in our company and I believe in our message. Investors write to me; I write them back. By the way, I found this to be very useful over the years. If just one person writes in, you learn something you don't learn from any damn (oops, I mean darn) survey. I don't care much for surveys. They are too impersonal.

This company was built on the simple notions. Really two principles. The first rule you learn in second-grade math. Gross returns − cost = net return. That is why index and low cost funds work. It's a truism. The shortest route to the top quartile in performance is to be in the bottom quartile in expenses. This is true for bonds, equities, whatever. Lower expenses equals higher yield. It's an absolute certainty. The following chart [Figure 4-1] shows two funds that earn the exact same investment return. Yet one charges 1.45% per year, the other, only .45%.

Assume that Vanguard charts roughly .28 basis points to our shareholders. Let's assume the rest of

Figure 4-1. How costs affect returns.

The Impact of Costs

	Fund A	Fund B	Fund C
Initial Investment	$20,000	$20,000	$20,000
Day 1	20,000	20,000	19,050
5 Years	28,994	27,764	26,353
10 Years	42,033	38,542	36,456
15 Years	60,936	53,503	50,432
20 Years	88,339	74,273	69,765

This example is for illustration only; it does not imply the returns available on any particular investment made today.

the industry averages a fee of 1.08. If Vanguard has roughly $300 Billion under management, it means we are saving our shareholders roughly $2.5 Billion annually!

The second principal is the Golden Rule. At Vanguard we have a special concern for human beings. And we don't just do it. We mean it.

[I must confess, I attended many business classes and seminars. Not one taught me the Golden Rule, or how to treat people. Mr. Bogle must have sensed my lost puppy-dog look.]

I recently gave a speech to a bunch of MBA candidates. I started out by asking them to solve a simple business theorem. I believe everyone got it right. I then asked how knowing and understanding human beings would help them in business. The only reply several awkward seconds later was from a student who asked what textbook that subject was covered in.

KS: *What books would you recommend to investors?*

JB: Many people have told me that my book, *Bogle on Mutual Funds,* is very useful. You should also read *A Random Walk Down Wall Street* [by Burton Gordon Malkiel]. Roy Hermansen and Walter Good wrote a good book on indexing called *Index Your Way to Investment Success.*

KS: *What does your daily reading consist of?*

JB: *The Wall Street Journal, The New York Times,* mutual fund magazines, *Forbes, BusinessWeek,* the *Institutional Investor.* I love reading the *Smart Money* and *Worth* articles when they print featured articles such as "The Fund That Will Beat the Index." I usually cut these articles out. They are most always wrong.

KS: *Do you have any heroes?*

JB: My English teacher Mr. Mason. He was a harsh editor. He taught me the correct way to write. I still do all my own writing.

      Walter Morgan. He was my first boss in this industry. He was a great mentor and is still a wonderful friend.

KS: *The big debate is passive (index) versus active management. Why are index funds so great?*

JB: Perhaps ask the question, "What makes a great fund?" The answer is the greatest fund is the one with the highest return with the lowest risk. An index is more efficient. Mutual funds can't beat market averages. It is a loser's game.

[Refer to Figure 4-2. This clearly illustrates that the index has historically outperformed the average mutual fund.]

KS: *If indexing is the "Holy Grail," why isn't it even more popular?*

JB: When we started indexing, everyone predicted that it would fail miserably. They said the returns would be poor. Our index fund started with only roughly $11 million. It is now well over $100 billion just in index funds.

The reasons why indexing is not even more popular are simple:

* ★ Indexing is counterintuitive.
* ★ Hope springs eternal.
* ★ Index funds must be bought, not sold.
* ★ There is not much profit in managing an index.

KS: *Would it be advisable for a person to have all of his or her money in an index?*

JB: Unequivocally someone coming into the mutual fund market should start off with the whole market and do it through an index. I say that for a few reasons. New investors are not used to risk. All of a sudden (by using an index) you strip two thirds of the risk. One risk is, of course, the market risk. That risk remains. You element style risk, i.e., buy a small cap fund and make more money over the long run (which may not even be true). And manager risk. Will your style cap manager manage the money better than an alternative manager or simply the index or risk more than other funds?

If you are not betting on managers and you are not betting on small or mid cap, you greatly reduce

Figure 4-2. General equity mutual funds that were outperformed by the Wilshire 5000 Equity Index. (The returns of the index have been reduced by 0.3% per year to reflect approximate index fund costs.)

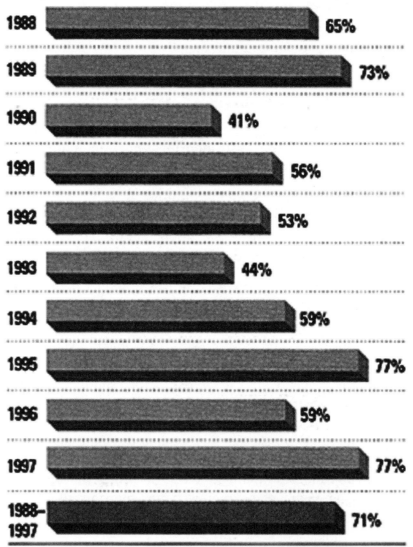

1988 — 65%
1989 — 73%
1990 — 41%
1991 — 56%
1992 — 53%
1993 — 44%
1994 — 59%
1995 — 77%
1996 — 59%
1997 — 77%
1988–1997 — 71%

the risk. You have a blend of small and mid cap. Furthermore because you own the entire market, what happens if a company does go out of business? It might represent .0001% of your portfolio.

There are two other important ingredients: costs and taxes. Index funds have lower costs and are more tax efficient. That is why indexes should outperform at least two-thirds of all mutual funds over an extended period. This is not making a big cap bet.

KS: *Why is an index fund more tax efficient?*

JB: Most mutual funds are not tax efficient. Inside a mutual fund, most managers buy and sell their stocks often, creating turnover. This turnover creates a great deal of capital gains tax. This tax will effect your performance.

It is unbelievable what mutual fund investors pay in taxes. Taxes incurred in the average mutual fund can cost the investor 2% or even 3% per year. Regular mutual funds already lag the index funds by roughly 2% or 3%. If you add taxes to this, nonindex funds just can't win. It's ludicrous. [See Figure 4-3.]

The index has very little turnover. You don't buy and sell. If there is a merger, it is usually done for stock. So it doesn't create a taxable event.

KS: *Other than index funds, how do you spot a fund that will have lower taxes?*

JB: By looking at funds with lower turnover. Furthermore, I am persuaded that those mutual fund managers that

☆ ☆ ☆ ☆ ☆ ☆ ☆ ☆ ☆ ☆ ☆ ☆ ☆ ☆ ☆ ☆

Index funds have lower costs and are more tax efficient. That is why indexes should outperform at least two-thirds of all mutual funds over an extended period.

☆ ☆ ☆ ☆ ☆ ☆ ☆ ☆ ☆ ☆ ☆ ☆ ☆ ☆ ☆ ☆

Figure 4-3. Assessing types of mutual funds for tax friendliness.

Type Of Fund	Potential For Taxable Income	Potential For Capital Gains
Taxable Money Market	High	None
Tax-Exempt Money Market	Very Low*	None
Taxable Bond	High	Low
Tax-Exempt Bond	Very Low*	Low
State Tax-Exempt Bond	None	Low
Balanced (Stocks and Bonds)	Medium to High	Medium
Growth and Income Stocks	Medium	Medium to High
Growth Stocks	Low	High
International Stocks	Low	High

*While income from tax-exempt money market or bond funds is not subject to federal taxes, all—or a portion—of the income may be subject to state taxes.

invest heavily in their own fund are more aware of the taxes. As a result these funds will have a lower turnover.

KS: *What about the idea of using a tool such as a variable annuity to defer taxes on a mutual fund?*

JB: It's brilliant. But most variable annuities use up in cost what they would have saved in taxes.

KS: *But you must acknowledge that certain funds and fund managers can beat the market.*

JB: Look. Everyone in this business from the reporters to the mutual fund rating services to the mutual fund managers says that. The problem is what are all these people going to do if everyone indexes? What is the *Journal's* headline going to say tomorrow if everyone is indexing? *"The index was up again."* Not very exciting is it?

    It is doable, but extremely difficult to find those exceptional managers that can beat the index. How many people knew Peter Lynch when he began managing money. Or John Neff when he began at Wellington?

I did a study to find out if the few funds that performed exceptionally had anything in common. I find that they did have things in common. We found seven funds that we thought were exceptional. First the funds had the same manager since the fund started performing well. And 5 out of 7 had low stock turnover (they didn't often buy or sell their stocks). All had relatively low cost.

Go for low turnover and tax efficiency. Go for low cost. Go for a portfolio manager that stays in place. Remember there could be spectacular funds. The problem is how do you, or an investor, find out about them in advance?

KS: *How do you feel about buying individual stocks?*

JB: I used to feel it was a fool's game. Lately, I am changing my mind. Buying individual stocks is really the only pure way to control taxes.

But to do it right, I think people should buy the 50 biggest growth stocks and hold them forever. I say growth not because I don't like value stocks. I say growth because if you want to control your taxes, you want lower dividends. Most value stocks have high dividends.

KS: *A few years ago you had a heart transplant. You have already made and given away more money than most people could dream of. You rarely take vacations. Why are you still here?*

☆ ☆ ☆ ☆ ☆ ☆ ☆ ☆ ☆ ☆ ☆ ☆ ☆ ☆ ☆ ☆
Go for low turnover and tax efficiency. Go for low cost.
☆ ☆ ☆ ☆ ☆ ☆ ☆ ☆ ☆ ☆ ☆ ☆ ☆ ☆ ☆ ☆

JB: I will never retire because I have an important mes-
           sage for the world. This industry has a long way to go
           to prove itself to where it wants (or should) be. Be-
           sides, what else would I do? My daughters live in the
           general vicinity. My wife spends a lot of time at the
           church. In the summer we go to Lake Placid.

KS: *How do you feel about asset allocation, modern portfo-
           lio theory, and efficient markets?*

JB: I think MPT and the efficient frontier is not right, for
           three reasons. Number one: It's based on return and
           on risk, which it should be, but they are weighted
           equal. Or, to put it another way, one percentage point
           in standard deviation offsets one percent in return.
           Remember that standard deviation is a way of mea-
           suring your risk-adjusted return. I say this unequivo-
           cally. A percentage point added to your long-term
           return is priceless. A percentage point added to your
           standard deviation is meaningless. To equate the
           meaningless to the priceless one for one strikes me as
           being absurd.
               Number two: Look at the efficiency curve [Figure
           3-2]. Don't just glance at it. What will you find? You
           will find that sometimes it is worth investing with a
           higher standard deviation. Most asset allocation mod-
           els over the last 10 years advised investors to have 20%
           of their holdings in international investments. I be-
           lieve I would have rather a higher deviation, and had
           no international exposure.
               Finally, remember that those charts and asset al-
           location models are backward looking. What is the
           point of backward-looking information?
               Those are three big strikes. Some might say you're
           out!

KS: *Then how do we asset allocate our portfolio?*

JB: We start off with common sense. Start with the likeli-
        hood that stocks will be better, if not too much worse,
        than other investments.

        If I were a young person, say investing in my
        401(K), I would not hesitate to be all in equities. If I
        were 65 and getting ready to retire, I wouldn't dream
        about having 100% in equities, but I would never have
        less than 30% or 35% in equities. Sure it's risky, but
        people are living a long time.

        To figure out what is right for you and to look at
        all the variables, I believe an adviser is worth their hire
        if their hire is for a fair price.

KS: *So the advisor is a good sounding board?*

JB: Don't look at an advisor as someone with the ability
        to outperform the market to help you beat the market.
        You should look at their cost for service. Cost for time,
        peace of mind. Cost of our knowledge. Helping getting
        you started. Being aware of your tax position. And
        helping allocating.

KS: *Do you try to forecast the direction of the market?*

JB: We are all market forecasters. What you have to do is
        discipline yourself. For years we have cautioned inves-
        tors regarding risk in the market. There is a lot of risk
        in the market. We have not told people to sell any-
        thing. Indeed we have told them to stay the course.
        However, you could read the Vanguard literature and
        what I have written for years as bearish as advice. And,
        in a sense it is. This is not a one-way street. It certainly
        has looked like a one-way street for the last three to
        three-and-a-half years, but does that mean we are
        wrong? If someone says I was wrong, I would just have
        to accept that. But I just think people are far too aware
        of reward and not of risk.

KS: *We live in the age of technology. Information is at our fingertips. Any information you have, I have as well. Good or bad?*

JB: What is the point of all that information if the index is the best bet? We have a lot of information. Fair enough. Is it leading to knowledge? I doubt it? Is it leading to wisdom, I can't imagine it!

I guess the definition of something is the reverse of a more common definition: We know less and less about more and more until we know nothing about everything. The old saying was, of course, the more and more we know about less and less until we know everything about nothing.

KS: *Do you play on the web?*

JB: Not much. I just don't have the time. I haven't book-marked many favorites yet. I do look at my e-mail. My family will spend part of the summer in Lake Placid. I hope one of my grandchildren will teach me more about the Internet.

KS: *How do you feel about international investing?*

JB: I don't believe we need to invest foreign. It's not necessary. I don't like currency risk. I know people will give me a hard time for this. They have been giving me a hard time for 15 years.

I will tell you a funny story that will be part of my next book: Abdul Raphad was an Arabian sheik. He went all over the ancient world looking for diamonds to increase his wealth. Finally, after years of searching he was frustrated and broke. He threw himself into the sea and died. Back at his former home in Persia, his successor was walking his horse. While drinking from a little stream, the successor noticed something dark. He pulled it out and it was a diamond. He had found acres of diamonds—the source of all diamonds—right there in his own back yard.

KS: *What do you think the future holds for us investors?*
      What advice are you giving your grandchildren?
JB: We are all frustrated. We all have opinions. The ticker
      is to not going to act on all your opinions. There is a
      point when you perhaps should not act. Today could
      likely be such a point. I will paraphrase from chapter
      27 of the original edition of *Securities Analysis* by Gra-
      ham and Dodd. The section talks about what went
      wrong in 1929:

> . . . . investing became so beautifully simple
> that research and analyzing statistical data has be-
> come unnecessary. The process consists merely of
> finding companies with a rising trend of earnings
> and buying their shares regardless of price. Hence
> the investment policy was to buy whatever every-
> one else was buying; a select list of highly popular,
> exceedingly expensive issues known as the blue
> chips. The idea of searching out the undervalued
> stocks in the portfolio consisted of finding the ac-
> tive and standard common stock. With slight exag-
> geration, the affairs of a investment trust could be
> administered by the intelligence and training of a
> actual laborer or a $30.00 a week clerk.

It sure sounds like the irrational exuberance that
is affecting our markets today. A few individual stocks
that everyone wanted to own have carried the stock
market over the last few years. The great majority of
the stocks greatly underperformed their respective indexes.
[Readers would do well to heed this excerpt. I inter-
viewed John Bogle before the market began to dip in
1998. He was, in a sense, comparing the stock market
of 1929 to our current market.]
Although the market is expensive today, I also question how much we should compare it to the past. You

want to know the past, you learn from the past, but it is never exactly the same.

KS: *Perhaps it as you said before—it's not an all-or-none question.*

JB: You are right. It is not all or none. People should hold investments. But even if everything looks great, even if the odds are 9 out of 10 that you will make money, an investor should not just look at the odds. Odds are not a living person. You are not a mathematical statistic. If you lose all of your money, even if the odds are only a 1 out of 10 chance, you are going to be an unhappy person if you are the 1 in 10 who does lose money.

KS: *Mr. Bogle, thank you for the interview and for fighting the good fight.*

Commentary

It sometimes takes good, old-fashioned practical advice to wake someone up. I think of this meeting and think of all the time and energy spent to pick better stocks, to find the best asset-allocation strategy. Then I look at Jack Bogle, a man who through "simple principles you learn in the second grade" has made millions and billions for himself and for the shareholders at Vanguard.

His investment approach is simple—almost *too* simple: Buy and index and hold on to it. The market will drop; it always does. When markets drop, it is a short-term opportunity, so be prepared to buy more. And don't invest more than you can afford to lose. The keys to investing include:

1. Keeping fees low

2. Keeping taxes low

3. Buying and holding

Can individual stocks or mutual funds beat the market? Sure, but it is very hard to forecast (guess) which ones will. So buy and index, and you'll immediately own a diversified, efficient basket of stocks.

Sometimes back-to-basics is more than just a cliché: It actually makes sense.

5

Mario Gabelli
Value to the Core

Name, residence	Mario Gabelli, White Plains, New York
Accomplishments	1997 Fund Manager of the Year; president and chairman of GAMCO
Hobbies	Spending time with family
Favorite reading	Benjamin Graham and David Dodd's *Security Analysis*
Influential figures	Roger Murphy, professor at Columbia University; Benjamin Graham and David Dodd, founders of Value-Based Investing
Quotable	"Conventional wisdom only results in conventional returns."
Investment style	Value, with a twist

Background

Mario Gabelli is a value investor. Period. Some of the other analysts and money managers you read about constantly change their models to keep up with Wall Street's changing trends. They continually search for a new and better mousetrap for locating the latest hot stock. Not Gabelli.

The proof of this steadfastness has been his long-term track record. Year after year Mario has been investing based on his true bottom-up, fundamental style of management. "Stick to your knitting," says Gabelli. Some years his returns are nothing spectacular, perhaps because the latest fad is Internet

stocks and all the money is going to the high-growth investments as opposed to value-based investments. Other years he
is the fund manager of the year. As he says, "If certain years
my style of investing is out of favor, all the better for me to load
up on cheap stocks." It's easy to say, but believe me, when you
have investors screaming in your ear, it takes nerves of steel.
Yet when the day is done, Gabelli and value investing always
seems to end up on top.

Although it is true that he does the same thing year after
year—bottom-up fundamental analysis based on the principals of value investing—he has done something previously
thought impossible. Gabelli actually improved on value investing by adding one critical element, the catalyst, which is explained in more detail later in the chapter.

What I enjoyed most about meeting Mario Gabelli is how
easy he makes value investing sounds. After interviewing certain individuals, my head was pounding, and I was a bit depressed. "Can I ever be a successful investor?" I wondered.
After meeting Gabelli, I was charged with enthusiasm and renewed vigor. "Yes." I thought, "I can do it too!"

I knew meeting Mario would be special. Although I usually
don't get nervous meeting someone, Mario's reputation is sure
to give anyone clammy palms. Mario Gabelli is one of the best-
known fund managers in the world. His mutual funds manage
more than $10 billion in investor funds. In 1997 Morningstar
rated Gabelli mutual fund manager of the year for his outstanding management of the Gabelli Asset Fund. Super Mario's funds enjoyed the best risk-adjusted return over the
longest period of time.

Mario Gabelli's involvement with the investment industry
dates back to 1967. He founded Gabelli Asset Management in
1977. Now over 120 employees call him boss. And he is in demand. He is regularly interviewed on CNBC, and he is commonly the subject of feature articles in *Barron's, Forbes,* and
Fortune. Why all the fuss? That's easy: Gabelli has an enduring,
nearly mythological track record for picking good stocks.

Mario Gabelli is the essence of value investing. Value investing is perhaps the oldest, most well-respected style of investing. He actually studied with the founders of value investing: Benjamin Graham, David Dodd, and Warren Buffet. In fact, Buffet and Gabelli both studied at Columbia University, where Gabelli earned his MBA.

Finally, word has it that Gabelli has no tolerance for incompetence. He is a man on a mission and won't wait for people that can't keep up with him. Knowing that he doesn't suffer fools gladly put me on my best behavior (and added to my nervousness at meeting a veritable oracle of value investing).

Preinterview Info

It seemed so appropriate for a day when I was going to meet a man whose success is founded upon going in the opposite direction of the momentum-chasing herd on Wall Street: To go to Gabelli, I went to Grand Central on a weekday morning and took a train bound for White Plains, New York. I thought it fitting that while everyone else was riding trains into Wall Street, I was bucking the trend and leaving the heart of the beast.

The rumors that he is demanding were true, to an extent. When I asked a foolish question, he told me so. I was trying to get him to tell me his secret on how he picks such good stocks. After asking this question 10 different ways he finally told me to go take a class or read a good book on value investing. He simply follows the original principles of value investing, and value investing is a well-documented and thoroughly researched topic.

I was looking to find Mario's special secret, but it wasn't until after the interview that it finally hit me. Mario's big secret is that he is disciplined, informed, and true to his colors. He sticks to his value investing approach, he turns over more rocks than the other guys and gals, and he is one of the most well-read individuals I ever encountered.

Mario is also practical—he knows how to make connections between the things he reads about and the events that unfold in front of him at any moment in time. For example, after I mentioned that I live in San Diego, Mario repeatedly used San Diego analogies to make various points. He told me about local companies, and he told me why El Niño has improved San Diego's fishing. Throughout our conversation I could see how Mario's success is built on his keenness to learn and listen, and the ease with which he applies his well-rounded knowledge to different situations.

Mario impressed me in other simple ways. Who knows what to expect from a man that has made so much money in the market? He took calls from his daughter during the interview. He personally drove me to the train station (not even a limo driver). After dropping me off he was going to pick his daughter up at a car repair shop. His offices are pleasant, but not extravagant. His personal office is just big enough for a couch, desk, and chairs, and it's decorated with baseball caps from various companies he has invested in. Value. Mario speaks it and lives it.

Mario's commitment to value is evident in his daily life—he walks the talk. His clothes were presentable but comfortably well worn—another sign of value. Mario grew up like most of us. He worked as a caddy and as a waiter in the Catskill Mountains. He paid his way through school, started his career as an analyst, took calculated risks, and worked his way up.

People warned me that Mario was harsh. While he is indeed direct, I interpreted his frankness as a sign of his love for his business—again, he won't suffer fools who would stand between him and his calling. That's one reason for his success.

As Mario was getting ready to leave the office, he picked up what looked to be a heavy carry-on bag. I asked him if he were going out of town, or if that were research. He opened the bag and showed me tons of reply cards. Mario explained that his company sent out an investor survey and, to his pleasant surprise, they received lots of responses. He wanted to read, and write back to, all of those that commented. Wow! That's a man who cares.

The Interview

KS: *Would you sum up your investment style for us?*

MG: I look for bargains. I look for the kind of investments you would want to participate in.

Conventional wisdom only results in conventional returns. Fads of investment and predictions of the next big thing come and go. Meanwhile, many companies have actual value already on the balance sheet and income statement, rather than potential value or possible future value. The secret is that some of them don't have it discounted in their capitalization—yet. Value stands the test of time.

☆ ☆ ☆ ☆ ☆ ☆ ☆ ☆ ☆ ☆ ☆ ☆ ☆ ☆ ☆
Conventional wisdom only results in conventional returns.

☆ ☆ ☆ ☆ ☆ ☆ ☆ ☆ ☆ ☆ ☆ ☆ ☆ ☆ ☆

KS: *Obviously it works. You are a great stock picker who seems to be in the right place at the right time. How do you accomplish this?*

MG: We miss a great deal of winners, too. We don't take chances on high-momentum stocks or certain technology stocks. We stick to our knitting and look for value with a catalyst.

KS: *You have done something people didn't think possible. You improved on value investing by adding a key ingredient—a catalyst. Tell us about that.*

MG: A company could be undervalued, but it probably will stay undervalued without a reason to unleash the price of the stock. That's the reason you need a catalyst.

People say "the market" is overvalued. But you can find bargains. However, you need an active ingredient, some event, to surface those values. Telecom reform in 1996 changes the entire telecom arena. This is an example of a catalyst. The drop in capital gains taxes. Management succession. What if the founder of Champion Spark Plug is old and might pass on? Perhaps the family will want to sell the company. These are all reasons that a stock might unleash value.

The theory of a catalyst helps take value investing, which is an academic discipline, and turn it into a practical discipline.

KS: *Give me something specific.*

MG: Regulatory changes. Banks had very strict requirements on what they could sell to the public. The rule was based on Glass-Steagall [Glass-Steagall Act of 1993]. This rule was recently relaxed. As a result, companies like Merrill Lynch could now buy banks. Banks could buy other banks. Banks could sell investments and insurance to the public.

KS: *So how would little ol' me capitalize on that?*

MG: You look at all banks selling less than two times book value, with less than $1 billion equity capital, and banks in a state that is going through deregulation. These banks could be good candidates. Either a takeover or increased earnings or something that would drive the stock higher.

KS: *Any other examples of catalysts?*

MG: Find hidden assets. There could be valuable land on the books of a company that the accounting is still showing at original costs.

One of my assistants bought a cat. We researched that spending on pet products is excessive. We researched population trends and saw that trends of pet ownership would probably continue. We researched the companies that should benefit the most from this trend. This research led us to buying a company called "First Brands."

Catalysts exist in many areas. Natural gas distributors are in a period of deregulation. There is a tremendous consolidation happening in film and entertainment stocks. Someone is buying these companies up.

KS: *But how do you know, how can you spot the next major deregulation or industry consolidation?*

MG: It's the ripple effect. By being aware of transactions in business. You can start seeing why multiples can increase. But even if there is a catalyst, don't overpay for the company. A good example is the radio business. Although this industry had deregulation, the price of the stocks went so far above the intrinsic value or private market value that the return was not worth the relative risk.

KS: *To do this you must spend time reading.*

MG: You bet. I read everything I can. If I am interested in a certain sector, I read their trade stuff. All big business magazines, the *Wall Street Journal.*

KS: *Mario, you are so close to Manhattan and Wall Street where all the action is. Why are we sitting here in White Plains, New York?*

MG: We do keep an office in Manhattan. However, this is our main office and it's terrific. First, the employees that live in the city, don't mind coming out to the suburbs. The hour on the train is economical and can be very productive. The employees are happy to be simply saving money on what it would cost them to park a car in the city.

I love it for the cost savings. What we save in rent by working out here basically pays for my entire research staff!

KS: *You're the essence of value! What's your day like?*

MG: I wear two hats. I run the Gabelli Value Fund, and I am the CEO of Gabelli Asset Management Co. Every morning the research department meets. I often sit in on these meetings. The research department talks about headlines and what is going on in the world today. They talk about companies. The various companies they are researching and what they think. By bringing it up in the entire group, two heads are better than one and someone else that is researching something similar might offer valuable insight.

Often companies and analysts host conference calls with the management of firms we are interested in. We will might listen in on these conference calls.

Our analysts are hands-on. We are often going in the field to meet with management of companies we like. We talk to the financial officers and top executives to get a feel for the company and the management running the company. It's important to meet important personnel and listen to what they say about the future.

KS: *What's the reason for your success: you or the people you surround yourself with?*

MG: You create an organization. My analysts bring ideas to the table; meaning I am looking for people to bring me ideas, not the other way around. I am strict in hiring only Ph.D.s.

KS: *You want all doctorates?*

MG: I want people who are Poor, Hungry, with a Deep desire to succeed.

KS: *Let's move on to the stocks you buy. It seems like you have been very influential in management. Do you buy stocks so that you can influence management?*

MG: No! You have it backward!

[Mario's response was so vehement that I thought he was going to throw me out.]

Start over. Management is extremely important to the franchise you are buying. It's like the prince kissing a toad. It's very tough for a toad to change its appearance. Good management will help accelerate the progress of a good business. I remember we liked a Pepsi bottling company very much based on their numbers and value. However, it was a great franchise with bad management. As a result, we didn't buy it.

Now, as far as our influence over management goes, we're large investors. We often invest in smaller companies that do not have a large amount of shares outstanding. So if we like a company and buy $20 million worth of stock, it could represent a large percentage of the stock outstanding. In that regard, our vote is a little more influential. But that is not why we buy a stock. I hope we are buying a stock with good management.

KS: *We live in the information age. Information is available to everyone, which challenges the preeminence of the Wall Street old boy's network. Your thoughts?*

MG: We all should be working in a fishbowl. Anyone should be able to see anything. The Internet literally changed the availability of information. I don't think too much information is bad; the hard part is finding the actual information you need. Really getting to the heart of it.

Think about this. If I want to shop for a new car, everything I need to know is right at my fingertips. My 14-year-old granddaughter can find information on the Internet better than anyone. Think about what that is going to do for their generation.

KS: *Many people say the market can't go down because too many people are investing—buying into the market causing stocks to rise. Can this trend continue?*

MG: It may continue, but I don't think it is necessarily good. It could create a huge backlash. What if, because of demand, it raises the dollar so high so as to be terribly detrimental. Our companies would not be able to export products as effectively. It would upset imports and exports, and then American companies would suffer if foreign companies didn't buy their products. The economy is very delicate and no easy answers exist.

KS: *Be careful what you wish for, because you just might get it?*

MG: Something like that.

KS: *What are your thoughts on indexing or passive investing?*

MG: The index approach has made money, and it's not a bad way to invest. But I don't think that the returns the index has experienced recently are the norm. Companies as a whole have been increasing their earnings more dramatically than the historical average. We have experienced an economy where everything came together—the sun, the moon, and the stars are aligned. We saw a period of declining interest rates, increasing company earnings, and powerful inflows of funds. This allowed companies to grow their profitability faster than the historical rate. All of this has allowed the S&P index to provide substantial returns.

If you invest in an index, you need to be happy with the return that the index grows at. I don't think many companies will do as well in the future. Over the next 30 years that very well may be an 8% or 9% annualized return. If you take the index and say GDP (gross domestic product) will grow at 2.5%, and inflation will average 3% totaling 5.5%, that is what stocks, on average, will grow at.

Furthermore, indexes lure mindless investors into buying into businesses without regard to valuation. I think many investors are unprepared for the time that the index actually starts to fall. I would caution those investors to be aware of the weakness.

What we do is entirely different than buying an index. Our goal is to earn a 10% real rate of return plus whatever inflation was. To do so we find companies that we think have hidden value with a catalyst that will unlock that value allowing the true value of the company to be realized.

☆ ☆ ☆ ☆ ☆ ☆ ☆ ☆ ☆ ☆ ☆ ☆ ☆ ☆ ☆ ☆

What we do is entirely different from buying an index.

☆ ☆ ☆ ☆ ☆ ☆ ☆ ☆ ☆ ☆ ☆ ☆ ☆ ☆ ☆ ☆

KS: *But it's practically the norm to compare a mutual fund's performance with the index.*

MG: I don't think it makes much sense. However, we started the fund in 1977 and the fund has averaged over 21% for more than 21 years. We don't compare ourselves to the index. Our benchmark is 10% real return plus inflation. Thus we strive at an absolute return not related in any way to the S&P 500 index.

If you compare us to the index, the S&P has had two down years while we had one. What's interesting is that we buy smaller/medium size companies (under $1 billion in market capitalization). We have handily beaten the Russell 2000, we beat the S&P, and we beat our own benchmark.

KS: *Some people think that analyzing the direction of the market is critical. Do you agree?*

MG: Analyzing the direction of the market is not so important to me. If you have a home, and three people are bidding on it, sooner or later it will come up in price. We are bottom-up stock buyers. We are looking for good value now—sooner or later the stock should have three buyers bidding up the price.

Some people chase fads or are looking for a quick run on their stocks. Our style works. We will not be in the top 10% (of investment returns) every year. However, over 30 years value investors will have one of the leading investment returns. You need stick to what you do. Run a marathon, not a short distance.

Other styles of investment selection are good too. Investors don't need to choose only one style. They can choose several, but they must stick with it— whatever style they chose. I remember a few years ago when everybody was buying earnings momentum stocks and the headlines read "Value Investing Is Dead." This talk is nonsense and people that chase the latest fad are usually unhappy investors.

KS: *When you look at a stock, what are you looking for?*

MG: I am looking at buying a business, not a piece of paper. When buying a business I study the fundamentals to try to determine the value of the business, not the stock price. This is what I call private market value (PMV), which is similar to the intrinsic value of the business. Our job is to determine if the stock price is above or below that PMV. There are a lot of great companies but the stock price is too high above the PMV.

☆ ☆ ☆ ☆ ☆ ☆ ☆ ☆ ☆ ☆ ☆ ☆ ☆ ☆ ☆ ☆

I am looking at buying a business, not a piece of paper.

☆ ☆ ☆ ☆ ☆ ☆ ☆ ☆ ☆ ☆ ☆ ☆ ☆ ☆ ☆ ☆

KS: *Let's talk a bit more about your fundamental criteria and how you determine PMV.*

MG: It's much easier when you think you are buying the business. You are going to look at the value of the franchise. You are going to look at what the cash-generating possibilities of that franchise are. Free cash flow is important. You will look at management, cash, receivables, inventory, the goodwill value of a company, earnings power, and so on. You want to look for revenue growth, net earnings growth, book value. Look for low but improving multiples.

The key, of course, is to find a business that is worth $2, is trading for $1, and that should grow to $10.

KS: *Tell me more about the multiples.*

MG: No hard-and-fast rule exists. We tend to buy leading companies that have a history of earnings rather than brand-new ones where we have to project. Often we will not start a new position in the fund if its price to earnings ratio is more than 30 times forward the 12-month estimated earnings. Often we will start selling once it reaches this target.

We like to analyze the balance sheet. Are receivables growing? We look at what assets the company has, minus the debt (called net). We want a lot of high net value. We also like to see cash flow. Statistically undervalued companies have lots of cash flow. With cash flow companies can do a great deal. Perhaps they will buy back their own stock, which usually triggers more demand for a stock. Or they might be a potential takeover candidate for a company that likes businesses that generate a cash flow.

KS: *Why is cash flow important?*

MG: If I were going to buy a company, the cash flow is critical. Many companies report great earnings, but if the cash flow is deteriorating, I would wonder why. Cash

flow could be important if a company is going to acquire other companies. It could be important as a
takeover candidate as many companies like to see the
companies they take over have cash flow.

*[See Chapter 2 and the end of this chapter for further
discussion on cash flow.]*

KS: *And then the catalyst?*

MG: Yes.

✵ ✵

Mario's Approach in a Nutshell

* Find the intrinsic value.
* Look for stocks Wall Street has forgotten about. Look for
  stocks that have fallen, low P/E stocks.
* When finding the stock, search for catalysts that will un-
  lock the stock's value.
* Look for stocks that have the potential for generating
  high cash flow.
* Don't buy and sell your stocks too often.

✵ ✵

KS: *Obviously for someone that is not as familiar with in-
        vesting as you, the market is confusing. What do you
        recommend to us normal people?*

MG: Read. Understand the fundamentals. Get that by read-
        ing Graham and Dodd [their *Security Analysis*]. Keep
        your eyes open. Or use professional management.

KS: *Thank you for a most enjoyable, educational time.*

The Value Approach to Investing

Throughout the interview, Mario kept insisting that he follows
the key principals of value investing. If someone wants to
know his secret, they need to become well versed in the rules
of value investing.

Gabelli's first step in locating a value stock is to find its intrinsic value. The following is a quick summary of the value approach to investing and how it relates to a stock's intrinsic value. As good as this summary may be, it is still no substitute for immersing yourself in careful study—something you may want to do if Gabelli's take on investing appeals to you.

Everyone wants a good value. The concept of value investing, however, focuses on what the company is worth right now—forget the future or what the company might earn next year. Is there a possibility that the company is worth more than the stock is trading at?

There is an age-old debate between efficient market theorists (proponents of index) and those who believe you can consistently beat an index. Value investors believe that anomalies exist that, when identified and exploited, allow you to beat market averages. They also believe that the market's pricing mechanism is based on faulty and frequently irrational analytical processes. Because of this market irrationality and inefficiency, the price of many securities only occasionally coincides with their true intrinsic value.

An example might be the price of gasoline. Suppose that the intrinsic cost of a gallon of gas (raw materials, refining, distribution, and retail profit mark-up) is $1 per gallon. Drive across the country and you'll probably end up paying anywhere from $.90 per gallon to $1.50 per gallon. Just as all sorts of forces—from regional gas station monopolies to snowstorms to city-specific driving habits—make the price of gas seem wacky and irrational, all sorts of idiosyncratic forces make the price of a stock wander far and wide from its intrinsic value.

In 1934 Benjamin Graham and David Dodd, the founders of modern security analysis, articulated the principal that inefficient markets create circumstances where fundamentally sound companies could become undervalued. This theory of investing in undervalued companies with dominant industry positions has provided consistently above-average returns through the majority of this century. Basically, the stock price sometimes does not reflect the true value of the company. Therefore the astute value investor should be able to buy an undervalued stock and have it go up when the market finally recognizes the value. History shows that if you have enough patience, value investing pays.

Key Principles of Value Investing

Intrinsic Value

Mario Gabelli referred to this as private market value (PMV). Although the definitions vary slightly, you are really trying to determine what the true value of the company is. To determine that value, look more at the facts: a company's economic value, the nature of its business, the investment environment, historical earnings, and current multiples. Basically everything we discuss from here forward is done in an effort to find the intrinsic value.

It is believed that, as a whole, companies have a well-defined life cycle. This cycle consists of three stages (Figure 5-1):

1. A series of struggles and setbacks

2. A halcyon period of prosperity and persistent growth

3. A final phase of maturity, characterized by a slackening of expansion and perhaps a loss of leadership or even of profitability

One of the keys to finding intrinsic value is to determine where on this life-cycle curve the company is. Evaluating larger com-

Figure 5-1. Company life cycle.

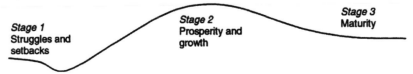

Stage 1
Struggles and
setbacks

Stage 2
Prosperity and
growth

Stage 3
Maturity

panies is somewhat easy as the numbers are concrete and there is a history to follow. Smaller companies in the early stages are harder to evaluate. Since more risk is involved with smaller companies, however, you should be rewarded better if the stock does go up.

Free Cash Flow

The money a company brings in is called cash flow. **Free cash flow** is important to value investors—it's what's left after the current assets pay off the current liabilities. Think of free cash flow as the earnings of the company apart from certain expenses such as interest, depreciation, and taxation. With free cash flow, companies can expand, buy back stock, or buy other businesses. Because all these uses of cash flow can affect a company's intrinsic value, free cash flow is critical to the value investor. Wall Street analysts will often use the acronym EBITDA (earnings before interest, tax depreciation, and amortization) instead of cash flow.

Capitalization Rate

The capitalization rate is the worth of a company at a given point in time. It is relatively easy to figure. Take all of the stock in a particular company that is outstanding and multiply it by the current stock price. For example Microsoft (MSFT) has 2.5 billion shares outstanding. If the price of one share of Microsoft is $100, the company's capitalization rate is $250 billion.

The prudent investor must ask if the company is worth $250 billion. The question is nebulous. Value investors will study first to see what the company should be worth today by making a reasonable assumption about the company's growth prospects and how it will do in the future.

Factors That Affect Capitalization Rate

So many factors can affect what a company is worth. Some analysts look to the economy and the product a company sells.

If the product is needed and expanding and if the economy is solid, an analyst can deduce that a company is worth more. If a company has a great deal of cash flow, this might be a reason for the company to be worth more.

Consider, for example, America Online. Assume that it shows annual sales in 1998 at $2.8 billion. A value investor might look at those sales and compare that figure to the capitalization rate. Further, a value analyst might figure that since America Online has 14.4 million subscribers it means an investor is paying roughly $1,685 per subscriber. I would think that based on what America Online earns per subscriber, this number is high.

The quality of management is important in trying to find the capitalization rate and the fair market value of a company. For example, if you knew Lee Iaccoca were going to manage the firm, you might think the capitalization rate deserves a higher multiple. Financial strength is also important to a company's capitalization rate. Take two companies having the same per share earnings. One is riddle with debt. The other has surplus cash, no debt, and pays a dividend. The second company is obviously more solvent and probably deserves a higher multiple.

Common Stock Analysis

Common stock analysis leads to a valuation of the stock. Once you have a valuation, you compare it to the current price to determine whether or not the security is an attractive purchase. This valuation, in turn, would ordinarily be found by estimating the average earnings over a period of years in the future and then multiplying that estimate by an appropriate capitalization factor.

A detailed value investor will attempt to find the value of a stock and compare it to the current price at which it trading. To find the value of a company, a value investor might attempt to estimate the average earnings over a period of years in the future and then try to determine what the present value of the future earnings is worth. Obviously this is not an exact science. So a value investor might try to create a risk premium based on how expected returns will fluctuate and how new products, new markets, and external economic developments will affect a company's intrinsic value. Although not an exact method by any means, the following formula is sometimes used:

Value = Current earnings × (8.5 plus twice the expected annual growth rate)

When looking at growth, consider looking ahead at least five years if not more. Remember, often such a projection can be found in services, such as First Call, that pool analyst recommendations.

Value investors love (or learn to love) crunching the numbers. If you love to do that too, learn how to read and interpret fundamental criteria including balance sheets and income statements.

Short-Term Anticipation

The difference between value investing and other investment strategies is that the others are often looking for short-term profits. They may do this a number of ways; for example, they may measure the earnings of stocks with the greatest quarterly earning momentum and thereby deduce that such stocks will have the quickest growth. And when the rate of change in earnings changes, it's time to sell. This approach is one major reason for volatility in the markets today. You will find that value investors typically hold stocks much longer than momentum-oriented investors. Short-term momentum is irrelevant when you are considering a company's intrinsic value and long-term prospects.

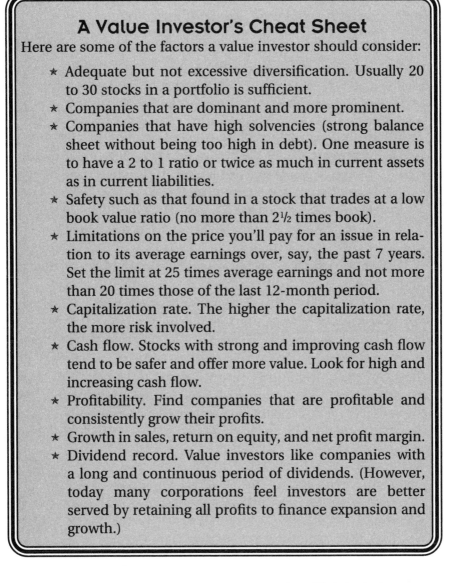

A Value Investor's Cheat Sheet

Here are some of the factors a value investor should consider:

* ★ Adequate but not excessive diversification. Usually 20 to 30 stocks in a portfolio is sufficient.
* ★ Companies that are dominant and more prominent.
* ★ Companies that have high solvencies (strong balance sheet without being too high in debt). One measure is to have a 2 to 1 ratio or twice as much in current assets as in current liabilities.
* ★ Safety such as that found in a stock that trades at a low book value ratio (no more than 2½ times book).
* ★ Limitations on the price you'll pay for an issue in relation to its average earnings over, say, the past 7 years. Set the limit at 25 times average earnings and not more than 20 times those of the last 12-month period.
* ★ Capitalization rate. The higher the capitalization rate, the more risk involved.
* ★ Cash flow. Stocks with strong and improving cash flow tend to be safer and offer more value. Look for high and increasing cash flow.
* ★ Profitability. Find companies that are profitable and consistently grow their profits.
* ★ Growth in sales, return on equity, and net profit margin.
* ★ Dividend record. Value investors like companies with a long and continuous period of dividends. (However, today many corporations feel investors are better served by retaining all profits to finance expansion and growth.)

Commentary

Mario Gabelli is a successful investor for three basic reasons:

1. He sticks to his knitting. He is a value investor and does not change his style.

2. He has incredible foresight. This foresight comes from being a student of people, from being well read, and from being "in the trenches." Much of the downfall of certain big-shot investors is that they perch too long in their ivory towers. They become out of touch and as a result can not accurately assess what is happening in the markets.

3. He has conviction. Sure he is demanding, takes a definitive stand, and is not afraid for people to know his thoughts. But this is not a vice. It is perhaps one of his biggest positives. Many investors have great ideas, but they second-guess themselves. They don't tell management or their employees exactly what they think.

Without these qualities you may still be a good investor, but, I doubt, a great one.

As for value investing, it is certainly not as sexy as chasing the fastest growth stocks or looking at the latest fad, but it works. However, I believe as long as I am alive that, over time, stocks will be priced according to what someone would pay if they were actually going to buy the company. Gabelli calls that private market value. And someone who studies value investing will have a better chance than someone who doesn't determine what the private market value is, and thus be able to pick winning stocks.

6

Marty Zweig
The World's Premier Forecaster

Name, residence	Marty Zweig, New York City
Accomplishments	Founder (and president) of Zweig Funds, one of the lowest-risk funds in the business; a regular panelist on *Wall Street Week with Louis Rukeyser*
Hobbies	Jogging, family, baseball
Favorite reading	*Reminiscences of a Stock Operator* by Edwin Lefèvre
Influential figures	Albert Einstein, Louis Rukeyser, Mother, Uncle Mart, J. P. Morgan
Quotable	"Hope for the best, prepare for the worst."
Investment style	Market forecasting and quantitative analysis

The interview with Marty Zweig primarily explores how to forecast the market. However, I am so impressed by the Zweig Funds' stellar stock picking that I also interviewed its chief money manager, David Katzen.

Background

Marty Zweig is a legendary investor known primarily for his market forecasting ability, which is continually rated among the best of the best. His success is built on his ability to first call the direction of the market and then decide where to in-

Portions of this chapter are reprinted from Marty Zweig's *Winning on Wall Street, rev. ed.* (New York: Warner Books, 1994).

vest. He appears as a regular panelist on the extremely popular PBS series *Wall Street Week with Louis Rukeyser*. Marty has been quoted in and has written articles and on the cover of our nation's most respected magazines including *Money, Forbes,* and *Barron's*. He first became famous for his first two newsletters that for a long time were top-rated by *Hulbert Financial Digest*. The newsletters forecasted the direction of the market, and got it right more than anyone else. He really came to fame during the market crash of 1987. At the time, Zweig published a very credible, well-followed newsletter. Just prior to the day of the market crash (black Monday), Zweig had alerted his investors to begin selling stocks and raising cash. The market lost 22.6% during 1987. Marty's model portfolio climbed roughly 9%.

The biggest surprise in meeting with Zweig was actually his organization. Sure Marty impressed me (or depressed, I am not sure which yet) as an individual, and an incredibly erudite individual at that. But aside from Marty, I found a first-rate organization. His chief money manager, whom you will hear from later, is David Katzen. David is a tremendous asset and an incredible money manager, and to back the two gems, I found a crack team of computer programmers, marketing people, and money managers.

Preinterview Info

It was a typical cold winter day in Manhattan, New York. The butterflies in my stomach told me I was going to meet an investor I truly admired. I left the hotel early to make sure I would make it to Marty Zweig's office on time. I found the building an hour prior to my interview, so with time to spare I ducked into the Barnes and Noble across the street. Leafing through magazines, I found numerous mentions of Marty Zweig. Confirmations of what I already knew—I was about to meet a heavyweight champion.

If you are awed by money, try this on for size. The Zweig
organization manages around $9 billion in assets, which trans-
lates into over $100 million in fees per year. It sounds great,
but don't forget he earned his money the hard way. No, he
didn't inherit it, he earned it over decades. Marty Zweig has
steadily demonstrated for almost three decades his skill in
managing money. *Forbes* magazine ("Living with the Bull, Pre-
paring for the Bear," April 6, 1998) called his transformation
the investment equivalent of apotheosis—the process by
which mortals become gods. Can you imagine receiving a
compliment like that from *Forbes,* a magazine that is much
quicker to rip someone apart than to offer a compliment?

The fact is, Zweig's ability is quite uncanny. Historically
he has proven to be one of the best at forecasting whether the
market is going to go up or down, and then having the conviction to act on that forecast. How has he become so good? I
believe one key to Zweig's success is his attention to the details. Once he finds a pattern that seems to work, he continues
to doubt it, test it, and retest it.

However, I never met anyone more afraid of losing money
than Marty Zweig. When I asked him about this, he agreed and
stated that he is constantly running scared. His entire exis-
tence consists of trying to determine the direction of the market. As you will learn, Zweig believes if you can call the
direction of the market, you have won more than half the investing battle.

To forecast the market, Zweig has probably probed, measured, monitored (Whew! Sounds like a doctor!), and created
more forecasting models than anyone you will ever meet. You
would think that his organization is filled with employees that
are money experts. Actually this isn't true. The organization is
filled with computer smart people and mathematicians. Zweig
would say that forecasting the market is not so much about
understanding money as it is about creating a model, about
finding a trend and sticking to it.

Another of the reasons for Zweig's success as a market

forecaster is that he isn't afraid to study history to find anomalies wherein the market will behave a certain way, a majority of the time, when certain conditions present themselves. His knowledge of history and market history is extensive. For instance, he could probably tell you where the market would be (higher or lower) six months after the market is up ten days in a row. Or declines lead advances for 10 days. Or what month is better for investing. When researched and measured, these vital clues become the core model to forecasting the market. He's the kind of guy who will research everything. If he thinks that there is a measurable correlation between the stock market going up on the days that Pluto goes into retrograde, he would probably explore that correlation to see if it were something measurable and worthy of adding to his model. Although this is a far-fetched example, you get the point. During the interview you'll learn exactly what his most accurate and important indicators really are.

I finally felt I was in a typical Wall Street–type firm. Even knowing all of this, I still didn't know what to expect. What I found were nice offices. The offices had great views, and the furniture was modern and new. Of all the interviews I have done, I finally didn't feel I was overdressed in my navy blue suit and red tie. Yet what did I find when I was ushered into Zweig's office? A regular guy! There goes my Wall Street image. Zweig was in sweats, he said, because of recent knee surgery. He was eating a salad out of a Styrofoam container and was cleaning off the floor salad dressing he had just spilled. He was recovering from knee surgery, and was nervous about his upcoming wedding.

The Interview: Part One

KS: *You have made it to the top of Wall Street. I am sure*
        many of our readers are anxious to learn how you got
        to where you are.

MZ: Hard work I guess. I came to New York to work as a finance professor at Baruch College. I was making about $14,500. I decided to write a newsletter hoping to make an extra few thousand per year. I started the *Zweig Forecast* in 1971. Although the newsletter gained in popularity I continued to teach until 1981.

KS: *Who helped you?*

MZ: No one!

[If I thought for a moment he was disinterested, after this question he raised his gruff, raspy voice and his eyes came back into focus.]

I started my newsletter in my apartment. I had no help and no money. I even licked the postage stamps and carried the letters in a postage sack to the post office.

KS: *You and your firm do so much research and analyze so much it seems quite overwhelming. Can an individual investor be a successful one?*

MZ: One person can sit in front of a computer all day, analyze a bunch of information, and buy terrible stocks. Another person may have a gift, a knack. This person can spend limited time, but invest very well. Overall, I think that if I were having back problems I would seek the best doctor to fix my back. If I wanted my money invested, I would seek the best money manager to invest my money.

KS: *What about doing what our parents did: Buy a stock and simply hold it?*

MZ: Not a bad strategy but it could blow up in your face. How many stocks that were a part of the Dow Jones are still a part of it? You should be invested in the best stocks, or cash, or bonds, or whatever. But only invest in the best ones.

KS: *We are in a very peculiar stock market environment. Is this the time to be investing?*

MZ: Because I forecast the market, I get that question a lot. Even when I am bearish on the market I still own stocks. It is not an all or none question. It is a question of degrees.

KS: *You are obviously a very busy man and are responsible for many employees, people's money, and a family. What's your basic philosophy?*

☆ ☆ ☆ ☆ ☆ ☆ ☆ ☆ ☆ ☆ ☆ ☆ ☆ ☆ ☆ ☆

I'm always nervous. In tough times I can't eat, I can't sleep.

☆ ☆ ☆ ☆ ☆ ☆ ☆ ☆ ☆ ☆ ☆ ☆ ☆ ☆ ☆ ☆

MZ: Managing money is something I take very seriously. Some people shrug it off. I'm always nervous. In tough times I can't eat, I can't sleep. However I have also gotten to a point that I try to do only the things I enjoy. When I was a kid I worked at a gas station. I hated the smell of gas on my hands. To this day I won't pump my own gas. It is worth it to me to pay for the service.

KS: *The other day I visited with Mario Gabelli. As you know he is a value investor. Everything in his life seems to be value. He was expounding on the amazing Internet and how he searched for cars on the Internet to determine best price, dealership, and so on. Do you do the same thing?*

MZ: I have two boys. We needed a big car. My 12-year-old told me what the best car was, a Ford Explorer. We went to the dealership and bought it on the spot. Did I pay an extra $2,000? Maybe. My time is more valuable than anything. I will always pay a premium for my time. Besides, who can argue with their kid?

KS: *Do you have time to read?*

MZ: I read a lot. Reading offers interesting insight. I read industry magazines and newspapers. I read major business magazines and lots of books. I love biographies. The last one I read was the one on Warren Buffet. I thought it was well done.

KS: *What are your thoughts on Warren Buffet?*

MZ: What a great investor. He has this uncanny ability to see where a company will be many years out. However, if I am smart enough to pick a couple of good stocks, I don't want to hold them through a bear market. He does.

KS: *Being in this business over three decades you see a great deal of change. How should that affect an investor's discipline for investing?*

MZ: Everything is always changing. We need to change with it. If the major stocks were agriculture and now they are manufacturing, you need to know that and make allowances for it. With all my indicators and computers I still realize that the game is always changing. This is not like chess where you have a fixed board and a finite number of possibilities. When investing, there is no substitute for judgment.

KS: *What makes you good at the subjective part?*

MZ: I always believe individual investors need to stay disciplined based on their indicators. However, there will always be something that you cannot factor into the model. Investors will need to determine how much of an impact that one thing will have on their investments. That one thing could be Asia or the year 2000 problem. These factors are where you must make a judgement call. You simply cannot know what the short-term effect will be. If you think that a strong possibility exists for your investments to go down, you might raise a bit more cash.

KS: *You keep coming back to the "proverbial bear market," yet the returns you and David have achieved are stellar. Unfortunately your mutual funds never will show as a best performer because you always have a portion in cash. If you were fully invested you might be a number one fund.*

MZ: We win by not losing. I am scared to death of a down market. Ultimately it's not what you make in bull markets, it's what you *keep* over the course of your investing life time that counts. [See Figure 6-1.] Not only is a bear market devastating, but, understand, just about everything goes down in a bear market.

KS: *But diversification will help in a bear market, won't it?*

MZ: Even if you are diversified, what safety does it give you? Virtually everything goes down! Look at this chart [see Figure 6-2].

KS: *What about indexing? Will that help absorb the impact?*

MZ: Take the last two declines, 1987 and 1990—look at the

Figure 6-1. Frequency and extent of market declines.

DJIA LOSS	Number of times in the past 96 years	Average occurrence	Time since last occurrence
-10%	65	every 1.5 years	6 years
-20%	39	every 2.5 years	6 years
-30%	21	every 4.6 years	9 years
-40%	11	every 8.7 years	22 years

Zweig Mutual Funds

Source: InvesTech Research. "Annual Risk" from one year's high to the next year's low since 1900.

Courtesy Zweig Mutual Funds

Figure 6-2. Effectiveness of diversification in a bear market.

Domestic Equity Fund Styles	8/25/87- 12/4/87	7/16/90- 10/11/90
Large-cap growth	-30.2%	-19.2%
Large-cap value	-25.4%	-16.0%
Mid-cap growth	-33.7%	-22.5%
Mid-cap value	-27.1%	-17.5%
Small-cap growth	-35.3%	-26.3%
Small-cap value	-32.0%	-22.0%

Zweig Mutual Funds

Source: Strategic Insight. Returns do not include sales charges. The performance data quoted represent past performance, which is no guarantee of future results.

Courtesy Zweig Mutual Funds

declines. The average growth fund was down more than the S&P 500, showing us that they (a) can lose money, and (b) can lose more than the index. Active management does not always lower your risk. [See Figure 6-3.]

Let's assume you had a large cap value fund. Do you really think you are emotionally equipped to handle a downtrend of 25% of your money?

Bear markets are frequent and I am scared. We take great pride in the fact that our mutual funds stress loss prevention, and we have done a great job of it. Our objective here is to reduce risk.

KS: *How much should a person have in stocks, bonds, and cash?*

MZ: If I believe a bear market is coming, I don't want to be fully invested in stocks. However, the amounts differ for everyone.

Figure 6-3. Bear market maximum declines.

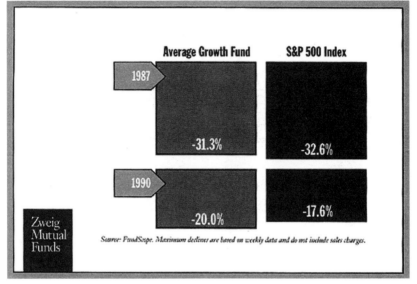

Courtesy Zweig Mutual Funds

What if I said that over the last 50 years, the stock index averaged 12%. However 37 of the last 50 years the market went up, meaning that there were 13 years when the market was down. How much would you want to invest in the market? One investor might say, "I don't need the money and if I can average 12%, I want to be 100% invested." Another investor might say, "This isn't a lay-up; 13 down years is tough. I only want 70% of my money in stocks."

KS: *Marty, how do you pick a stock?*

MZ: Whatever works. I will test anything. The President's being impeached. I would study the moon's alignment to the earth if I thought it would work.

How Marty Times the Market

[At one point in our conversation, I posed the question, what creates a bull market?]

MZ: For a raging bull market, you need falling interest rates, probably an economic recession (that helps the Fed to loosen up and rates fall), lots of cash on the sidelines, good values. Namely, low P/E ratios. And a great deal of pessimism, because pessimism means the market should rally very strongly, and the first rally of a bull market is the best.

KS: *Marty, your whole premise is that a successful investor moves in and out of the market. This, in essence, is timing the market. Experts say timing the market is dangerous. Just by missing the best days, you can kill a good return.*

MZ: Look, stocks provide a far better return over time than bonds and cash. You can't argue that. People will often say there is no need to time the market, because if you just hang in there, that wealth bestowing long-term returns will be yours. However, the truth is, investors can't stomach the downdrafts. They bail out and keep their money in cash. It is actually one of our indicators that we will discuss later. We do try achieving growth in our funds, but with much lower volatility.

People have been critical of timing the market. People often state that if you miss the best days in the market, your return will be greatly reduced. Although statistics show that investors do give up a lot by being out in an up market, look at this figure [Figure 6-4]. It shows what happens to your holdings in a down market.

We don't simply market time and pull out of all our money; the process is gradual. Assume one of our indicators becomes bearish. I might say, "Let's cut our holdings by 5%." David might say, "Today's a weak day in the market, let's do half now, half tomorrow."

KS: *It's been said that you'll analyze just about anything.*

MZ: All in all we have 70 different factors in our market model. The most important indicators are the *mone-*

Figure 6-4. Promotional piece from the Zweig Group supporting timing the market.

The Myth of "The Forty Best Days"

As usual, Mark Twain said it best:
There are three kinds of lies: Lies, Damned Lies and Statistics."

Here's a *statistic* from the "buy-and-hold" school:
Average Annual Return: 17.6% (S&P 500: 1980-1989)

But if you missed the *best*	Your average annual return fell to
10 days	12.7%
20 days	9.6%
30 days	6.9%
40 days	4.4%

Source: Ned Davis Research, Inc.

This "study" purports to tell you to buy-and-hold forever and always, because if you miss good days, bad things happen to you. At Zweig, we politely ask:

What if you missed the bad days?

If you just managed to miss the *worst*	Your average annual return soared to
10 days	26.6%
20 days	30.5%
30 days	33.8%
40 days	36.9%

Source: Ned Davis Research, Inc.

Nobody's encouraging you to miss good days. But at Zweig we say: **The key to success in equity investing is being out of harm's way on the really bad days!** And that takes active risk management from Zweig.

Oh, and by the way...
Even if you missed the best and worst days, you outperformed the heck out of "buy-and-hold" **with a much, much smoother ride!**

If you missed both the *best and worst*	Your average annual return was
10 days	21.1%
20 days	21.4%
30 days	21.4%
40 days	21.3%

Source: Ned Davis Research, Inc.

Courtesy Zweig Mutual Funds

tary indicators. Next are *sentiment indicators* (flows into mutual funds). Finally, *momentum indicators* need to be looked at. [emphasis added]
   Our model has 100 points. If we reach 100, we are 100% in stocks. If we reach a terrible rating on our model, 0, we would probably be about 40% in stocks.

Monetary Considerations

Monetary considerations deal primarily with interest rates. I always say; don't fight the Fed, and it's true. If interest rates are going up, it's almost always bad for the stock market. When interest rates are going down, it's generally good.

The Federal Reserve is really the bank that controls all banks. It has a board, and this board decides the direction of interest rates. If it feels the economy is overheating, it raises rates, and vice versa.

One of the easiest ways to watch interest rate movements is through the prime rate. Most major publications such as the *Wall Street Journal* and *Barron's* have prime rate information. The prime rate doesn't change every day. One of the prime rate's virtues is that it lags beyond other interest rates. It usually falls only after a drop in federal funds rates or in the yields on certificates of deposit. Changes in interest rates *lead* the market. The graph in Figure 6-5 clearly illustrates that market trend over a long period of time. As interest rates trend higher, the stock market trends lower. The reverse is always true. The graph spans three decades yet the indicator almost always works.

Sentiment Indicator

The crowd tends to follow the wrong signs near market tops and bottoms. . . . Let's start in the depths of a bear market. The economy is usually in a recession or worse, business profits are tumbling, and investors are punch-drunk from suffering

Figure 6-5. Comparison of stock market and prime rate trends: 1968–1998.

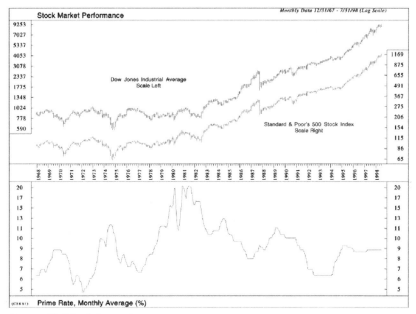

Courtesy Ned Davis Research

huge losses during a year or two of falling prices. Bad news is making headlines; good news is not even a dream at this point. Conditions have been so awful for so long that most people can see nothing else but the downtrend continuing. It's amid such doom and gloom that bear markets bottom and bull markets begin, meaning that the vast majority of people are wrong, precisely at the bottom.

At this point the Fed will probably lower interest rates. Stocks gain value. The economy will probably lag for a little while longer; however, stocks will begin to move up.

With the following indicators, remember one thing: Beware when the crowd is too one-sided. If everyone thinks the market is rising, I'm nervous, and vice versa.

To track sentiment indicators, try watching the mutual fund cash to asset ratio (see Figure 6-6). This statistic is often found in *Barron's* Market Laboratory section. It tracks mutual

Figure 6-6. Forecasting record of mutual funds based on cash/ assets ratio: 1954–1993.

Date	Cash/Assets Ratio Extreme Optimism	Extreme Pessimism	Dow[a]	Dow Change to Next Funds' Extreme	Funds "Predictions" Right	Wrong
July 1956	4.7%		516	− 29 points		X
June 1958		7.2%	487	+148		X
April 1959	4.4%		635	− 57		X
September 1960		6.6%	578	+123		X
December 1961	4.3%		701	−128		X
September 1962		7.0%	573	+296		X
November 1964	4.5%		869	− 60		X
October 1966		9.7%	809	+ 70		X
September 1967	5.2%		897	+ 1	X	
March 1968		9.2%	898	+ 38		X
December 1968	6.1%		936	−191		X
July 1970		11.8%	745	+217		X
April 1972	4.6%		962	−307		X
September 1974		13.5%	655	+282		X
September 1976	4.9%		937	−124		X
March 1978		11.3%	813	+ 25		X
September 1978	6.9%		838	+ 32	X	
May 1980		10.4%	870	+136		X
March 1981	8.0%		1006	−177		X
June 1982		11.7%	829	+430		X
December 1983	7.5%		1259	−158		X
June 1984		10.3%	1101	+166		X
March 1985	8.1%		1267	+168	X	
October 1985		10.4%	1435	+334		X
February 1986	8.4%		1769	+ 68	X	
September 1986		10.2%	1837	+439		X
March 1987	8.6%		2276	−323		X
April 1988		10.9%	1953	+198		X
January 1989	10.9%		2289	+415	X	
February 1990		12.5%	2704	+279		X
June 1991	8.0%		2983	+299	X	
January 1992		9.6%	3282	+ 61		X
February 1993*			3343			

Dow points gained on funds' predictions: +983
Dow points lost on funds' predictions: −4,796
Net points lost on funds' predictions: −3,813

*Dow price is third Friday of following month when cash/assets data are available.

funds that are either raising or lowering cash. When they are raising cash, you would think that would be bearish, but this is a contrary indicator and it is in fact bullish.

Momentum Indicator—The Trend Is Your Friend

Momentum indicators are examples of technical indicators. Any calculation using price and volume is part of technical indicators. There are two important measurements of stock momentum: price and volume.

Price

When forecasting the market, the advance/decline indicator [A/D] becomes very important. Advances comprise the total number of stocks that rise on a given day. Declines are those that fall. If 1,000 stocks are up on the day and 500 are down, the advance/decline ratio would be 2 to 1. Of course, advances dominate when the market does well, and declines predominate when the market does poorly. It is a sign of very strong momentum when advances overwhelm declines for a significant span. And vice versa.

There is a great truth that strength in the market leads to greater strength. I recommend tracking the A/D ratio over a 10-day period. If, over this period of time, advances beat declines by a ratio of 2 to 1, this is very bullish. Critics might say, if you invest after 10 days of strong market movement you are getting in too late. Actually statistics show if you had bought after this, you would have made abnormally large profits.

[Recall Figure 2-6, which shows the Dow Jones as the top graph and the advance decline line below it. This is what Marty is referring to.]

In fact, this is such a powerful indicator, that since 1953 there were only two incidents that the market went down within six months after the advance decline had a ratio of 2 to 1 for over 10 days. Any other time in the past there were 10 days with twice as many advances to declines, it was very bullish.

Volume

A second momentum indicator uses the ratio of up volume to down volume. Up volume comprises the total volume of all stocks that rise on a given day, and down volume totals all that decline. This can be found in *The Wall Street Journal* or *Barron's*.

Research suggests that when 90% or more of the volume is on the upside in a given day, it is a significant sign of positive momentum. In other words, when daily up volume leads down volume by a ratio of 9 to 1 or more, that tends to be an important signal for stocks. It only occurs roughly twice a year.

In fact, every bull market in history, and many good intermediate advances, have been launched with a buying stampede that included one or more 9 to 1 up days. Two within a relatively short period of time is extremely bullish.

As great as these two technical indicators are, they are limited in practice. They seek tremendous bursts of momentum, and this occurs only occasionally—thus the buy signals are rare. In addition, these indicators are not extremely useful in giving sell signals.

The 4% Model

The 4% model was developed by Ned Davis. This model will not provide for an investor if the market has spectacular returns over a short period of time, but it is a truly awesome model for providing consistency for long-term market direction.

The main ingredient of the 4% model is the Value Line Composite Index. This index is an unweighted price index of approximately 1,700 stocks. Many publications, including *Barron's,* publish the Value Line Composite Index. You only need the weekly close of the composite. This trend-following model gives a buy signal when the weekly Value Line Index rallies 4% or more from any weekly close. It then gives a sell signal when the weekly close of the Value Line composite drops by 4%. [See Figure 6-7.] This is a great indicator because it helps you stay with the trend as opposed to fighting it. You never want to fight the trend. The trend is your friend.

Since 1966 there were 50 buy signals, while only 28 were profitable (56%). However they produced an average profit of 14.1% per trade. Conversely, the 30 losing trades lost only 3.5% per trade. This is a perfect example of cutting your losses short and letting your profits run.

Figure 6-7. The Value Line Composite Index.

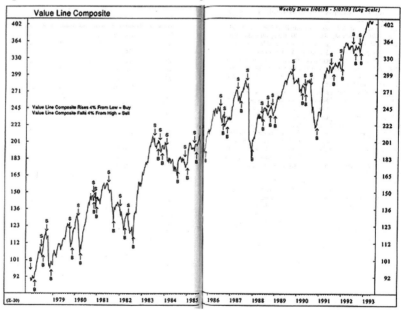

Courtesy Value Line

The Interview: Part Two

KS: *You are famous for creating a few proprietary indica-*
        tors of your own. Here we are late in 1998, and people
        are wondering about a possible bear market.

MZ: One reason why I don't think we will have a bear mar-
        ket is because everyone is very bearish.

KS: *All right, I'll bite.*

MZ: Contrarian indicators work extremely well. Meaning if
        everyone were bearish, I might be bullish. We created
        an indicator of where the direction of the market is
        going by polling investment analysts and asking if
        they were bullish or bearish (market sentiment).

        In the 13½ years we have been doing this, 13
        times the investment analysts were overall pessimistic
        on the market. In 12 of the 13 times, the contrarian
        indicator worked and the market moved up. There
        have only been 3 other times when the analysts we
        polled were as pessimistic as they are now. In all three
        instances the market was at a bottom and surged
        higher.

KS: *What parting advice would you give all the aspiring*
        investors?

MZ: First, never put all your money in stocks. Second, stick
        to whatever methodology you use. It might be that
        you have a certain model including ratio analysis. For
        example, you will not buy stocks with ROE less than
        20, or a P/E ratio higher than 10, or earnings growth
        less than 15% annually. Understand that more impor-
        tant than what you put in the model is that you stick
        to the model you choose. Third, know how much risk
        there is in investing and how much you are willing to
        lose (your risk tolerance).

        Marty Zweig is the ultimate market forecaster, but it is also
        important to note that his organization has picked great stocks

as well. Heading up the stock-picking department is David
Katzen.

Individual Stock Selection—
Meet David Katzen

David Katzen buys stocks based on quantitative analysis. His
style is similar to Louis Navallier's (see Chapter 10), but they
differ in how they use quantitative analysis. Utilizing **quantitative analysis** is basically a form of investing that is based on a
very specific set of indicators, numbers, and measures. It
would differ from, say, Mario Gabelli and value investors who
are more subjective. For example, they want to get a feel for
management, which is not something that can be measured.

David joined Marty in 1986 after a career that began in
1980 working for Value Line. (Value Line is still considered the
premier service for fundamental research ranking stocks.)
David is all numbers. His background is math, his masters degree is in math, he is math.

KS: *Tell me how you invest.*

DK: My goal is growth. We want to add value. If that is
       measured by beating the index, then we want to beat
       the index.

       We use a quantitative research model to pick win-
       ning stocks. Quantitative research is basically any-
       thing that consists of a well-defined strategy for
       picking stocks. To do this we have built a computer
       model. Our goal and what we have done successfully
       is to turn the odds slightly in our favor. Similar to ca-
       sino odds. Because they play thousands of hands, they
       can turn the odds. It's the same as buying hundreds
       of stocks.

KS: *Do you own lots of stocks?*

DK: Yes, our average portfolio probably owns over 200
       stocks. I am confident in our model, but not overly

confident in any one particular stock. What we find is the stocks that move up, tend to move way up. Many don't move much in either direction, and the ones that go down don't go down nearly as far as the ones that go up. Overall we might only have 55% winning stocks at any one time.

☆ ☆ ☆ ☆ ☆ ☆ ☆ ☆ ☆ ☆ ☆ ☆ ☆ ☆ ☆ ☆
Our average portfolio probably owns over 200 stocks.
☆ ☆ ☆ ☆ ☆ ☆ ☆ ☆ ☆ ☆ ☆ ☆ ☆ ☆ ☆ ☆

KS: *It sounds like an index fund.*

DK: No way! Too many stocks in the index would never fit our model. If we are able to capture the best stocks in the index, and avoid the worst, we should consistently beat the index. Our stock picking in fact has consistently beat the index. Our mutual fund usually does not beat the index because we keep a great deal of cash. If you look at our risk it is much lower than the index. Further, look at our fund's performance in the down years. While many other mutual funds and the index get hit hard in down markets, our funds have historically performed well in down periods of the market.

Our model includes over 1,500 large and mid-cap stocks. This is the most liquid segment of the market. The top 10% (150) stocks, the model says, are the most likely to outperform—thus the buy list.

KS: *With so many people investing today, it seems that stocks are more expensive than ever. How can you find good deals?*

DK: Whenever I look at the universe of stocks I look at the stock's history. I compare it to the stocks in that sector, and compare it to the stock's history. Then I compare it to the market as a whole. So earnings have grown and the price to earnings ratio (P/E) has grown as well. It's all relative.

Assume a stock's P/E usually trades at a 20% discount to the Standard & Poor's 500 Index. However, now it is trading at the same multiple as the S&P Index. That could be a sign of full value. So I might conclude that that stock is expensive relative to every other stock in that universe. This should work regardless of new market models or paradigms. So I don't say stocks trading at 30 times earnings are expensive. I look at the relationship of this stock compared to the market. This works regardless if the market is trading at 50 times earnings or 5.

For example, in the 1970s and 1980s banks sold at 50% of the then going market multiples compared to the index. Now they are at 90% market multiple. Therefore one might conclude bank stocks as overvalued. So if bank stocks traded at a P/E of 5 and the market averaged a P/E of 15, and now bank stocks are trading at a P/E of 14, one would conclude that they are fully valued.

KS: *You created a stock picking model. Tell us about it.*

DK: I think we look at the same plain vanilla indicators as many others. The reason our model is so complex is a result of what we see and how we interpret it. In all, our model is probably looking at 15 different major concepts.

You will probably find that many other money managers use similar indicators. The key for our model is how they relate to each other. And that is truly the "secret." Determining at what point what looks favorable. When is a lead unfavorable? To determine this you must compare the stock to historical norms, then the sector's history, and the stock. This is not a Graham and Dodd value approach. Our approach is not to find long-term investments to hold for years and years. Our approach and our model is designed to find stocks that should beat the market over next 6–12 months.

For example, in 1992 we bought McDonnell-Douglas. At the time the stock had only average growth characteristics. It was trading at a low valuation (low P/E, price to book, and price to cash flow) and it was at the low end of a 20-year historical range relative to the market. The stock had moved with the market for the year. All of a sudden earnings growth improved and profit margin widened. Our model spotted its valuation as so compelling. We were surprised by this event because, as you may remember, in 1992 nobody was buying defense stocks. With the cold war ending, what need was there? Like your friend Mario Gabelli, in order to buy a stock we want a reason why it will go up, a catalyst to get it going. In this case we found that its profits were expanding in a dead industry because it cut costs. We decided that if it can grow profits in a bad industry, think what it can do if the industry turns around. Further, we like buying stocks based on risk versus reward. This stock has a low risk compared to the reward. We bought it and made a terrific profit over the next several years.

[The reader should find it interesting that Katzen bought a stock in an unloved sector (defense). This is almost exactly opposite of something that William O'Neil, for example, suggests doing.]

KS: *It must have been tough buying a stock in a dead industry.*

DK: Yes, that is the hardest part. The hardest part is not building the model, it's the discipline. It takes mental discipline. You must stick with your model.

KS: *Does your model include talking to management?*

DK: No. Although talking to management may be impor-
        tant to some people, I believe I can add the most value
        by overseeing and continually improving the model.

☆ ☆ ☆ ☆ ☆ ☆ ☆ ☆ ☆ ☆ ☆ ☆ ☆ ☆ ☆ ☆

**Although talking to management may be important to
some people, I believe I can add the most value by
overseeing and continually improving the model.**

☆ ☆ ☆ ☆ ☆ ☆ ☆ ☆ ☆ ☆ ☆ ☆ ☆ ☆ ☆ ☆

KS: *What about buying stocks that are hitting their new
        highs compared to their new lows?*

DK: I have bought stocks that have hit new highs and new
        lows. However, if I had a choice, I would always take
        the new high list to buy stocks.

KS: *That must mean you are taking more risk, that you
        have more exposure to the downside.*

DK: We did a study on that, and ironically it's opposite to
        what you would think. Our stocks tend to have a low
        price to earnings ratio but a growth rate higher than
        the industry and the market as a whole. Our stocks are
        growing at faster rates than their historical norms. Our
        style seems to buy a stock in the early stages of a profit
        acceleration/growth cycle. So although we may buy a
        stock hitting a new high list, we usually hit it at the
        early stages of the cycle.

KS: *Do you have an objective when buying a stock?*

DK: We want to beat the market with less volatility risk.

KS: *Have you accomplished this?*

DK: Our stock portfolio over the short- and long-term has
        consistently beat the Standard & Poor's Index. The
        reason why our mutual fund does not beat the index
        is because we can't stand volatility, and as a result we
        hold lots of cash.

KS: *When do you sell?*

DK: Once in the fund, the stock stays there until it falls into
       the bottom half of the universe, based on our model.
       If a fund is not in the top decile in our model, even
       though the stock might still be better than many other
       stocks, we don't want it. We only want the stocks that
       reach the top of the universe of stocks we are tracking.
       There is no compromising with that discipline.

✫ ✫

David Katzen's Stock-Picking Secrets

★ Lowest P/E ratios relative to the stock's history and rela-
  tive to the market
★ Stocks consistently increasing their return on equity
★ Strong earnings growth
★ Strong sales
★ Buying by corporate insiders
★ Looking for lower debt
★ Insider trading
★ Tracking the analysts (We like to see stocks where ana-
  lysts continually revise their numbers upward.)
★ Surprises (We like stocks that beat the analysts' expecta-
  tions.)

✫ ✫

The Zweig/Katzen Strategy Put to the Test

If I were following the Zweig/Katzen strategy, this is what I
would do:

1. *Track the market.* Use the indicators and charts Marty
   gave us. Use *Barron's,* the *Wall Street Journal,* and *Investor's Business Daily* to track the indicators that Marty

suggested. Increase my holdings if the market heads up. Go all the way down to 25% stock exposure if I think the market is heading down.

2. *Screen stocks for an acceleration compared to their norm.* I would go to one of the Internet sites such as Microsoft Investor or Quicken.com and look at a stock that has a growth rate faster than its norm, that is increasing profits faster than its norm. I'd also look for increasing return on equity and increasing cash flow.

3. *Look for a change in analysts' projections.* Again, I would go to a site such as MS Investor Investools or First Call to screen stocks about which the analysts have revised their earnings numbers upward.

4. *Find the stocks that still have relative value.* This means the valuations based on price to earnings, price to sales, or price to cash flow have not increased as fast as the potential increase in the stock's price.

5. *Look for other positive indicators.* I would look for insiders of a company that are buying stock in their company or a company decision to buy stock back. These are terrific examples of stocks that have positive indicators.

Commentary

The time I spent with Marty Zweig and David Katzen was priceless. Although they have powerful computers and numerous indicators, I found that I could follow many of the more important steps.

Tracking the market trends does seem important. Figure 6-4 illustrating what happens if you miss the worst days in the market proved this to me. Watching the advance/decline and monetary indicators, such as interest rates, and watching the direction of the major market indexes seem to be fairly easy yet extremely helpful in calling the direction of the market.

Furthermore, although David Katzen's stock-picking model is quite elaborate, I found that he does make mistakes and still makes a great return on his stocks. He stated that its not uncommon to have as much as 40% of his stocks down at any given time. In addition, his indicators are not extremely exotic or hard to find. Looking for high growth with low multiples doesn't seem too hard. Try to find stocks that will beat analysts' expectations, look at companies that are buying stocks back, and simply use other commonsense factors to achieve successful quantitative analysis and market forecasting.

7

William J. O'Neil
Ambassador to the Individual Investor

Name, residence	William J. O'Neil, Los Angeles
Accomplishments	Editor/owner of *Investor's Business Daily*
Hobbies	Running, working out, reading, baseball, and politics
Favorite reading	Gerald Loeb's *Battle for Investment Survival*; Jesse Livermore's *Reminiscences of a Stock Operator*; Bruce Jenner's *Finding the Champion Within*; Dale Carnegie's *How to Stop Worrying and Start Living*
Influential figures	Thomas Edison, Abraham Lincoln; also the sort of positive-thinking people covered in the "Leaders and Success" column of *Investor's Business Daily*
Quotable	"Success in a free country is simple. Get a job, get an education, and learn to save and invest wisely."
Investment style	Growth/momentum—CAN SLIM system—with a heavy technical bias

Background

He has already thought of it, researched it and, if he deemed it worthy, added it to his repertoire. Everybody in the money business knows of William J. O'Neil; his unique personality, his incredible research, and the various companies he owns. O'Neil literally supplies stock research to the biggest and best on Wall Street. If you ever wonder where to find certain information such as stocks with the greatest momentum, percent of institutional ownership, or stocks with the biggest change in volume, you should look no further than O'Neil's publications.

Companies under O'Neil include Daily Graphs, Investor's Business Daily, and O'Neil Datagraphs, as well as research services to institutional clients (such as mutual funds). In addition to his companies, O'Neil created the famed CAN SLIM method of stock picking, the essence of his investment style.

I believe William O'Neil would be successful regardless of his vocation. Similar to other all-stars, his top management is fiercely loyal to him. They completely and totally stand by him and make his cause their cause. I got a feel for this as I talked with his employees. You can hear and see the respect and admiration while talking about him. They tell vivid stories about how they all know what they will be in for when he is gone for a day or two. Without fail, O'Neil will have three or four completed yellow pads of paper with notes and ideas for them to put into reality. They suspect that he doesn't sleep.

In a nutshell, I attribute his success to the following characteristics:

* He possesses tireless energy.
* He researches his convictions and isn't afraid to take action. He was one of the first to compile an extensive database to track stocks, and he has written many books on the subject.
* He is always looking for ways to improve.
* He is logically and efficiently organized.
* He has the ability to affect change immediately (the bullet approach).
* Discipline and hard work are pillars of his success.

Preinterview Info

William O'Neil is a true entrepreneur. I think of an entrepreneur as someone that has a great idea and capitalizes on it. As in the case of most of our all-stars, O'Neil is not only a great investor, but he is very strong minded, a good teacher, and greatly respected by his employees. He has definitive opinions regarding Wall Street, stock picking, and the future of America. Perhaps because of his success, or perhaps because he has shunned the "good old boys" network, Wall Street has not made it easy for him. Many of those on Wall Street thought his investment ideas were ludicrous. They thought his idea for another business and investment paper were ludicrous. His critics have been harsh.

All of this knowledge about O'Neil made me that much more excited as I was driving to his office in Los Angeles. At first I thought he would be in a high-rise in downtown Los Angeles with a picturesque view of the city. But as I was driving up from San Diego it become clear that I was not headed toward downtown, but, rather, toward Marina Del Rey, which is in the Santa Monica area. I figured that his offices must be in one of those "Ocean View Suites." Much to my surprise, the directions led me not to an ocean view suite but to an industrial park. If it were not for the little sign on the building that said *Investor's Business Daily,* I would have sworn I was in the wrong place.

I walked into an unpretentious waiting room. The paneling was pure 1970s, and the chairs were probably as old as me. Where was that Wall Street image I was looking for? The glitzy offices? The unmistakable traces of money? These all-stars have *money* because they are smart; they know how to spend it, and how to make it. Like the other all-stars, I believe O'Neil abhors spending money on anything that won't return him more than what he put in.

The Interview

KS: *Tell me a little about your past, your background, and how you got to where you are.*

WO: I was born in Oklahoma City and raised in Texas to a

lower middle class family. I graduated from Southern Methodist University. My father died at a young age, which made life a little tougher. Perhaps that is where my work ethic started. I worked hard. I went and joined the Air Force and worked my way through college. Once I finished college, I began my career as a stockbroker. The stock market always fascinated me. I used to watch the tape (still do). So deciding to be a stockbroker seemed natural to me. By the time I was 30, I was pretty successful at investing, doing so well on a stock called Syntex that I was able to buy a seat on the New York Stock Exchange.

Back in the early 1960s, the investments I made as a stockbroker did very well. The problem was it seemed I spent more time selling than actually doing research. Yet my personal portfolio from 1962–64 increased around twenty-fold. So I decided to make a change and move to California. I figured California was a place to succeed.

By this time, I really started tracking, studying, and researching stocks. Basically, I wanted to know why certain stocks continued to do well. And I wanted evidence. So, I started the first database in the securities industry. Currently this database has information on over 10,000 publicly traded companies. This database helped me create models of the greatest stock market winners.

Today this research is bought by hundreds of institutional firms, brokerage and money management firms. Much of this is published in many of our publications and services including *Investor's Business Daily, Daily Graphs,* and *WONDA.*

KS: Investor's Business Daily (IBD) *is what you are best known to the public for, but you were doing well selling your research to mutual fund companies and the like. Why start* IBD?

WO: In 1984 I started *IBD*. I was frustrated and upset that
       the public did not have a simple resource to help
       choose stocks. *IBD* is designed to create an efficient,
       organized source for making investment decisions.
           Originally I thought our major source of readers
       would come from senior management of major com-
       panies. To my surprise *IBD* has turned into an indis-
       pensable tool for individual investors. It is designed to
       give an investor all the pertinent information in order
       to make informed stock picks. The paper allows a
       reader to screen a great deal of information, in many
       different ways, making it easy and quick to find what
       you are looking for.
           We must have done something right. It is now
       America's fastest growing business newspaper and the
       only serious competitor to the *Wall Street Journal.*

KS: *A real David and Goliath Story?*

WO: Well, the paper makes sense. And since we began we
       have now branched out. The paper promotes certain
       causes, we have a New America Page, and other seg-
       ments the readers love. But the bottom line is every-
       thing that I discuss in CAN SLIM for picking a stock
       can be found in *IBD*. We have been back-testing and
       building our database for 30 years. What a great, and
       inexpensive, way for investors to tap into this data-
       base resource.

KS: *You publish your own paper. You are not financed by
       billion-dollar Wall Street brokerage firms or huge mu-
       tual fund empires. So how did you manage to succeed
       in such a tough world?*

WO: Read the beginning of my book *How to Make Money
       in Stocks*. There I say, "Success in a free country is
       simple. Get a job, get an education, and learn to save
       and invest wisely. Anyone can do it. You can do it."

KS: *That's wonderful, but easier said than done. How do you do this practically? Even your employees are so loyal. Many have been with you over 10 years.*

WO: To have a growing firm, you must have the ability, rather it's a necessity, to change directions immediately. Further we have created a horizontal organizational structure. Really it's an environment that promotes idea generation and eliminates ego problems. There is an open door policy, even mine.

    The firm is also excellent at what we do. We have excellent research and ideas. Many of our ideas are beta tested for up to a year before we will open them to the public.

    Successful firms must have a quick response to customers.

KS: *What books would you recommend for individual investors?*

WO: *How to Make Money in Stocks* and *Investor's Business Daily's "Guide to the Markets"* both by William J. O'Neil.

KS: *Do you watch CNBC?*

WO: Only to look at my advertisements.

KS: *What about a hot story idea from CNBC?*

WO: Hot stories could be detrimental. I follow a system using fundamental and technical indicators. Other stimuli could lead me astray. All of that can taint your system. To be successful you must stay very disciplined.

KS: *What about regular reading?*

WO: If you are looking for ways to pick stocks, I believe there is nothing better than reading *Investor's Business Daily* regularly.

KS: *Prior to interviewing you, I did my research. I read your paper, I've seen you speak, and now speaking with you*

18

today reaffirms my early suspicion. You are incredibly optimistic about so much. I see so many negative and possibly drastic events that are looming over the horizon. How can you stay so optimistic?

WO: We won the cold war. We are in times similar to the 1950s, the United States is dominating, we are on top. There is an incredibly high demand for our technology. Further, an enormous amount of wealth exists in our country. For those that can learn a simple easy-to-use system for profiting in the stock market, it shouldn't be too difficult to make lots of money.

KS: *Would you say that anyone or anything helped make you more successful?*

WO: So many people have been strong influences. Thomas Edison, Abraham Lincoln, and many more. It does not matter that I have not met these individuals personally. If people can follow strong, positive examples, you can beat the odds and become successful. Actually this is the exact reason why we created the "Leaders & Success" column in *Investor's Business Daily.* Each day it covers the lives of people who have made it, and discusses how they got there.

       To be successful, people can follow great examples, and people should strive to think right.

KS: *What do you mean by thinking right?*

WO: Believe in your success. Have the right attitude. Choose to be successful and you will be. Thinking right is the key to achieving one's goals. For my company I often bought positive thinking libraries for many of my associates to help make sure they think right.

       Quite simply, one person cannot influence your life. It is a compilation of hundreds of examples of success. You can think your way towards a very productive and successful life.

KS: *As we speak, the stock market keeps climbing; up, up and away. When will it end?*

WO: We are living in a system that is self-adjusting. Study the recessions that the United States has experienced. You will find that their severity is seriously diminished from years ago. I believe now we will see more in sector rotations. Even as the market reaches new highs, many sectors, and countries for that matter, have already experienced their own bear market.

William J. O'Neil's Secret Investment Style

KS: *Let's talk about your style of investing. What are you? How do you do it? [I always ask that question with a smile.] It's interesting, of all of those I have interviewed, your style is one of the easiest to follow. You offer very specific do's and don'ts. Further, the indicators that you track are easy for the average investor to track. [One other important point to note regarding William J. O'Neil. He does not invest money for individuals, nor does he own a mutual fund or money management firm. He and his firm provide research and information. I find this a plus, as he is less biased toward any one thing. He has no vested interest in any specific stocks or mutual funds. He collects no fees or commissions for recommending a particular stock or fund.] To start, how should we get ready? What kind of research will we have to do?*

WO: It's really simple. You need *Investor's Business Daily*. Possibly *Daily Graphs*. That's it. The information is all there, it's just a matter of using it.

        Our method of stock picking came by using our historical data dating back to the early 1950s. Through exhaustive research and ongoing analysis, we wanted to find similar traits of the best winning stocks. We found certain criteria kept appearing in the most successful stocks. So we devised a formula, a system for buying stocks with the criteria most important in picking a good stock. This system has an acronym called CAN SLIM. Each letter in CAN SLIM stands for one of the seven key factors that all of these past superwinners have in common.

Too many other investors take an academic approach to investing. Academics might state, "Stocks with low P/E and low book values are technically undervalued and should go up in price." This is not academia—this is what has worked and should continue to work.

[The reader will find it interesting that many other all-stars profiled in the book use P/E a great deal.]

KS: *If this research began in the early 1950s, have not times changed? Isn't the criteria for picking stocks changed?*

WO: Actually the principal doesn't change. Perhaps in the 1950s one of my criteria would have been earnings growth. In the past I might have found that the best performing stocks had earnings growth of 20% annual growth. Today, I still look for earnings growth, but I might look for 30%.

KS: *The CAN SLIM system uses a great deal of earnings growth and earnings momentum. Recently this type of investing has been quite popular. However, hasn't this method also produced huge casualties with the stocks getting crushed?*

WO: In any bear market you will give some money back. Stocks will go down. But you should also be looking at the market. If you watch the market averages, you will notice certain market averages and the relationship to each other should be more accurate with knowing which are overvalued. I don't think I have missed a bull/bear market by more than five days. While one

sector is having a bear market, another could be having a bull market.

KS: *I noticed in studying CAN SLIM that you don't use one
of the most popular ratios for determining if a stock is
under- or overvalued, The price to earnings ratio
(P/E)—it's not there.*

WO: So many investors use P/E ratios inappropriately. You
don't need P/E to evaluate stocks. Factual analysis of
each cycle's winning stocks shows that P/E ratios have
very little to do with whether a stock should be bought
or not. Back-tested studies prove that percentage increases in earnings per share are much more important in determining if a stock will advance than the
P/E ratio. Further studies prove that the stocks that
grew the most grew their P/Es as well. A stock that
started out with a 20 P/E could ultimately grow so
that the P/E is 45.

KS: *Before we study CAN SLIM, any other last minute
words of wisdom?*

WO: Do not project into the future. Statistics and readily
available information should be used to make your
investment decisions.

Be disciplined following the rules of CAN SLIM.

Never let emotions enter into decision making. Be statistical and stick to the basics of equity trading.

Finally, start small. On the cover of *IBD* is a quote,
"For people who choose to succeed." You can
choose to succeed.

★ ★

CAN SLIM

Fundamental to O'Neil's approach to investing is a system represented by an acronym, CAN SLIM. CAN SLIM is a system
made up of seven factors. This approach is very thorough, as
it includes both fundamental and technical analysis for picking
stocks:

1. Current quarterly earnings growth

2. Annual earnings increase

3. New products, management, highs, more people trading the stock

4. Supply and demand

5. Leader or laggard

6. Institutional sponsorship: a little goes a long way

7. Market direction: how to determine it

☆ ☆ ☆ ☆ ☆ ☆ ☆ ☆ ☆ ☆ ☆ ☆ ☆ ☆ ☆ ☆ ☆ ☆ ☆ ☆

Current Earnings

O'Neil believes that current earnings could be the single most important element in stock picking. "I am continually amazed by how many people buy common stocks with the current reported quarter's earnings flat (no change), or down. There is absolutely no reason for a stock to go anywhere if the current earnings are poor."

The following clipping [Figure 7-1] is from *Investor's Business Daily*.

WO: We regularly publish the earnings of a company as it reports them. Every day an investor can look at which companies reported the best earnings. I believe knowing the companies with the best earnings will go a long way toward finding successful stocks.

Earnings per share are calculated by dividing a company's total after-tax profits by the number of shares outstanding for that company. For example, if you have a company with a million shares outstanding and with earnings of $100,000 you would have earnings per share of $10 per share (1 million divided by 100,000).

The common stocks you select should show a major percentage increase in the current quarterly

Figure 7-1. A sample of the "Earnings News" column from
Investor's Business Daily.

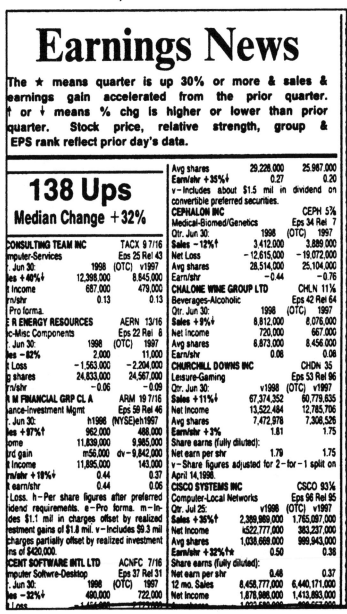

earnings per share (the most recently reported quarter) when compared to the prior year's same quarter (i.e., June and last June). The question is how should it increase? The answer is the highest increase for the time. If in the 1970s the best companies were growing their earnings by 15%, and in the 1990s the best are growing by 30%, you want the best for the time, but at least 20%.

It is also suggested once you find a stock that has an increase in its quarterly earnings, look at other stocks in the sector. It is believed that if the sector is "hot," the stocks will go up faster than if you have a star performing stock in a weak sector.

Conversely, other stocks and sectors are weak. One of the most important factors in finding a stock, and possibly a good sector, is to look at the stock's relative price strength. The **relative strength** measures how well it performs against the benchmark, the Standard & Poor's 500 market index. The relative strength is measured from 0 to 100. If your stock had a relative strength of, say, 80, it would mean it does better than 80% of all of the stocks in the index. This is very good. I believe that strong stocks and strong sectors are the sectors to be in. Stocks beating the market are strong. I would be hard pressed to recommend a stock that has a relative strength of at least 70, and would prefer 80 and above. I want that stock to outperform 80% of all the other stocks in the index.

KS: *But isn't it expensive to buy stocks that are doing better than the index?*

WO: Stocks that are going up, tend to go up more. I am always amazed when someone says, "Wow, look at these oil stocks, they are so cheap. They have lost all this money, have a really low P/E ratio, and are way down. I think this is a value so I should buy it." Dogs usually stay dogs. Investors could do better by looking at the hot sectors, the ones that some might find expensive, and find the best stocks in that sector. Good stocks can get better.

[In fact, Figure 1-2 in Chapter 1 illustrates this point.]

For this reason we publish the sectors that are the weakest. Investors should tend to avoid these sectors. We also publish the stocks that are hitting new price highs. The belief is that stocks that are hitting new price highs are doing so for a reason. If it is hitting a new price high, it is because of something significant. Research suggests that investors could make more money buying stocks off the list of stocks that are hitting new highs, rather than new lows.

[See Figure 7-2, which shows a list of stocks losing relative strength. The lower the number, the less the strength, which means fewer people are buying the stock. If fewer people are buying the stock, the price of the stock will not rise as easily as one that has many buyers.]

KS: *Not buy low and sell high?*

WO: Buy high and sell higher.

[Figure 7-3 clearly illustrates stocks that are hitting new highs. According to William J. O'Neil's research, stocks that are hitting new highs tend to keep moving higher. Stocks hitting new lows tend to keep moving lower. Thus it is better to buy high and sell higher than to buy low.]

One of the most popular research tools that our readers use from *IBD* is the table entitled "Where the Big Money's Flowing" [see Figure 7-4]. This table is filled with an incredible amount of useful information.

(text continues on page 173)

Figure 7-2. A sample of stocks with few buyers.

Falling Relative Strength Stocks

(Stocks were above selected categories of 70, 50, or 30 the previous 6 months)

Below 70		Mid Coast Bc		Greatr Del Vly	
Analysis&Tch	AATI	MCBN			ALI
Progressive	PGR	**Below 50**		Skytel Comm	SKT
EnergyRsrch	ERC	Rexall Sun	RXSO	GardnerDnvr	G
Party City	PCTY	Metals USA	MUI	BEA Systms	BE/
EnhanceFinl	EFS	Paging Ntwrk	PAGE	Oglebay Nort	OG
Spartech Cp	SEH	BonTonStors	BONT	Interim Svcs	
Boole&Babge		PulaskiBk	PULB	**Below 30**	
	BOOL	Center Bncp	CNBC	SevenSeaPet	S
NACCO Inds	NC	Haven Bncrp	HAVN	Wausau Mos	WI
Windmer Dur	WND	CitizensCorp	CZC	Sola Intl	S
Mecon	MECN	Tab Products	TBP	GardenRidge	
Electro Rent	ELRC	Royce Value	RVT		GRI
Superior Tele	SUT	CommerceGr	CGI	Station Casin	S
Whole Foods	WFMI	Brass Eagle	XTRM	Dover Corp	D
Union Bnkshr		RelianceStl	RS	I C N Pharma	I
	UBSC	ConcrdFabA	CIS	GS Financial	GS
Prime Bncp	PBNK	OfficeMax Inc	OMX	GoldenStBcp	G
Hillenbrand	HB	NorthAmerSc	NASI	Starmet	ST
Buckle Inc	BKE	Digi Intl	DGII	Tava Tchnlgy	TA
RaymJames	RJF	Pillowtex	PTX	Vical	V
Edwards AG	AGE	Luxottica Gp	LUX	Ubics	U
Financial Sec	FSA	FirstKeystn	FKFS	Ezcorp Inc A	EZ
BedBathBey	BBBY	CMAC Invest	CMT	Russ Berrie	F
				Phys Relianc	PH

Courtesy *Investor's Business Daily*

Figure 7-3. A sample of stocks hitting new highs.

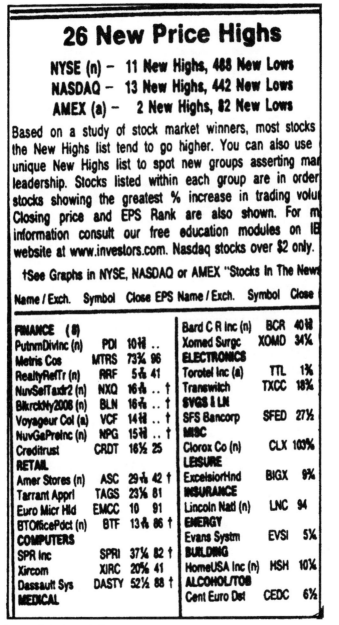

Figure 7-4. A sample of "Where the Big Money's Flowing" from *Investor's Business Daily.*

Where The Big Money's Flowing

Stocks $18 and higher, with at least 1/2 point price chg & 60,000 (if Vol % Chg. is +300% or more, must trade 75,000 shares). For stocks up in price, the EPS + RS must be 110 or more and next year's earnings estimate 17%+. Stocks w/o estimates are included. Stocks rated 80 EPS and 80 Rel Str. or higher are boldfaced.

E P Rel Grp M Acc 52-Wk S Str Rtg R Dis High	Stock Name	Stock Symbol	Closing Price	Price Change	PE Ratio	Float (mil)	Volume (1000s)	%Change In Vol.
5058 89 AAC 66	Baxter Intl o	BAX	58⅞ +	1⅞	24	251	3,061	+183
78 53 BAD 59⅝	Knight Ridder o	KRI	44 +	1	17	74	543	+166
70 58 BBD 37½	First Data Corp o	FDC	25¾ +	3¼	17	442	5,785	+163
96 91 CAA 47	**Manitowoc Co**	MTW	38⅞ +	2⅞	14	17	140	+160
89 93 ABB 68¾	**Gateway 2000 Inc o**	GTW	51⅜ +	1⅞	26	64	5,377	+156
83 76 B .B 32½	Bell & Howell Co o	BHW	27¾ +	1⅜	21	17	159	+154
85 65 CAD 39⅝	Department 56 Inc o	DFS	28¼ +	⅞	12	18	115	+104
50 67 B .B 29⅝	Shurgard Strg Ctrs o	SHU	25⅜ +	⅞	18	27	62	+83
61 71 AAB 49⅞	Torchmark Corp o	TMK	40 +	½	16	139	448	+50
59 95 ACC 65⅛	Quaker Oats Co o	OAT	62⅞ +	⅞	27	132	762	+40
53 82 CCC 47⅛	Great Lakes Chem o	GLK	40 +	1	19	58	381	+32
63 87 A .B 72⅝	F P L Group Inc o	FPL	61⅝ −	3⅝	16	179	3,847	+425
56 27 ABD 57⅝	Dole Food Co Inc o	DOL	29⅜ −	5	12	46	1,475	+414
84 46 CAD 37⅜	Hon Industries Inc o	HNI	22⅜ −	2⅜	13	54	301	+263
78 74 DBC 55⅜	Newell o	NWL	43½ −	¾	22	154	3,091	+257
61*40 DBD 40⅝	Gtech Hlds Corp o	GTK	23⅜ −	2⅛	11	41	470	+244
30 27 CBC 42⅝	LaSalle Re Hldgs Ltd	LSH	22⅜ −	⅞	5	11	72	+185
48 80 ACC 30⅝	Northern State Pwr o	NSP	26⅜ −	⅞	15	150	1,040	+160
9 98 AEB 61½	Cox Communic o	COX	56 − 5		..	258	813	+156
55 42 ABB 40⅝	MasTec o	MTZ	19⅝ −	1¼	35	11	159	+147
90 67 CBB 37⅝	Crane Co o	CR	28⅜ −	⅝	15	61	397	+140
86 48 ECC 52	Pillowtex Corp o	PTX	27⅝ −	1⅞	22	8.6	152	+131
84 73 CAA 31¼	Tredegar Industries	TG	22½ −	½	14	22	79	+124
99 91 BAC 55½	Abercrombie & Fitch o	ANF	38⅝ −	2⅛	32	54	1,724	+107
72 67 CBE 59⅝	UNUM Corp o	UNM	45½ −	1½	17	136	943	+106
46 61 CCA 34½	Alcan Aluminium o	AL	25⅜ −	⅞	13	228	796	+101
92 38 DAC 66⅝	Ethan Allen Interiors o	ETH	32⅜ −	1¼	13	26	546	+100
95 97 DAC 52	Symbol Technology o	SBL	45⅛ −	4⅝	32	47	648	+98
97 98 BAD 92⅜	Nokia ADS Pfd A o	NOKA	85⅜ −	⅞	32	594	3,576	+90
37 68 CCB 64⅝	Varian Associates o	VAR	38½ −	½	16	28	314	+88
96 48 CAC 37⅝	Dollar General Corp o	DG	21 −	1⅝	28	144	1,872	+85
34 46 DCE 60¾	C S X Corp o	CSX	37⅝ −	1⅝	12	210	1,074	+83
90 40 CAB 57⅞	Franklin Resources o	BEN	33¼ −	3⅛	17	159	1,485	+81
98 48 BAB 39⅛	Buckle Inc o	BKE	18⅝ −	1¼	15	7.5	126	+79
37 31 CDD 52⅞	Philips Electron Nv o	PHG	52⅝ −	2⅝	11	365	1,603	+79
82 71 ACB 39⅝	St Jude Medical Inc o	STJ	28 −	⅝	19	81	762	+75
51 89 ACD 44⅝	B E C Energy Hldg Co o	BSE	40⅛ −	⅞	14	47	258	+74
69 39 B .D 31⅞	Tanger Factory Outlt	SKT	21⅞ −	⅝	13	7.7	67	+72
23 95 AEC 50⅛	MediaOne Group Inc o	UMG	42 − 2¼		..	603	2,779	+66
59 63 ABE 81⅞	Boston Scientific Crp o	BSX	54½ −	2⅝	35	135	1,936	+63
82 58 ACD 98⅞	Lincoln National Co o	LNC	70⅝ −	3⅝	14	99	556	+57
95 83 ABE 65⅝	AirTouch Commun o	ATI	50⅝ −	3⅝	54	568	3,337	+56
43 63 BDC 89⅜	Aetna	AET	66⅝ −	⅞	13	143	917	+52
84 _ 47⅝ U S _	o	USB	35⅞ _		20	706	2,8_	
_⅞ N_		NUE			14	85		

Courtesy *Investor's Business Daily*

The very left column shows the Earnings Per Share Rank (EPS). We usually like over 80%. The same is true for the next columns, Relative Strength and Group Rating (relating how this industry group is doing compared to the market). The SMR, or Sales + Profit Margins + Return on Equity, is an indicator that was recently added. Finally, the Accumulation Distribution column is important to look at as well. Stocks that are being accumulated have an A or a B rating. For a stock to go up, people need to be buying it. Those five ratings are named *IBD SmartSelect*™ Corporate Ratings, and are the five most often used characteristics by analysts today.

The "20 Most % Up in Price" information [see Figure 7-5] is important as well. Stocks that are hitting new highs tend to do better than stocks hitting new lows. Add that information to the other indicators included in this research and this listing is a great research tool.

Annual Earnings Increases

WO: Each year's annual earnings per share for the last five years should show an increase over the prior year's earnings. A company should grow its earnings by at least 25% per year, at a minimum. By looking for the stocks that have the highest earnings growth, you will weed out at least 80% of the undesirable stocks that have lackluster growth.

What O'Neil would do is to look in his paper for the fastest sector of earnings growth, and then look for the company with the best earnings growth. You can also find information in many stock analyzing programs such as Investools. You can do a search of the sectors with the best performance and then of the stocks with the best performance in that sector.

Figure 7-5. A sample of stocks that had the largest percentage increase from the previous day.

20 Most % Up In Price (Stocks Over $12)

EPS Rnk	Rel Str.	Stock Name	Closing Price	Net Up	Group Str.	Volume (100s)	Vol. % Change
80	68	B A Merchant Svcs	15 11/16	+ 2 1/16	B	700,6	+932
66	58	Tesoro Petroleum	14 7/16	+ 1 7/8	C	513,9	+297
70	58	First Data Corp	25 13/16	+ 3 1/4	B	5,784,6	+163
91	35	I C N Pharmaceutcls	22 1/8	+ 2 11/16	A	1,129,1	+53
45	19	Banco Latinoamer E	18 5/8	+ 2	D	123,5	+170
70	77	E G & G Inc	24 13/16	+ 2 5/8	C	188,9	-10
76	92	Intrstate Johnsn Lan	33 7/8	+ 3 9/16	D	21,8	+106
38	77	Autoliv Inc	31 11/16	+ 3 5/16	D	100,2	+69
92	35	Wolverine Wld Wide	13 11/16	+ 1 1/4	D	542,8	-1
49	48	Heller Financial Inc	23 5/16	+ 2 1/8	B	278,8	+11
76	35	Affiliated Mgrs Grp	21 5/8	+ 1 7/8	C	31,3	-56
56	22	Panamerican Bev A	19 5/8	+ 1 5/8	B	570,3	+38
32	91	Telcm Italia ADS CIA	54 1/2	+ 4 1/2	A	6	-65
19	21	Bankers Trust N Y	66 7/8	+ 5 1/2	E	4,485,2	+113
10	28	Polaroid Corp	25 11/16	+ 2	C	953,5	+101
83	40	P M I Group Inc	50 1/4	+ 3 11/16	C	235,2	+16
85	43	Ametek Inc	19 5/8	+ 1 3/8	D	128,4	+15
58	39	Guilford Mills Inc	16 1/8	+ 1 1/8	E	28,1	-55
57	85	Administaff	31 9/16	+ 2 1/8	E	25,4	-59
61	82	Telecom Italia ADS	76 1/4	+ 5 1/8	A	83.6	-21

Courtesy *Investor's Business Daily*

Whoa! Didn't you and I always learn to buy stocks low and sell high? O'Neil as well as many other of our all-stars would rather buy a stock hitting a new high than a new low list. Buying a stock as it reaches new highs is important as it helps tell *when* to buy a stock: as the stock emerges from its price adjustment phase and slowly resumes an uptrend, approaching new high ground. It should be bought just as it's starting to break out of its price base. O'Neil says, "What seems too high and risky to the majority usually goes higher and what seems low and cheap usually goes lower."

New Product, Management, High Price

It's very important for a company to have something new. This will help grow the stock. New can refer to new product, new management, or even a stock's new high price.

Supply and Demand

Many of us were brought up to believe that big stocks are better. O'Neil states that as an investor you actually want less shares outstanding as it will create more demand. Big is not always better.

To further create more demand constantly look for companies that are buying back their own stock.

Having a smaller float (due to the fact that the company is buying back shares), should provide scarcity and more people seeking to buy fewer available shares.

Leading Stocks

As O'Neil puts it, there are leading and lagging stocks, Why not buy the leader? Investors that continually buy the best two or three stocks in the industry do better. These top stocks can have tremendous growth while the other stocks do a whole bunch of nothing. Sometimes the investor sees a stock in the industry group that is not in the top three, however it is trading "cheaper." You end up buying the cheaper stock. This is called a sympathy buy. You might feel it is safer, or that you are getting a real bargain.

How do you know if you have a leader or laggard? O'Neil looks for a stock's relative price strength. The relative price strength of a stock measures the stock's price performance against the price action of a market average (usually the Standard & Poor's 500). If you have a relative strength of 70, for example, it means the stock outperformed 70% of all stocks in the market. O'Neil suggests only buying stocks with a relative price strength of 70 or better, preferably over 80.

Institutional Sponsorship

According to William O'Neil, in order for stocks to go up, you need lots of buyers. The biggest buyers are institutions such as mutual funds and pension plans. I would look for companies that institutions own and are continuing to buy, thus increasing their percentage of ownership in the stock.

Market Direction

O'Neil is a practical man. "You can be right on the stock, but if you are wrong about the general direction of the market, three out of four stocks will slump," so he says. For that reason, he asserts that investors need to know if you are in an up or down market. Further, you need to know if the market is in the early or late stages of an up or down market.

A 33% loss in portfolio of stocks requires a 50% gain just to get back to breakeven. For example, if a $10,000 portfolio declines to $6,667, the portfolio has to rise $3,333 (or 50%) just to get you even.

"Too many investors try to argue a market trend. If you can spot a market trend you don't really need many other tools. Recognizing when the market has hit a top or bottom counts for over 50% of your success in investing."

KS: *So, how do you determine if a market is topping out?*

WO: Study the general market chart every day. Look for any
       reversal of a trend. Most important would be to watch
       the daily price chart and volume chart. If you see the
       price of the Dow or the S&P 500 start to fall while vol-
       ume starts to increase, that could be the sign of a mar-
       ket top. Heavy volume without further price increases
       is not good, and usually means a stock (or the market
       as a whole) can drop further. Even if a major index
       is rallying, it means nothing if the advance/decline is
       negative. This would slow the entire market down. An-
       other sign of a market top would be if the Federal Re-
       serve Board changes the discount rate higher.
           Look at how the leading stocks are acting when
       the general market begins dropping. If the leading
       sectors and stocks in those sectors begin to fall, this is
       a bearish signal. Also, usually right before a market
       top, everything is running up. When small, low-quality
       stocks begin to run up it is considered a market top. If
       we are entering a market top, raise at least 25% in cash
       and sell the worst of the stocks you own.

Conclusion

KS: *When do you sell a stock?*

WO: Bernard Baruch, a famous market operator on Wall
       Street and trusted adviser to U.S. presidents said, "If a
       speculator is correct half of the time, he is hitting a
       good average. Even being right 3 or 4 times out of 10
       should yield a person a fortune if he has the sense
       to cut his losses quickly on the ventures where he is
       wrong."
           Never use what you paid for the stock as your rea-
       son to sell. It doesn't matter if you have a profit or a
       loss. You sell a stock if it drops 7% or 8% immediately

after you buy it. You sell a stock when the factors change. A factor could be a bad quarterly or annual earning report. If something changes for the worse, don't bother waiting around. Get out.

The whole secret to winning in the stock market is to lose the least amount possible when you are not right.

KS: *If a stock that you own goes down, will you average down and buy more?*

WO: What for? If the stock is going down, it is going down for a reason. Cut your losses and move on.

Commentary

William J. O'Neil's CAN SLIM method has many terrific attributes. It is easy to follow, specific, and makes sense. Further, if the investor is using *Investor's Business Daily,* much of the information is instantly at your fingertips.

However, I believe that this method of stock picking is aggressive and that the stocks that you buy will be volatile. Compare this method to Louis Navellier's (Chapter 10). Many similarities exist, but Navellier attempts to keep risk in check by providing a formula to weed out extremely aggressive stocks. The concept of buying leaders with the best earnings will probably lead an investor to many excellent stock buys. But without looking at key ratios, I believe these stocks will be feast or famine stocks (not many stocks in this portfolio will simply do nothing).

8

Ron Elijah
Looking at the Market—Backwards

Name, residence	Ron Elijah, San Francisco
Accomplishments	Managing director of Robertson Stephens Investment Management; VP portfolio manager for its value and growth fund
Hobbies	Being father to his two boys: "All my time out of work is spent with them."
Favorite reading	Harry Dent's *The Great Boom Ahead* and Jeremy Siegel's *Stocks for the Long Run*
Influential figure	Parents; anyone who has managed money (for a living) for a long time, and survived
Quotable	"Greed makes people blind."
Investment style	Top-down, growth

Background

Robertson Stephens Investment Management, head-quartered in San Francisco, is perhaps one of the best small firms for investment banking research and managing institutional money. It became a leader in this field by identifying emerging business trends and providing incisive institutional research. When you hear statements either in this book or while reading or watching TV about stock analysts—what they said, their predictions, and so on—this firm is one of the more important firms cited.

In 1987 Robertson Stephens decided to apply its expertise to mutual funds. It launched some of the best performing mutual funds available. Some of its well-known funds include Robertson Stephens Value + Growth, Robertson Stephens Information Age, and Robertson Stephens Contrarian. In 1995 the Robertson Stephens Value + Growth fund received a Five Star Morningstar rating.

Preinterview Info

When you imagine how the professionals buy stock, you probably envision one of our all-stars feeding a list of set criteria into a computer. The computer would then match the stocks that fit the preset screen. Any matches would be potential buy candidates. For many investors, this method is widely used. It's called bottom-up stock analysts. Ron Elijah, on the other hand, does it backwards. He is a top-down manager who's looking for themes. This approach means he first wants to identify the sectors of the market that are most appealing and then look for a company that might fit his investment criteria.

You may wonder why those who have already made their mark (and their millions) still come to work. The offices of Robertson Stephens are plush, with a beautiful view of Alcatraz and the Golden Gate Bridge. Just to stare out the window would be at least some incentive to continue coming to work. Yet Ron Elijah's personal office is unpretentious. He does most of the research himself with help of one or two research assistants. He still goes to analyst meetings, crunches numbers, and reads annual reports, and it is he who ultimately decides what stock is bought or sold. Elijah is in the trenches, he is not a figurehead.

One of the most enjoyable aspects of Ron Elijah's personality is that he is very humble, or, rather, there is an absence of the big ego that is often too common among Wall Street elitists. He actually asked *my* opinions. He talked about *mistakes* he had made, and how he tries to get better. While humility is a key to his success, make no mistake—Ron Elijah is a fighter and a thinker, and totally committed to improvement.

The Interview

KS: *How do you like managing money?*

RE: I love it. It is stressful at times. But it always changes. I continue to improve and get better. I don't make the same mistakes I did 5 years ago. I love a job where every day is different.

KS: *What do you like least about managing money?*

RE: I hate it when my brother in-law comes over for dinner and tells me he bought one of the stocks I recommended and wants to know why it's down—way down.

KS: *Tell me the essence of your style of management.*

RE: Find a theme, look for fast growing leading stocks, sell fast if you are wrong.

I look at various groups of stocks and then I look at a stock. I ask myself why this company is important. What do they have that I need today, and will I need it, even more tomorrow? That need could be shoes, it could be semiconductors, it could be computers.

KS: *It's a treat to talk to a top-down investor. Most investors look for great stocks first, and will then try to determine if it fits into the market as a whole.*

RE: Finding the right theme is critical. At any given time, a certain industry or sector is experiencing significant economic and social changes. We attempt to identify the specific sectors that will benefit from these changes.

Everything is about demographics. Demographic studies show that most people are entering their peak earnings years now [see Figure 8-1]. Furthermore we have the highest level of discretionary income ever. If

Figure 8-1. Projected change in the U.S. population: 1995–2005.

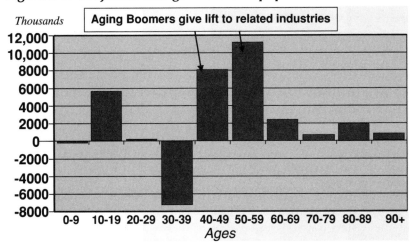

Source: U.S. Census Bureau; Elijah Asset Management, LLC

household income is averaging $44,000 annually, and discretionary income is representing about $20,000, that means consumers have about $60 billion extra to buy something. That will drive purchases, investing, and a myriad of other trends.

Look at baby boomers. Think to yourself, this is the largest segment of the population and they are now entering their 50s representing their peak earning years. Ask yourself what they are going to need, what they are going to buy. By the year 2000 it's projected that the 50+ age group will control more than 75% of the nation's wealth.

Look at the two big spikes [in Figure 8-1]. As they march along you can see the baby boomers are now in their 40s and 50s—these are peak earning years. Ask yourself what will they buy with all this extra money? Ten years from now, what will they be buying? If you can identify this trend, it's half the battle.

KS: *Tell me about another trend.*

RE: A major trend is the aging of America. The U.S. Census

Bureau estimates that the number of people over the age of 85 will more than double by the year 2010. Again, think to yourself, what will this group of people be apt to buy and spend money on?

KS: *What are your favorite themes right now?*

RE: Technology, retail apparel, financial services (baby boomers save for retirement), and health care.

KS: *Tell me about technology.*

RE: Very rarely do you have an industry that will cause a drastic and profound change. I think of the combustion engine and the industries that resulted from that. I think of electricity. And now we have technology. Look at this chart [Figure 8-2]. This clearly illustrates that compared to the population and compared to the gross domestic product (GDP), the United States is investing more in technology than any other country. This is huge.

KS: *You make a compelling argument. However, haven't*

Figure 8-2. Global technology investing as of 1995, with a $557 billion technology market, a $28.3 trillion global GDP, and a 5.7 billion world population.

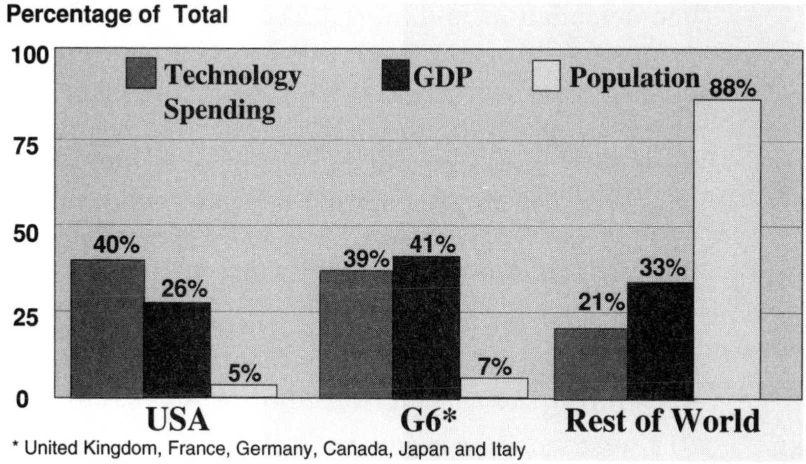
Percentage of Total
100
75
50
25
0
Technology Spending
GDP
Population
40%
26%
5%
39%
41%
7%
21%
33%
88%
USA
G6*
Rest of World
* United Kingdom, France, Germany, Canada, Japan and Italy

Source: IDC; Bear Stearns; Elijah Asset Management, LLC

many technology stocks such as the Internet ones al-
ready exploded to ridiculously high prices?

RE: Ridiculous compared to what? This is one of the most
        dynamic and fastest growing industries in the world.
        And today it is still in its infancy stage. How can one
        use historical valuation approaches to determine the
        value of these? As an investor, wouldn't you want to
        be part of that trend?

KS: *How about retail and apparel?*

RE: Numbers show that persons between the ages of 45
        and 55 are at their highest earnings and discretionary
        earnings years. Further study shows that a big chunk
        of their discretionary spending goes to apparel.

        I didn't even understand retailing until last year.
        But now that I analyzed it, I found women's apparel is
        a huge, profitable industry. Styles constantly change
        and someone is making big money off of this.

KS: *Why health care?*

RE: Health care is a huge and compelling story. We have a
        greater need now for health care than ever before. As
        today's need turns into tomorrow's need as the baby
        boomers mature, and, wow, do you have a trend.

        I have this great graph that shows drug prescrip-
        tions and the population cycle. Look at this chart [Fig-
        ure 8-3]. It's amazing that the age groups of 55
        through 75 are very small but their prescription drug
        use is way up. Think about if it is so far up today what
        will happen to that trend when baby boomers move
        into their 60s and 70s?

KS: *OK, OK. These are all great, growing themes. But*
        doesn't everyone else know this and are not stocks par-
        ticipating in these themes already expensive as a result?

RE: Of course stocks may get ahead of themselves. But ask
        yourself, will this industry still grow? And can the stock
        still grow in that industry? Find the sector that you

Figure 8-3. A graph showing the relationship between drug prescriptions and the population cycle used to illustrate a health-care theme for investing.

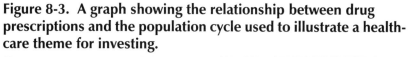

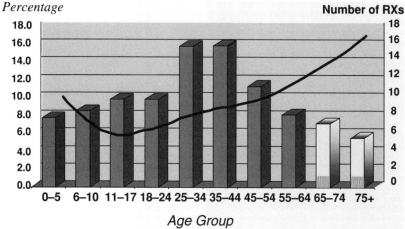

Age Group

Source: U.S. Census Bureau; Walgreen Co. estimates (1995); Elijah Asset Management, LLC

think will have five years of explosive growth. Even if the stock appears expensive based on historical standards, Wall Street will still drive stocks of the fastest growing industries higher. Just look at the Internet stocks. These stocks are trading expensive based on historical means. However, if you had invested in this group, you would probably have made money.

Watch the volume numbers that show which sectors of the market people are investing in. The fundamentals are important for showing valuation and which stock in an industry group you want to invest with. But picking a winning stock is more than just looking at the fundamentals. You can look at balance sheets and P/E ratios all day and miss a ton of great stocks. I'll bet a lot of investors out there say, "Well, I will screen all the stocks that are trading 'cheap' with P/E ratios of 10 times earnings. I will buy those and wait for them to go up." Chances are you will be sitting around waiting a long time for many of those stocks to go up, and many never will. This method of buying stocks is backward. Forget historical valuations when you find your theme.

Instead, find your theme and buy stocks that have excellent growth potential. You may have to pay a higher price. However, chances are those stocks will go higher. Many of our stocks won't even make money for many years. But if you grow revenues, profits of a company should follow.

It is more important than anything else to get a feel for the psychology and behavior of Wall Street.

KS: *I hear what you are saying, but some of the stocks are trading at such high multiples, there has got to be an accident waiting here somewhere.*

RE: First of all look at the history of the market in general as shown in this next illustration [Figure 8-4]. It proves that any time long-term interest rates and inflation were low, the market could support a higher P/E ratio. So if you use that as some sort of market barometer, than I still want to find the fastest growth sectors.

Figure 8-4. Valuation historical considerations as of 8/21/98 with the S&P Industrials at 1,290.80.

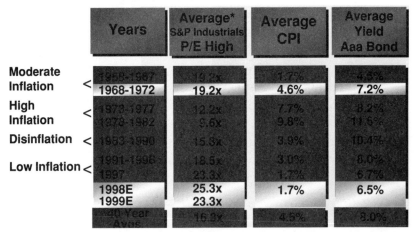

Years	Average* S&P Industrials P/E High	Average CPI	Average Yield Aaa Bond
Moderate Inflation < 1958-1987	19.2x	1.7%	4.5%
1968-1972	19.2x	4.6%	7.2%
High Inflation < 1973-1977	12.2x	7.7%	8.2%
1978-1982	9.6x	9.8%	11.6%
Disinflation < 1983-1990	15.3x	3.9%	10.4%
Low Inflation < 1991-1996	18.5x	3.0%	8.0%
1997	23.3x	1.7%	6.7%
1998E	25.3x	1.7%	6.5%
1999E	23.3x		
40 Year Avgs	16.2x	4.5%	8.0%

*S&P Industrials P/E before extraordinary items.
Source: Standard & Poor's; Goldman Sachs; Elijah Asset Management, LLC

We talked about the drug sector. The wave of pre-scriptions is huge. Look at the pipeline of people who need those drugs. As an investor, you can decide to look at the makers of drugs (Pfizer), distributors (Johnson and Johnson), or the retailers (Walgreen's).

If the industry is accelerating, then so should its margins (profit margins), which will ultimately drive the stock higher. So find stocks that are growing their revenue and growing their profit margins. This could be more important than looking at net earnings or a price to earnings ratio.

[Note how different this advice is compared to someone like Mario Gabelli in terms of the valuations that Ron Elijah is willing to spend. However it is very similar in the fact that they are both looking for, in some degree, a catalyst to drive the stock price higher.]

KS: *I wonder if the readers are getting a feel for just how darn optimistic you are?*

RE: The future is bright but it does not tell you what stocks to buy. Find the right sector, then find the right growth stocks in that sector. In other words buy the industry first, than look at the company. If industry accelerates, margins should go up.

KS: *Which leads to my next question. I'm glad to know the theme, but now what stock?*

RE: The theme is the most important.

When looking for stocks always ask yourself, "What do they do, why do they exist, why does the world need them, will they need more next year?" We pound the pavement looking for stocks. We go to conferences when management is giving a talk. We crunch the numbers, we visit management, we talk to their competitors, we do a ton of work before buying a stock.

KS: *Do you always buy the industry leader?*

RE: No. You don't need the number one company. If you
        pick the right theme and there is a force in the indus-
        try, many of the stocks will do well. As a result con-
        sider loading up on those stocks that you really like,
        but don't limit yourself to one.

KS: *I noticed in your fund that you seem to take big bets on
        a handful of stocks instead of owning a whole bunch of
        stocks. Couldn't this create a great deal more risk?*

RE: If I am going to go ahead and buy a little bit of tons of
        stocks, it sounds to me like a closet index fund. If you
        want to beat the market, your portfolio can't look like
        indexes. If you are confident with certain sectors and
        certain stocks, you will need to take big bets.

KS: *In the mutual fund business, many investors look at
        turnover, which means how often you buy and sell your
        stocks. The turnover in your funds are high, meaning
        you don't keep stock very long. Why?*

RE: I buy stocks with the intent on holding them a long
        time. And some stocks, like a Dell Computer, we have
        held for years. But, it's true, I am a fast seller of stocks
        once I decide I am either wrong about the stock, or
        the time to own it. I would much rather get rid of the
        stock fast, take a tax loss, and buy it back cheaper.

        I remember vividly the fall of 1997, the market
        began to tank. When a sector starts to sell off, all the
        stocks in the sector will sell off regardless of whether
        it is a good stock. So I needed to limit our downside. I
        sold a whole bunch of really great stocks—and I fully
        intended (and did, in many instances) to buy the
        stocks back cheaper. If I don't limit my losses and our
        fund starts to significantly drop, our investors are not
        going to wait around. They will bail.

KS: *Yes, I can understand that kind of active trading for a
        mutual fund, but what about for your personal stock
        holdings? Do you trade as much?*

RE: We have very strict requirements on how often and

how many days before or after I can buy or sell a stock for the fund, when I can buy or sell for my own account. Besides, much of my personal investments are in my funds. But even if they were not, I would use primarily the same discipline for my own holdings.

KS: *Please continue with your high-turnover discussion.*

RE: I used to weather every downturn. I would say to myself don't panic. But what I also found was that certain trends exist. I use these trends to either buy more at a cheaper price, or to hold off on a purchase.

    Charting the market reveals extremely useful information. This graph [Figure 8-5] shows me that the NASDAQ usually has a significant correction on average twice per year. So I often refrain from buying into a rally that's long in tooth. Rather, I would like to buy in after one of these corrections. So I say to myself, what does this mean? Often it's just people taking profits. The longest rally lasted about eleven months, the shortest was two months. So when I think a downtrend is coming, I don't mind selling and buying back cheaper.

Figure 8-5. A graph of the NASDAQ Composite showing all corrections over 10% in the 1990s.

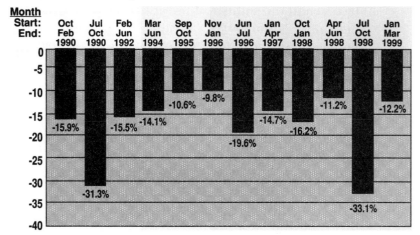

Source: Instinet; Elijah Asset Management, LLC

KS: *What sort of signs are you looking for?*

RE: I think overall that stocks get ahead of themselves. Greed makes people blind. If we are invested in a certain sector and analysts begin to lower their earnings expectations, it is usually a bearish signal. Investors should pay close attention to this. But usually analysts stay at the party too long. They tend to be a little late, meaning the stock is already experiencing a downtrend and then the analyst lowers expectations.

You really need to listen to what the company is saying. If you don't go to analysts meetings, then look up what they are saying on the Web. Actually go into the company's Web site and read what the press releases are saying. Read the tone of their press releases.

One of the most important things we do is talk to competitors and suppliers. They will tell you if the company has slowed orders, are not buying as much product, and so on.

Before we buy a stock we crunch the numbers.

KS: *What does crunching the numbers mean to you?*

RE: We want the stocks that stand out. We want the stocks that are growing their revenues, earnings, return on equity, and profits faster than their market as a whole, faster than the industry they are competing in. If the personal computer (PC) business is growing at 15% per year, I want to find the stocks growing at 20% per year. But you have to be careful because management can often manipulate these numbers.

KS: *How?*

RE: For example, many analysts like to see same-store sales growth. If Nordstrom's does not grow an existing sales year over year, an analyst might not recommend the stock. Although it is true that same-store sales growth is important, more important is the profit and the revenue growth. If Nordstrom's wanted to have an increase in same-store sales growth, it would just put on a sale. A sale might not necessarily be good. It could bring down profit margins.

If a company has a quarter of lower same-store sales growth, many analysts will not recommend buying this stock. This might cause the stock to sell off. I will look to see if its profits went up. If its profits went up but the stock is down, I might look at this as a buying opportunity.

To me profit growth is more important than earnings growth.

KS: *Do you care if the price to earnings ratio exceeds the growth rate for the company?*

RE: No, I don't. Profitability and growth prospects for a company are much more important.

Assume that the average stock in the Standard & Poor's Index experiences growth at 7%, and the index has a price to earnings ratio equal to 20 times earnings. Assume next year Compaq (CPQ) has the potential to grow earnings by 25%, but this year it only grew earnings by 10%. Compaq is trading at a price to earnings ratio of 18 with a return on equity of 28%. CPQ is more profitable than the market, and is trading at a discount to the market.

KS: *If it is not an industry or market correction, what would motivate you to sell a stock?*

RE: Oftentimes a stock will become overvalued because of price appreciation.

KS: *I thought you said you would buy a stock that has historically high valuations?*

RE: So long as everything is great. I can't afford the littlest hiccup or possible problem if I am going to spend a great deal of money on stocks. I am not going to tolerate my kid's Nike shoes falling apart in a day if I am going to spend $50 on a pair of shoes.

If the fundamentals deteriorate in any way, I sell. If the company growth begins to slow below what we (or all the analysts) targeted as its growth rate, I sell. Even if a short-term problem occurs, I sell.

✮ ✮ ✮ ✮ ✮ ✮ ✮ ✮ ✮ ✮ ✮ ✮ ✮ ✮ ✮ ✮

Selling is based on valuation, but not on historical valuation.

✮ ✮ ✮ ✮ ✮ ✮ ✮ ✮ ✮ ✮ ✮ ✮ ✮ ✮ ✮ ✮

Selling is based on valuation, but not on historical valuation. Many investors will sell if the stock exceeds its historical valuation, meaning if the stock usually trades at 15 times earnings and now it is 25 times earnings, it is higher than what the stock historically trades at, so these investors would sell. That's not why I sell. For what I do, selling based on historical valuation is silly because it has nothing to do with the next 10 years. I am buying stocks with great growth potential, they should sell at a premium. But when it gets ahead of its future growth rate, then I start getting nervous.

KS: *What would be an example of a short-term problem?*

RE: Increasing receivables. If the receivables continue to grow that means to me their clients are having a harder time and not paying on time. This could mean sales for the company I have invested in could slow. Which could mean to me huge problems down the road. Again, if I am going to pay a high multiple everything has to be perfect. I will not allow anything to change, I'll be out of the stock.

       If receivables are increasing faster than revenue growth you have a problem.

KS: *Do you meet with management?*

RE: You bet.

KS: *I'm looking at your software and notice it has informa-*

tion about receivables. It has graphs. It seems like it has all you need.

RE: The software is called Baseline. It's new for me and I'm just getting used to it, but so far I like it.

Commentary

Ron Elijah's basic secrets, then, include focusing on an expanding market (the whole theme idea) by looking for growth in a growth industry and being prepared to pay for that growth. They also include looking at companies with new, improved, and upgraded products that will help drive up revenue and profit margins and get Wall Street to sit up and take notice.

In addition, he likes to get a glimpse at a company's future earnings by checking out its receivables and book to bill ratio. It's not a good sign if receivables are expanding because that indicates slow incoming payments or fewer sales. He'll talk to vendors, clients, and competitors, even call the company. He'll read analysts' reports and Internet sites.

Finally, his secrets include always being prepared for the downside by knowing the risk/reward ratio and by being willing to act appropriately when faced with a negative situation.

Ron Elijah's Approach of Top-Down Investing

★ *Find the themes I want to invest in.* Quite frankly I really like the themes Ron has identified. You might read certain demographic books and find a new theme for baby boomers, or international investing, or generation X. However, I will argue for his themes as the best choices for successful investing.

★ *Print a search of the stocks in the theme I like.* For example I would go to Value Line and read the report on the stocks in that theme. I would go on the Web and look to Quicken. com, Yahoo Finance, or Microsoft Investor and compare all the stocks in the industry. At this stage I would forget ratios such as P/E. I would look for the companies that are growing their earnings faster, growing profits faster, and so on.

I would look on a company's Web site for their press releases. When you can interpret and read the tone of these press releases, you can get a feel of the future.

★ *Read all historical news.*

★ *Create a chart.* I would do a 50-day moving average, and compare it to industry or sector to get a feel for how it trades.

★ *Look for a standout.* Based on Ron's approach I would want to pay for something special. So I'd look for something like a new product launch.

★ *Look for the best candidate.* After tracking the stock for a couple of days, I would decide what it's worth to me.

★ *Buy the stock already.*

Ron's approach is a good, solid approach. I like his theme idea. I like the fact that he asks why a company is important, and whether we will need their product or service in the future. I would also concede that the type of stocks targeted using Ron's approach do deserve a higher valuation and that historical valuations are not as important when buying stocks Ron's way.

I would, however, caution the conservative investor that this method will be volatile. If markets do slow down, you better be prepared to do what Ron does: either bail out of the stock or get ready for a rough ride.

9
Foster Friess
The Best-Kept Secret on Wall Street

Name, residence	Foster Friess, Wyoming, Arizona, and Pennsylvania
Accomplishments	Money manager, Brandywine Fund; chairman, Friess and Associates
Hobbies	Charity work, family, picking up trash
Favorite reading	*The Bible* and Andrew Tobias's *Beyond Wall Street*
Influential figures	Parents; Jesus; family
Quotable	"I am a recovering perfectionist."
Investment style	Growth, at reasonable prices

Background

Why do certain money managers "have it," while others don't? As you read through this book, commonalities appear among successful money managers. They are the ones who have a long-term track record, keep cost in perspective, and are willing to take big bets for big rewards. Foster Friess is no exception to these all-star characteristics.

Foster Friess and Associates manages the $6 billion Brandywine fund, a fund that seeks high growth, and has beaten the market. Friess, and his Brandywine Fund, is the best-kept secret on Wall Street. I say this tongue-in-cheek. The advertising budget for the Brandywine Fund is a big fat zero. You have never seen an advertisement or solicitation for the Brandywine Fund. Despite this fact, the fund is really no secret. Ask anyone who knows money management, and he or she will tell you that Foster Friess, owner of Friess and Associates and manager of the Brandywine Fund, is a great stock picker, and that the Brandywine Fund is among the best of the best. It constantly performs among the top 1% of all funds.

Friess has a superconsistent track record of methodically and predictably picking superior stocks and providing investors in his fund a return superior to both many other funds and the S&P Index. Not only does this fund have stellar returns, it has done so without experiencing a down year (except for 1988) since its inception in 1985. This is hard to do in of itself, but even harder for a fund like Brandywine that looks to invest in rapidly growing companies. In a 1997 article, *Money* magazine calls Brandywine "a fund you can count on." Even the employees of Morningstar, the fund rating service (see Chapter 11), often choose to invest in Brandywine for their 401(k) plan. Tell me that's not a huge compliment!

Foster Friess is one of the most dynamic, interesting chaps I had the pleasure of getting to know. As with all of our all-stars, his views are strong. But his views are different, very different. He is different on everything from family to business to success. I am almost inclined to write a book entitled "Friess Psychology." Forget the fact that he is a great stock picker. Anyone who could learn how to have the harmony and balance that Foster and his family seem to enjoy, would have a truly priceless gift. The fact that his return is an envy among the all-stars is icing on the cake. So read on and learn the secrets of being a great stock picker, a great employee, and a great person.

Preinterview Info

Déjà vu all over again. Another busy morning in Manhattan and I am boarding a train to go out of the city to find a money manager. I'm going to . . . Delaware? You bet. That is home (or one of the homes) for Friess and Associates.

The train ride took just over an hour and it was pleasant enough. I arrived at the office and was showed around. Judging from the pictures on the wall, Friess looks equally as comfortable in cowboy attire out west, playing golf, or holding high-level meetings with senators and congressmen. His tall, athletic build is at once intimidating yet inviting. I could just bet he gives his sons, daughters, and wife (all three beautiful and successful in their own right) great big bear hugs. Shoot, by the end of the day, I thought he was going to give me a big hug.

Obviously Friess is an important man. The walls in his office are lined with pictures of him with senators and congressman and playing golf with President Bush. There are covers of many magazines with Foster's mug plastered on them. Foster on his farm with Wilbur, his Pig (you will learn soon enough about Friess's pigs-in-the-trough theory). Friess looking like a cowboy at his home in Jackson Hole, Wyoming. Friess playing golf near his Arizona home. Friess helping the homeless near his Pennsylvania home. Wait a minute. Where does Foster Friess live? Everywhere! Arizona, Wyoming, and Pennsylvania. He says it gives him a better perspective on life, and it's better for stock research because different parts of the world have different perspectives.

I also noticed in talking to the associates working at Friess and Associates that something was out of the ordinary. Employee tenure is long. Indeed, as I rode in a converted minivan complete with phones, faxes, and so on from the train station to their office in Delaware, the driver talked about company loyalty. He told me that all the employees, including the driver, get to go to Jackson Hole for a holiday party. But what impressed the driver most about his employer was when one of the other drivers was sick and in the hospital last year, even the senior staff went to visit him.

There's very little stress in the office. I didn't see frantic stock trading. There was no advertising director, but there was a whole department of charitable activities: specifically, determining where and how they would spend their money on charitable activities. Even the investor relations department consisted of only a few people. However, you will be happy to know, everyone was in business dress. Even Friess had donned a suit.

The Interview

KS: *As I talk to your employees, I hear crazy stories. Stories about no-sit-down meetings. I hear about company trips—where everyone gets to go. Separate truth from myth for us.*

FF: We run things a little different. You see, I am a recovering perfectionist.

KS: *Excuse me?*

FF: Perfectionists abhor error. They strive to eradicate mistakes. Persons that strive for excellence on the other hand, love error. They find error an opportunity to adjust. We at Foster Friess are committed to excellence.

First, our employees know their priorities; God, family, Friess and Associates (and our clients). We don't believe in trying to correct people's weaknesses. Rather, we focus on their strengths and try to get them to buy into our philosophy. We have no company hierarchy. We have team members. The job of our team leaders is to get people to buy into our philosophies.

KS: *Your driver said you pay for everyone to go on vacation once a year. That must be expensive.*

FF: A firm is only as good as its team members. It's a small price to pay for their loyalty.

If I get a fax from someone at, say, 7:00 P.M., I need to counsel him or her. They should be with their children at that time.

Since the beginning of time there have been four basic issues: fear, guilt, love (relationships), significance. People constantly look for solutions such as using alcohol or working late to feel important. Running away is a solution. We recognize this and help our team members find better solutions. One of the best solutions is a strong family unit.

KS: *I heard that you don't allow your assistant to buzz you on the phone.*

FF: Everything is time sensitive. Our eyes are faster than our ears. The tongue is faster than the pen. If my assistant buzzes me on the phone I either need to write down what she is saying or try to remember it. Both are not efficient. If she faxes me, I can quickly make a comment and fax or e-mail her back. Or I have a hard copy to keep with me.

Further, we rarely even write our faxes. Instead we call a transcription company that transcribes it for us, and then faxes it. So if I am off in the wilderness and need to tell my assistant something, I will call the transcriber, tell them the message, and they will fax it.

I see so many inefficient companies that voice mail someone, then they voice mail back and two days later you talk. Either e-mail or fax me. I e-mail or fax a direct response. I rarely talk on the phone during the day.

KS: *How do you feel about meetings?*

FF: Meetings are a waste of time, so very rarely will we have one. If we do it is standing up, and short. A meeting should be to honor or recognize someone in the office. It is not for brainstorming. Usually a meeting takes too long, and does not include the people that should be in on it anyway, and those people who are there are bored, inefficient, and could be doing something productive.

Every person in the office has a project management database (PMD). This includes all long-standing and short-term projects. I pull a copy of this every morning. I respond to what I need to respond to, and the meeting is over.

If we are deciding where to have our Christmas party this year, we don't need a meeting. The person in charge of that project asks everyone through e-mail where they want to have it. She gets the responses and makes a decision. No long meeting required.

KS: *What books would you recommend?*

FF: *The Bible,* of course.

KS: *How about financially related?*

FF: *The Bible* deals with significant issues. It deals with success, relationships, mental health, and of course, finance. For something purely financial I like Andrew Tobias's book called *Beyond Wall Street.*

KS: *What are the periodicals that you read regularly?*

FF: *The Economist, Wall Street Journal, Investor's Business Daily, Business Weekly, Financial Times, Forbes,* and anything else I can get my hands on.

KS: *Let's talk about stock picking. Where do you get ideas?*

FF: Ideas can come from anywhere, at anytime. I could be on a walk, at restaurant. From people we talk to at other companies whose stock we own. We even have a person in our office that gets ideas by watching the financial channels all day.

But when we do get an idea, we act. I am never without my beeper or my phone. I call the transcription company that faxes the message to the person who I want to follow-up on the idea. The same occurs for everyone that has ideas.

KS: *How did you get started?*

FF: In 1961 I attended the University of Wisconsin. While there I met members of the Brittingham family who have operated a financial investment firm. They managed money for the funds of the Nobel Foundation. They gave me a job and I moved to Delaware. Ten years later I started my own investment firm and part of Nobel portfolio came with me.

KS: *You are a 56 years of age and could probably retire comfortably today. What motivates you?*

FF: Oh man! The investment business is so exciting, so dynamic, so compelling. It's intellectual stimulation. People you interact with are exceptional. The people behind the companies we invest in are shaping the world.

But don't forget, as excited as I am about managing money, or you may be at what you do, you shouldn't lose sight of family. We need more mentors. We have lots of children without parents that need mentors. Always give back. If more of us gave back, this country could be so much better.

Changes are constant. Population, inflation, technology, even politics. The challenge of a money manager is to have an antenna tuned to what are those changes and how to get out in front of them. That's not easy. It's the intellectual challenge that stimulates me.

KS: *In a nutshell, tell me your approach to investing.*

FF: Unlike other companies, we have one brand, one flavor. That flavor is vanilla. Our fund is the Brandywine Fund. We want our fund to be the best and find the best companies to invest in. We look for fast growing companies that have the potential to surprise us; meaning we want earnings to come in even better than expected. And we don't like to overpay for the companies; meaning if the earnings ratios are too high, it usually will not fit our model.

Not only do we want great earnings growth, but also we like to see an increasing rate of earnings growth (momentum). So if a company earns 15% one year, we might want to see 20%. We also want to look at the validity of the earnings; meaning we tear apart the balance sheets and net-worth statements. We don't like companies that do funny things with their accounting—funny things like showing a great profit because their tax bracket was lowered. We also don't like to see companies with too much debt.

Finally, we like companies that are solving problems or changing our society in some way.

KS: *And I want world peace. Everybody wants what you have delivered. Let's start with earnings. How can an individual investor find stock with strong earnings?*

FF: There are so many different ways that individual investors can find these types of companies. For example, why not look in a newspaper like *Investor's Business Daily* or the *Wall Street Journal?* Often these papers will show stocks that have reported earnings growth. A stock that reports strong earnings growth one quarter might be the beginning a trend.

You interviewed William O'Neil for this book. He has great research. Look at his daily graphs. Look for stocks that have slowly chugged along with steady volume and steady price. Then look for a change. Look for a pickup in price and/or volume. Chances are someone knows something.

An investor can ask their broker for analyst's reports on various stocks.

We even look in the papers for stocks hitting new highs. Stocks that are hitting new highs are doing so for a reason. Studies show that stocks and sectors hitting new highs can consistently beat stocks and sectors that are "cheap" or hitting new lows. Most papers also publish stocks that have hit new highs versus new lows [see Figure 9-1].

KS: *Sounds like an expensive way to go.*

FF: Would you rather buy stocks on the new low list, trading at under book value? Again, it sounds like a great value, but those stocks are dogs. They usually have poor earnings growth and the stock won't move.

KS: *So ratios such as a low price to earnings ratio are not important?*

FF: Oh, they are very important. We don't want to overpay for the growth. We have found that by not overpaying, or by buying stocks with lower P/E, it takes a great deal of the risk out. If a company is growing at 40% a year, we don't want to pay for a P/E of 40. We would rather pay 16 times earnings for a stock we think is going to grow its earnings by 20%.

Figure 9-1. High and low stocks.

KS: *With a lower P/E and insisting on earnings, don't you miss good stocks?*

FF: Sure we do—lots of them. I'll bet great biotechnology stocks exist with wonderful ideas and new products. We will miss those stocks that are still great ideas, without earnings to back them up. Conversely, we will often miss great companies like Home Depot where we think the P/E ratios are too high.

☆ ☆ ☆ ☆ ☆ ☆ ☆ ☆ ☆ ☆ ☆ ☆ ☆ ☆ ☆ ☆

. . . if we love the management or the balance sheet, or if we believe in a great new product, we will bend and pay a little more for the stock. However, on average we don't like to pay more than 15–18 times next year's earnings for a stock, depending on the industry.

☆ ☆ ☆ ☆ ☆ ☆ ☆ ☆ ☆ ☆ ☆ ☆ ☆ ☆ ☆ ☆

We look at the price to earnings ratio and we compare it to other stocks in the industry. We compare it to the stock market as a whole and the growth rate of that particular company. Also understand that if we love the management or the balance sheet, or if we believe in a great new product, we will bend and pay a little more for the stock. However, on average we don't like to pay more than 15–18 times next year's earnings for a stock, depending on the industry.

KS: *Do you only buy smaller or mid-size companies?*

FF: Absolutely not. We buy whatever stock fits our criteria.

KS: *How do you spot a trend?*

FF: There are so many trends. Take health care for example. Companies are coming up with better drugs. Companies are creating better diagnostic tests, and they are doing it cheaper. Distribution of products is even better. Consider the category killers like wholesale warehouse clubs. We are buying our products cheaper and more efficiently—even old products such as shoes. We have come up with new ways to market and make shoes. We have seen a trend change from people wearing sneakers to hiking boots. This is a trend.

Corporations and individuals are buying airplanes at tremendous rates. Think of what this will do for all the ancillary businesses from airline parts to service contractors. People have more leisure time. Look at the cruising companies, golf companies. The demographics on golf are incredible. This must be a true play on aging.

KS: *What else makes your style unique?*

FF: Once you buy a stock you *must forget two things.* Forget when you bought it and what you paid for it. By strict sticking to this discipline, it will allow an investor to add to a stock that is up 50%, or stock that is down 15%. I know it is hard, but we could care less what we paid or where the stock was priced last year. Simply force yourself not to look at the price. Instead focus on where the stock is going from here and where is it going compared to other stocks you can buy.

KS: *You also talked about finding stocks that will do better than people expect. How do you find these companies?*

FF: Be perceptive. Look for companies that have a new product that will have a tremendous impact. Look for companies that are acquiring interesting investments, or divesting themselves of bad investments. And, of course look for good management.

When we buy new stocks, we talk to management. We find out who they buy things from, their suppliers. This will give us ideas for other stocks. We talk to suppliers. Go into a computer store. See which ones are selling and why. Is Nokia selling more than Motorola? Ask yourself what companies will have a slowdown if Asia has a serious recession.

We recommend that investors go to trade shows. If you are interested in computers, go to computer trade shows. Find out what products everyone is talking about. Who is getting all the attention. These steps provide investors with valuable insight.

KS: *Sometimes it is hard for individual investors to do research, such as talking to management.*

FF: Regardless of how big or small of an investor you are, you should call the company. Talk to the person in charge of investor relations, or the chief financial officer (CFO).

However, even if you don't talk to management you can get hints. That's why I look at stocks hitting new highs. Chances are someone knows something and that's why the stock is going up. Stocks hitting new highs are ones that are having unusually strong earnings growth, or new management, or selling a bad company—all the things we look for in a good investment.

We like finding a stock that is gaining on competitors. Perhaps it was one of the top 10 companies in a particular field, and now it is number 7. We want the number 7 company moving to number 2 or 3.

KS: *Not number 1?*

FF: Usually the number 1 stock is just too expensive.

KS: *You talked about earnings. But many companies have strong cash flow or revenue but no earnings yet. Will you buy companies without earnings?*

FF: Generally no. We don't like to buy on hopes. We like to see earnings now, and try to find companies that will have even stronger earnings (and profits) tomorrow. It's the earnings that we believe allow companies, and ultimately their stocks, to grow.

KS: *How important is talking to management?*

FF: Very.

KS: *What do you talk to management about?*

FF: We want to know what the analysts are projecting the company will earn. We want to know if the company agrees with the analyst's projection. Is it too low? Why?

We always call the company's customers. We ask if they are happy with the proposed company. We ask them why they buy this product. We ask them if they could do without the product or service. Basically we need to know why they need this company. We ask if they also buy from the company's competitors. We ask them to compare the two.

Furthermore, when we talk to management, we always get at least three ideas for a new stock. We ask them who their suppliers are, who their competitors are, and what products and services they can't do without.

I remember doing a survey of a coupon system that drug stores and grocery stores used. There was a total of three competitors in the market. The one that was number 3 was quickly adding new grocery stores and beating their competition. So we called the grocery store and they told us this new company was better and more aggressive. Ultimately this stock grew the most.

KS: *Some critics say you have a great deal of volatility, which creates risk. Usually you bet heavily on certain sectors, which, again, creates risk. How do you respond to this?*

FF: For example, let's assume that I own a large percentage of technology stocks. It's not that I am in love with technology, but it's these companies that fit our criteria of rapid growth at reasonable prices. Further, these companies are the ones that we think will do better than the analysts expect.

Risk has its rewards. We pare down long-term risk by buying what we think are good growth companies at reasonable prices. However, I have long believed that higher volatility brings better long-term returns.

You really need to define risk. Is risk volatility? I am not sure I agree that this is true.

KS: *How do you define risk?*

FF: People define volatility as a surrogate for risk. Risk is risk. Volatility is volatility. I think the case can be made that volatile stocks like Cisco, Dell, and Microsoft could be better investments with lower risk than less volatile stocks such as stock in a utility that has a nuclear power plant. So the assessment of risk is more of an art form and not usually quantifiable. When discussing risk you need to consider a myriad of other factors, factors such as ease of entry, ability to raise prices, raw material supplies, marketing concepts, accounting issues, goodwill, depreciation, ability of management to get new financing, and about 15 other criteria. The industry does not have computer systems that easily quantify risk. So we fall back on a too-simplistic approach such as volatility.

KS: *When looking at stocks, do you look at the stock's alpha or beta?*

FF: I just don't see that as being as important when we invest. Could you imagine the great industrialists like J. P. Morgan or Carnegie or Vanderbilt asking the beta or alpha on a business?

Alphas and betas are statistical measures that define historical volatility and performance compared to an index. These measures just don't include the fundamental research we feel is important.

KS: *Do you lose on many stock purchases?*

FF: Oh yeah. At any time we could be down as much as 40% on the stocks we own.

KS: *Do you buy lots of stocks?*

FF: You bet. We might own several hundred at any given time.

KS: *Over the last several years you sold many of your stocks and simply parked the money in cash. Are you market timing?*

FF: Going to cash is an overstatement. We try to be fully invested. However, when something hits that nobody could see coming, that's different. Markets don't do well in periods of serious uncertainty. Asia is a great example. Overall, long-term we are very bullish. But short-term events can cause huge price swings. My absolute first goal is to make my clients money. It upset a lot of people when we went to cash. But we felt it was right thing to do.

Most importantly, we do a great deal of fundamental research before buying a stock. We believe this is the best way to pick good investments over the long term.

However, the market is not driven by fundamentals. It is driven by perception. And if the perception is something extraordinary, something drastic is going on in the market, why should we sit and wait for all the stocks, including ours, to get hammered?

✯ ✯ ✯ ✯ ✯ ✯ ✯ ✯ ✯ ✯ ✯ ✯ ✯ ✯ ✯ ✯

The market is not driven by fundamentals. It is driven by perception.

✯ ✯ ✯ ✯ ✯ ✯ ✯ ✯ ✯ ✯ ✯ ✯ ✯ ✯ ✯ ✯

KS: *What happened in 1998 that caused you to increase your cash position?*

FF: I remember a stock, Oracle, lost $9^1/_2$ points in one day. After that we started hearing a great deal of bad or negative information. Suppliers overseas were reporting that sales were falling. We noticed that Asian air-plane flights were carrying fewer passengers. So in January (1998), I pranced around Japan, Korea, Tai-wan and Hong Kong. I came back convinced that it was worse over there than what the United States thought.

I think everybody was talking about everything except the negative financial reports that Japanese companies were reporting. I raised cash feeling that their problems would spill over to the United States.

In the beginning of 1998 you had companies trad-ing at close to 35, 40, even 45 times earnings yet the companies are only growing 15% per year. How do you explain that?

KS: *Another rumor has it that you have a strict sell disci-pline and you use a colorful allegory to help us under-stand it.*

FF: Our sell discipline is based on the "Pigs-in-the-trough" theory. Remember, I grew up on a farm in Wisconsin. If you watch the pigs, you will notice that when a pig approaches a group at the feeding trough, it has to shove aside a weaker or less hungry one to get in.

The same survival of the fittest philosophy holds true for the stronger stocks that replace the weaker ones. In that regard, usually we will sell a stock when a better one comes along that we want to buy. We might own a stock trading at 40 that we think will be going to 50. However, if we found another stock we could own that we think is going to 60, we will sell the one we already own to buy a stronger one. So we often sell good companies.

KS: *What are your thoughts on active versus passive man-agement (indexing)?*

FF: I have never been able to understand the logic behind owning an index. When we buy a stock we are making a judgment where a stock will be going only after intensely scrutinizing each fundamental criteria of each stock. If you buy a stock simply because it is part of index, you are buying it because of past successes. This tells you nothing about the future of the stock. Simply, you are making a judgment based on hope.

Tearing Apart a Balance Sheet— A Quick Lesson

The best way to follow the approach of tearing apart a balance sheet is to first obtain a balance sheet. Requesting a copy from the company can do this. Also, most of the web-sites mentioned have a copy of the company's financials. You can also contact the company and ask them to send you research reports that analysts may have written about the company. Your broker or money manager should also be a good source of this.

Let's analyze the accompanying balance sheet and income statement survey on XYZ Company (see Figure 9-2). Realize that this is a summary illustrating the past four years. Either the full balance sheet and the annual summary or the quarterly summary could be easily retrieved from the Internet.

In looking at the cash column, notice that cash for the past two years is significantly higher than the previous year. This helps financial solvency and current and quick ratios. However, you want to know why cash is up. Look in the footnote to the balance sheet or call the company. Ask if they are planning on buying something, or if they just sold a major business. If they just sold a major business, don't add that to normal revenues as it artificially inflates the revenue and earnings number and allows the company to appear to be doing better than it really is. Events such as the sale of a business should be placed aside into a one-time events category.

Also notice that receivables are going down. This is good if it means that the company's customers are paying quickly

Figure 9-2. Balance sheet and income statement survey for XYZ Company.

XYZ Company Balance Sheet Summary	Dec 1997 US $ (12-MOS)	Dec 1996 US $ (12-MOS)	Dec 1995 US $ (12-MOS)	Dec 1994 US $ (12-MOS)
Cash	4102	4165	1463	1180
Securities	5,825	3,829	995	1,230
Receivables	3,503	3,791	3,173	2,010
Allowances	65	68	57	32
Inventory	1,697	1,293	2,004	1,169
Current Assets	15,867	13,684	8,097	6,167
Property and Equipment, Net	18,127	14,262	11,792	8,516
Depreciation	7,461	5,775	4,321	3,149
Total Assets	28,880	23,735	17,504	13,816
Current Liabilities	6,020	4,863	3,619	3,024
Bonds	448	728	400	389
Preferred Mandatory	2,041	275	725	744
Preferred Stock	0	0	0	0
Common Stock	3,311	2,897	2,583	2,306
Other Stockholders' Equity	15,984	0	0	0
Total Liabilities and Equity	28,880	23,735	17,504	13,816
Income Statement Summary				
Total Revenues	25,070	20,847	16,202	11,521
Cost of Sales	9,945	9,164	7,811	5,576
Other Expenses	2,347	1,808	1,296	0
Loss Provision	0	0	0	0
Interest Expense	27	25	29	57
Income Pre Tax	10,659	7,934	5,638	3,603
Income Tax	3,714	2,777	2,072	1,315
Income Continuing	6,945	5,157	3,566	2,288
Discontinued	0	0	0	0
Extraordinary	0	0	0	0
Changes	0	0	0	0
Net Income	6,945	5,157	3,566	2,288
EPS Primary	$4.25	$5.81	$4.03	$5.24
EPS Diluted	$3.87	$0.00	$0.00	$0.00

for the product. But be careful if there are fewer orders coming through. One good indicator is to see what future shares are. Call the company and ask what sales are already booked for the next quarter. This figure is sometimes called book-to-bill numbers.

The recent trend is to show lower inventory. If you have inventory building up, it means you are not selling your product fast enough. This balance sheet shows inventory down from 1994 and 1995 levels but on a trend. It would be advisable to find out why.

This balance sheet shows property and equipment on the rise. Why is it on the rise? Look at the footnote. Perhaps land was reappraised. Analyze all the property if think they understated the real value of their property. You might have stumbled on a true find if the property is undervalued.

In regards to the income statement, the revenue has been steadily climbing. Another bullish sign is the fact that cost of sales is not increasing as fast as revenues.

The income tax in this balance sheet appears to be in line with what you'd expect. A lot of tricks occur here. If the company had a tax loss from previous years, it might be able to offset that in future years. While this is good, it artificially increases the earnings. Conversely, if it got clobbered in taxes this year, it might be an isolated event. Yet the tax will affect its earnings. This would be a great way to spot a possible jump in earnings for the next quarter or year when this tax is no longer an issue. This company had significantly higher taxes. The footnote would probably show why.

Also look closely at its earnings, more closely than we did here. Find out if it has significant earnings or losses from events that are not part of its daily business. For example, let's assume this company sells blue jeans. But assume it lost big money in currency devaluation when it sold overseas. This will not last forever. Or what if it had a big jump in earnings and, with extra cash, bought stocks that made a lot of money? This would artificially increase earnings.

Don't be afraid to tear apart the balance sheet. Look at the latest one. Read the footnotes. Ask for analyst reports. Call the CFO. Such research will help you make the right investment decisions, especially when following Foster Friess's style.

Commentary

If you couldn't tell, let me say that I thoroughly enjoyed meeting Friess and the people at his organization. I believe he and his family are good people. As a result, they find good people to work with. I never thought trading stocks could be done with minimal stress until I met Foster and his gang. Here's a recap of Friess and Associates' stock-picking criteria:

* Rapid growth through earnings growth and momentum
* Modest P/E
* A trend that will boost a company's earnings to more than expected
* New products, good management
* Management's opinions about analysts' projections
* Stock ideas from a company's management and its customers
* Clean accounting (e.g., don't buy a stock that has a great earnings quarter because of a move to a lower tax bracket)
* Strong top-line sales growth
* Ability to forget what you paid for the stock and when you bought it

In regard to his stock picking, you can't argue with success. I believe his style is one of the most commonsense styles yet. He has definitive parameters, yet he isn't totally rigid. I like a manager that says the market is expensive, and that some extraordinary circumstances could cause a serious market correction, so let's increase cash. I also like a manager who is not averse to making bigger bets on certain sectors or stocks in which he or she feels confident.

To me, it makes a great deal of sense to have the primary objective of finding stocks with strong earnings growth and that are not too expensive (as measured in the ratios such as price to earnings, price to sales, and price to cash flow). I like this method even more because I believe these are easy criteria for individual investors to research.

But be ready. I do find that Friess's mutual funds tend to be somewhat volatile. Friess takes bigger bets both with individual stocks and by buying stocks in certain sectors, thereby weighting the portfolio heavily in one or two particular sectors. His reason for doing this, he says, is that it seems when he finds a stock that fits his criteria, generally many more in that same industry seem to start popping up. Often you will see heavy exposure to specific sectors such as technology or health care. If you are investing for yourself, if you are as good as Foster Friess, over the long-term these bets could pay off. Understand that you will take risk in the short-term.

If you decide to follow Friess's philosophy, I would recommend that you start reading the local papers. Find stocks that have heavy volume on one day, or those where the price pops up unexpectedly. *Daily Graphs, Investor's Business Daily,* the *Wall Street Journal,* and *Barron's* are all excellent sources to spot these trends. Many of the popular financial Web sites have programs that allow you to screen stocks in this manner as well.

Also look for ideas when you go into stores. Find out what is selling, who has the best service contracts, and the like.

Finally, do your fundamental research. Most important to this style of investing is anticipating who is going to surprise us with better than expected earnings. Once you compose a list of candidates, weed out the most expensive ones based on P/E ratios.

10

Louis Navellier
A Man Who Has Beat Them All

Name, residence	Louis Navellier, Lake Tahoe, Nevada
Accomplishments	President of Navellier and Associates and the editor of *MPT Review*
Hobbies	Playing golf with wife and spending time with wife and children
Favorite reading	Peter Bernstein's *Capital Ideas: The Improbable Origins of Modern Wall Street,* and *Against the Gods: The Remarkable Story of Risk*
Influential figures	Harry Markowitz and William Sharpe for MPT; his wife and children; and Peter Bernstein
Quotable	"If any of my employees ever love or hate a stock, I have to fire them."
Investment style	Quantitative analysis

Background

While earning his MBA in finance at California State University Hayward, Louis Navellier started a research project to prove that it's possible to beat the stock market with modern portfolio theory (MPT). In 1980 he started publishing his research. From that point forward his career has been moving like a rocket, and he has never looked back.

If you recall from Chapter 3, the theory behind MPT is that the market is efficient. To beat the market, you have to in-

The illustrations in this chapter serve as examples. They change month to month.

crease risk. Well, Navellier takes the theory behind MPT and uses it to actually beat the market. As for risk, that's covered in the interview portion of this chapter.

Something that impressed me a great deal regarding Navellier is that he publishes his research findings. He actually tells you exactly what stocks he is buying, selling, and holding. This information is published in a newsletter called the *MPT Review*. Hulbert Financial Digest, the premier rating service of newsletters, has rated the *MPT Review*'s model portfolio the highest return from 1985 through 1997. This is not a subjective rating; rather, it is calculated based on the cold hard facts of which newsletter had the best return.

Aside from publishing his findings, Navellier manages money. Through private accounts and various mutual funds he manages billions of dollars. Oh, and by the way, he is one of his own largest clients.

Navellier implements quantitative analysis to pick stocks. This approach is similar to the approach of David Katzen (money manager for Marty Zweig, Chapter 6). Quantitative research requires heavy computer firepower to test and backtest theories. Although quantitative analysis is not new, what is new is how Navellier has used his computer to build a model unlike anything I have seen, and certainly different than any other quantitative analyst's. His model is not stagnant; it's ever changing. His philosophy is based on identifying and exploring inefficiencies in the stock market, with the objective of finding stocks to outperform overall market.

Preinterview Info

Prior to meeting Louis Navellier I had never been to Reno (America's biggest little city). The cabby was all too happy to tell me about the city, the changes, and the future of Reno. He pulled up to one of maybe two quasi–high-rise buildings. Although I had been surprised by how casual and relaxed offices of the other all-stars I had previously interviewed were, I still put on my uniform (blue suit, red tie) even though I thought for sure that I would be overdressed here. To my surprise, everyone was dressed. Even Navellier had a tie on.

I did not, however, find a typical (whatever that means) Wall Street money management firm. It was a relaxing, perhaps computer think-tank atmosphere. The pace was slow and I wondered if that is how Navellier chose Reno. (I later found out one of the main reasons was taxes.)

I arrived for my appointment early, and his kind staff allowed me to wait in his personal office. This office consisted of a big conference table and desk. I knew immediately that the conference table was not for conferences. Although I really wasn't sure, it looked as though the table had a mahogany finish. It was hard to tell because the entire table was stacked with books, charts, and graphs.

The rumors about Navellier are that he is a hard worker (often working seven days a week), is terribly analytical, and is passionate about his work. Knowing this, I wasn't sure what to expect. I found a very low-key family man. Twice during our interview he took a call from his wife. She wanted to remind him to pick up her mother from the airport.

The Interview

KS: *What do you do here?*

LN: We manage money. Our goal is to beat the market. If we can't beat the market, why are we here? We also publish, which is something we've been doing for over 18 years. We publish the *MPT Review, The Blue Chip Letter,* and *The Mid-Month Bulletin.* We manage a series of private managed accounts and mutual funds under various names.

We manage over $2 billion with a staff of roughly 55 people. One of the accomplishments I am most proud of is that we very rarely lose accounts. Over the last 13 years we are averaging an annualized return over 20% per year, net of all fees.

Although we manage money, really we are a computer think tank. We build a model that tells us what stocks to buy or sell. We don't sit around deciding if we should buy or sell a stock. Many investors will use quantitative analysis to show them a list of stocks, and the manager might buy what the research suggests. We follow our model exactly.

It just happens to be that we use our research to crack the code of picking winning stocks. Our office doesn't have analysts and researchers. We have computer-smart people. We don't listen to hot stock picks. We don't go to research meetings, or chase a hot initial public offering (IPO). We crunch numbers all weekend. By Sunday night we get a list of stocks that our model says to buy or sell. Over the coming week we carry out what the model suggested we do.

KS: *Your success at managing money speaks for itself. You have beaten most major stock indexes.*

LN: It's not just beating it. It's consistently beating it and how much risk you are taking to beat it.

KS: *And you do this how?*

LN: In today's day and age computer power is awesome. We can try out and test and backtest just about anything we can think up. What we do is find the market inefficiencies. As a result, we tend to capture most of the upside when a market is rising with roughly 20% of the downside. Our system is very dynamic. It changes constantly.

The hard part is not finding the right stock, but matching the right stock to the investor's risk tolerance.

KS: *I thought your newsletter, the* MPT Review *stood for "modern portfolio theory," which means the markets are efficient and individuals, over a period of time, can't beat the market?*

LN: You can beat the markets. We actually use some of the math from MPT. This math shows us what an efficient market is; we then analyze this math further in an effort to beat the market. Our job is to find the stocks that are not efficient.

I will suggest that certain markets are very efficient, markets like the Standard & Poor's 500. I believe it is possible to beat this index, but investors might have to incur more volatility risk. For example, everybody kept talking about how it was impossible to beat the S&P 500 stock market index. It's true, the S&P is very hard to beat. But we did a bunch of backtesting to figure out how to load up on the best stocks in the index in order to beat it. To beat it we take a little more risk volatility risk, but we beat it. What is interesting is that we beat it and our model blue chip portfolio is only 67% correlated with the index.

Modern portfolio theory suggests that the stock market is extremely efficient and almost impossible to beat using the MPT model. Therefore, in 1977 I decided to prove that you could indeed beat the stock market and started my own very ambitious research project. After building a database of approximately 300 over the counter (OTC) stocks, I started calculating alphas (return independent of the market), betas (market sensitivity), and standard deviations (volatility).

After selecting the top 10 percent of the OTC stocks with the highest alphas and lowest volatility between 1977 and 1979, I was shocked by the outstanding performance! Three years of research proved that high alpha stocks outperformed the market. So I used the principals of MPT to beat the market.

KS: *You are perhaps most well known as a small-cap momentum investor.*

LN: We do track a stock's momentum, but we track many other things as well.

KS: *What would you read?*

LN: I'm an academic who is constantly looking for better systems. I like math and statistics. I would not be a good person to ask what they like to read. What I would advise individual investors to learn about different styles of investing. Begin tracking these and find out what style you like. Certain styles you will like some you will not. For example, I respect value investors, but I could not be one.

How I invest has no impact on what I read. I might read *Forbes* for pure enjoyment or personal edification; however, we invest like one would fly a plane in a storm—just on the instruments.

KS: *Tell me a little about the market environment.*

LN: This market environment seems to be rewarding the 50 biggest stocks and many other stocks are not doing much at all. In fact, small stocks have been going down. In the early months of 1988 the earnings momentum of larger stocks was accelerating. So everyone was bullish on the future of corporate earnings. Earnings are easy to track. You could find this, for example, in the *Wall Street Journal.* Every quarter they publish the earnings outlook.

Then, we slowly watched earnings growth fizzle. Much of this had to do with a strong dollar. Multinational companies have a hard time selling overseas when the dollar is so expensive. The early warning signs were when stocks such as Boeing (BA) and Eastman Kodak (EK) came in with lower than expected earnings.

At this point many investors, including big Asian

and other overseas investors wanted quality and kept pouring money into big, blue chip stocks. So blue chip stocks kept going up because people were buying, although warning signals were going off everywhere that earnings might be disappointing. Ironically, the smaller and middle size stocks were going down, when perhaps they actually have better earnings and reasons to actually go up.

KS: *Let's get into your approach to investing, starting with risk.*

LN: Look at the temperature chart [Figure 10-1]. Risk is usually measured in volatility. I don't believe the stock market is that risky of a place if you properly diversify. Nothing will protect you from a market crash, but diversifying properly will make a portfolio less volatile than say if you had 100% of your investments in the S&P 500.

Something that is very important in measuring risk is covariance [see Chapter 3 on asset allocation]. One of the best ways to reduce risk is to balance your see-saw. Covariance basically measures how investments move in relation to one another. The bigger the covariance, the more investments tend to move in opposite directions. Often, depending on the type of market, investments move in opposite directions.

KS: *Your system is based on quantitative analysis. That means you have a clearly defined model. Teach me.*

LN: We start with an initial universe of roughly 9,000 stocks. We weed these stocks out in three main steps: quantitative, fundamental, and optimization. Our quantitative screens pick basically the top 5% of stocks, about 450 of them. Then we apply our fundamental research to these stocks and pick the top 2%. This leaves us with 150. From here we will pick the top 1%, which basically is our portfolio.

Figure 10-1. The reward/risk factor.

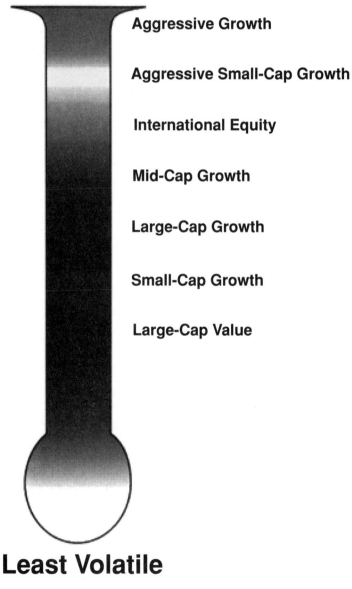

Most Volatile

Aggressive Growth

Aggressive Small-Cap Growth

International Equity

Mid-Cap Growth

Large-Cap Growth

Small-Cap Growth

Large-Cap Value

Least Volatile

Courtesy Navellier & Associates

KS: *Does your model of technical or fundamental indica-*
        tors ever change?

LN: Absolutely. Our model tracks what works on Wall
        Street. We are not looking at buying good businesses
        or anything else like that. If I were looking at buying a
        company to own or to do a leveraged buyout, I would
        probably analyze the company differently. However, I
        care about stock performance. We want stocks that
        will go up. Based on that we will weight our indicators
        to the indicators that are currently the most important
        to Wall Street analysts.

        Three or four years ago people loved stocks with
        free cash flow, then they loved stocks that had the
        highest incremental earnings growth (momentum),
        then they loved stocks that beat analysts' expectations
        (earning surprises). My job is to find best stocks.
        Today nobody cares about cash flow.

        The market is ever changing. Sometimes analysts
        are looking for growth indicators, other times it is
        value. In 1997, value beat growth by the most dra-
        matic margin in 19 years. So instead of guessing what
        works on Wall Street, we build our model according to
        what worked on Wall Street based on the preceding
        one- and three-year basis.

        So, for example, stocks with high return on equity
        (ROE) beat the market over the last three years, but
        did not beat it over the last year. As a result we will
        not use ROE as much in our model.

        The best part about our system is that it is fully
        automated. If a stock hits our radar, great; if not, we
        don't even consider it.

        [These statements and Louis's philosophy are very
        interesting. Much of what he says sounds like he is
        chasing a fad, something we recommend avoiding.
        However, he does stick to his discipline; it's just that

the indicators in his discipline change as the market changes. You will also note how this is truly the antithesis of value investing or Mario Gabelli's approach. Gabelli does the same thing year after year and measures things like ROE and cash flow. Over a period of time he averages a pretty good performance. Louis does the opposite and is similarly successful.]

KS: *Let's talk about your quantitative screens. What are they?*

LN: The quantitative screens are pretty simple and easy to follow. We rarely change them and the purpose is to maximize the reward versus risk ratio. The following is what we measure:

1. *Alpha—excess return independent of the market.* Figure alpha by assuming the return in the market is zero. If this is so, the alpha would be zero. The higher the alpha, the better your return would be, over and above the market. Just buying high alpha stocks could be risky though. Stocks that have high alphas tend to also have high betas. Beta is a measure of risk volatility. The higher the beta, the more volatile the stock is. High volatility often translates to high risk. So what we do is try to bring this down with a few other statistics.

2. *Standard deviation—measure of stock volatility.* The higher a stock's standard deviation, the more risk you would incur. So if we can find the stocks that have the highest alphas with the lowest deviation, it is the best of all worlds.

3. *Reward/risk ratio.* This simple formula is what gives us the best of all worlds. We want to find the stocks that have the maximum possible reward with the lowest risk. To do this we divide the alpha by the standard deviation. By doing so,

the stocks that have the highest reward-versus-risk ratio are systematically weeded out.

By performing all three steps we are left with the best 5% of the stocks based on reward versus risk.

KS: *It sounds like an impressive theory, but how do we know it works?*

LN: We test how effective this strategy is going back one year, and also bring back three years.

Look at these graphs [Figure 10-2]. This proves to me that the markets are *not* totally efficient because I get a downward slope. Look at the chart and notice that the bar column in section one is higher and continues to deteriorate to the 19th column. This is a very good test, proving to me that low reward/risk stocks underperform the market, and that high reward/risk stocks beat the market. So lower reward/risk stocks have the lowest return.

The graphs prove it. In both the three-year test and the one-year test, the stocks in the first column include the ones that are currently on our buy list. The next three columns include stocks we are currently

Figure 10-2. Graph depicting reward versus risk for 3-year and 1-year tests of the S&P 500 and the U.S. Russell 2000.

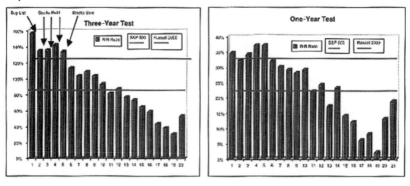

Courtesy Navellier & Associates

holding. The fifth column is stocks on our sell list, and the remaining bars are other stocks in the universe.

Understand, you can just buy high alpha stocks and think you have a winning strategy. We track alpha and the momentum of the alpha; that is, has alpha increased over the last six months?

KS: *Let's talk about your fundamental indicators.*

LN: Our goal is to find the fundamental statistics that are best at driving prices higher. We study and backtest, again based on one and three years, the value and growth screens that have worked the best. Depending on which indicators worked the best, we weight the statistics to show that one statistic might be more accurate and more important than another.

KS: *How do you know the statistics you are looking at work the best?*

LN: We test indicators. We start with the top 10 and go all the way down to 30. As soon as the statistic does not work anymore, the results decay. When the results decay we stop using the indicator. Every quarter we test what works and update the system accordingly.

KS: *Give me an example of all of the indicators that you might track at any one time.*

LN: I'll give you a list of all our indicators. The weighting of these indicators change, but we can discuss this later. [See Figure 10-3.]

KS: *Give me an example of an indicator that seems to work well over both a one-year and a three-year period.*

LN: If you look at a company's earnings growth, it is a good indicator. Companies over the last three years that have had the best earnings growth had done very well. Over one year this method has still worked, but not as well.

So what we did is we searched the stocks that had the best earnings growth divided by the price to earn-

Figure 10-3. Current screens tested for Navellier's system.

■ 1. Alpha	■ 19. 6-Month IBES Earnings Est. Change
■ 2. Alpha Momentum	■ 20. Liquidation Value per Share
■ 3. Error Adjusted Alpha (Alpha - Error)	■ 21. Forward P/E
■ 4. Error Adjusted Alpha (Alpha/Error)	■ 22. P/E Change
■ 5. Reward Risk Ratio (Alpha / Std Dev)	■ 23. Price / Book Latest Twelve Months
■ 6. 6-Month Alpha	■ 24. Price / Earnings
■ 7. 6-Month Alpha Momentum	■ 25. Price / Net Working Capital
■ 8. 6-Month Error Adjusted Alpha	■ 26. Present Value Growth Opportunities
■ 9. Sharpe Ratio	■ 27. Quarter Earnings Per Share Growth
■ 10. Book to Price	■ 28. Reinvestment Rate
■ 11. Free Cash to Market Value	■ 29. Return on Equity Change
■ 12. Earnings Growth / PE	■ 30. Sales Momentum
■ 13. 12-Month Earnings Change	■ 31. Standardized Unexpected Earnings
■ 14. Earnings Momentum	■ 32. Sustainable Growth
■ 15. Earnings Change	■ 33. Year to Year Earnings Growth
■ 16. Historical Growth Rate	■ 34. Price / 50-Trading Day Average Price
■ 17. 1-Month IBES Earnings Est. Change	■ 35. Price / 2-Year High Price
■ 18. 3-Month IBES Earnings Est. Change	■ 36. Dividend Discount Model

Courtesy Navellier & Associates

ings ratio (EPS divided by P/E). The stocks that had the lowest multiple have performed excellent over both one and three years. [This no longer works on a one-year basis.]

This figure [Figure 10-4] proves it. Stocks in our universe that we would consider buying or are holding are in the first three columns. These stocks over one and three years consistently beat the market.

KS: *When you research stocks and backtest the top performers, are there any commonalities that actually surprised you?*

LN: I am always surprised by what works on Wall Street. However, what I do is accept what works and don't question it. One example of something that surprised me is that companies that reinvest back into their companies, in land or equipment, in buying back stock, etc., tend to do much better. Many computer software programs track a company's reinvestment

Figure 10-4. Graphs depicting earnings per share growth/price-to-earnings ratio multiples using the Russell 2000 stock index.

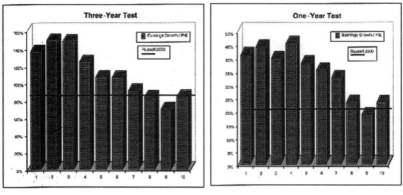

Courtesy Navellier & Associates

rate so it would not be too hard to track. I can show you in a graph how the stocks with the highest reinvestment rate and lowest P/E perform as compared with other stocks. [See Figure 10-5.]

KS: *Depending on if you are buying big stocks or small stocks, does your weighting change on the fundamental models?*

Figure 10-5. Graphs depicting how stocks with the highest reinvestment rates and lowest P/E's perform as compared with other stocks.

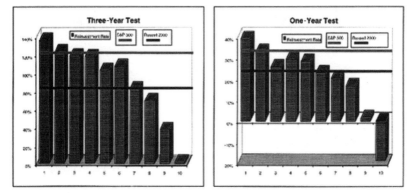

Courtesy Navellier & Associates

LN: Yes. Different fundamental statistics work depending on the type of stock. Although we change our models regularly, here is an example [Figure 10-6] of what a typical fundamental model would look like.

KS: *Once you find the stock, how do you maximize it?*

LN: Great question. We call that portfolio optimization. When we find stocks that fit our criteria, many of the stocks in the same category or industry come up. If a sector is doing well, many stocks in that sector will do well. Stocks run in packs. Good examples of this include technology, pharmaceuticals, etc.

        Well, if we overweight a portfolio with too much in one industry it would increase risk. [Recall the dis-

Figure 10-6. Example of a typical fundamental model in Navellier's system and what each indicator represents.

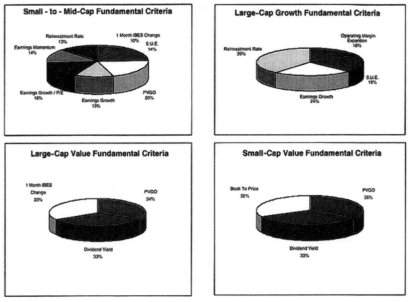

Courtesy Navellier & Associates

cussion of covariance in Chapter 3.] That is where we employ the critical work of modern portfolio theory. The whole goal is to maximize return and minimize risk. So we do the math and look for stocks that are negatively correlated.

You could take our model and push to try and get a higher return, but you would be increasing your risk. We have never had a down year, so the system works.

☆ ☆ ☆ ☆ ☆ ☆ ☆ ☆ ☆ ☆ ☆ ☆ ☆ ☆ ☆ ☆

We have never had a down year, so the system works.

☆ ☆ ☆ ☆ ☆ ☆ ☆ ☆ ☆ ☆ ☆ ☆ ☆ ☆ ☆ ☆

KS: *How do you do this?*

LN: We want to zig when the market zags.

KS: *What do you mean?*

LN: For example, if oil stocks are going down, it might help boost airline stocks because airlines will get their oil prices cheaper. This is negatively correlating the stock.

KS: *But how does the portfolio reduce risk—in English?*

LN: We take several steps. First we monitor standard deviation. If the standard deviation is high, you will be taking more risk. What standard deviation does is show us a probable range in which a stock may move up or down compared to the market. This is called unsystematic risk. If a stock moves within its trading range and does not exceed its standard deviation, this is normal and acceptable risk. The stocks that exceed their standard deviation increase this risk. The measure of standard deviation is perhaps the most important indicator in measuring a stock's potential risk.

Our fundamental criteria is strict as it looks for the best growth stocks, with the lowest risk. The same is true for our quantitative research. We find the best potential growth stocks with the lowest volatility measures.

Finally we have a strict sell discipline. If either the quantitative or fundamental criteria deteriorates, it's out of the portfolio. We only keep the top stocks.

KS: *Elaborate on your sell discipline.*

LN: Our sell discipline is simple. If a stock falls out of the top 20% of our reward versus risk criteria based on the quantitative screen, we sell. If the stock falls out of the top 70% of the fundamental screens, it is sold.

Commentary

At first glance, you might think it would be difficult to implement Louis Navellier's approach. However, in actuality, his approach might be the easiest investing approach there is. You don't sit by a stock trading screen; research does not take all of your time. In fact, Louis himself crunches all of the numbers over the weekend and on Monday comes up with his buys.

Now it's true that you don't have the computer firepower that Louis has, but you do have access to it. Here is what you do:

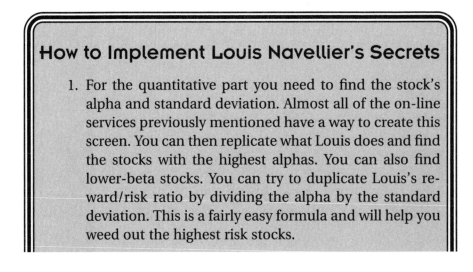

How to Implement Louis Navellier's Secrets

1. For the quantitative part you need to find the stock's alpha and standard deviation. Almost all of the on-line services previously mentioned have a way to create this screen. You can then replicate what Louis does and find the stocks with the highest alphas. You can also find lower-beta stocks. You can try to duplicate Louis's reward/risk ratio by dividing the alpha by the standard deviation. This is a fairly easy formula and will help you weed out the highest risk stocks.

2. The same is true for the fundamental research. Just create a screen. You can decide how much you want to weight certain screens, and how often you wish to change them.

3. If you still think you need more guidance, here is a novel idea: subscribe to Louis Navellier's newsletter. This way you can continue to track what he is doing and how he changes his models, and do so in a relatively affordable manner.

11

Don Phillips
Everything You Always Wanted to Know About Mutual Funds but Were Afraid (or Didn't Know) to Ask

Name, residence	Don Phillips, Chicago
Accomplishments	CEO of Morningstar, which he built; tireless advocate for the mutual fund industry
Hobbies	Family, music, and sports (he's a Chicago Cubs season ticket holder)
Favorite reading	John Train's *The Investment Masters* and Benjamin Graham's *The Intelligent Investor*
Influential figures	His father; Sir John Templeton; Louis Rukeyser; and Jo Vinsweto
Quotable	"The unlived life isn't worth examining."
Investment style	Quantative and subjective research to find the best mutual funds

What You Don't Know About Mutual Funds Can Be Dangerous

Thousands of mutual funds exist. Many have terrible performance. Many others are too expensive. How do you find not only the best funds, but the best funds for you?

Nine Things You Need to Know About Your Mutual Fund—Or You Are Forbidden to Invest

1. *Can you trust the mutual fund advertisements?* Advertising can be manipulated. Advertisements might state that a particular mutual fund had a long-term average. Remember, it is easier to have good performance over the long-term. Furthermore, be careful if an ad tells you it is a "best performing fund." What is it best in? The index? The sector? As declared by a rating service, and if so which one?

Be careful of tricky statements. A mutual fund advertisement might suggest that its fund has returned a certain percentage since a certain time. For example, "Since the market low of 1987, we are a best performer." What did the fund return before the market low? Chances are the return was dismal and that is why the advertisement says "since" the market low, as opposed to "before" the market low.

2. *What is the fund* really *doing with your money?* You would think that a government bond mutual fund would have all, or a vast majority, of its assets in government bonds, but that's not true. I called many government bond funds and found that these funds invested in everything from Ginnie Maes to Treasury futures.

What if you thought you had a large-cap growth fund, only to find out the fund was investing a great deal in small-cap international stocks?

Many mutual funds buy futures, options, and derivatives. Some mutual funds do this to reduce risk. Most do it to increase return, which really increases the risk of the fund. Many seemingly conservative bond funds use these strategies to provide a little higher yield to the investor. Question the higher yield and find out exactly what the mutual fund's position is regarding futures, options, and derivatives.

You must read the prospectus and find out what the mutual fund bylaws state it is allowed to do with your money. Then call the mutual fund company and ask the following questions: What are the current sectors it is invested in and what is the weighting in each sector? What are the top ten holdings and the percentage of the fund in each holding? How much cash is the fund currently holding?

3. *Who is the fund's manager?* Before buying a mutual fund, obtain biographical information on the mutual fund manager. Think of it as interviewing someone for a job, because you are. You are interviewing for the most important job—someone to manage your money.

Your fund might have been performing great for the last five years, but recently the fund manager left the company, and now some new person is managing the fund. Always ask how long the person was managing the fund.

Find out how the mutual fund manager gets paid and earns his or her bonus. I am a big believer that the bonus be tied to the net return *after taxes and expenses.*

4. *How much money is the mutual fund* really *making for you?* This seems like an easy question to answer but it's not. First you need to figure out the gross return of the fund. Then figure the return net of all fees and expenses. Finally, determine how much the fund made for you after taxes (see question 5).

Lots of mutual funds use averages. "Our fund has averaged 15% per year, over the last five years." Never look at the return based on an average. An average is too easy to manipulate. If markets are doing well, so would the mutual fund averages. I would rather you look at the return every single year, year in, and year out. This will also help get away from a closet index fund—one that basically follows the index, but probably charges you more (see question 7).

5. *How risky is your fund?* Investing is about risk versus reward. Even if your mutual fund has enjoyed a positive return, it still might not be worth the risk it is incurring. To maximize the return while minimizing the risk, find returns with a low

beta, high alpha, and low standard deviation. This information can be obtained by calling the fund or on a most mutual fund reports prepared by a rating service, such as Morningstar.

All of these measures compare the proposed fund to a benchmark, usually the Standard & Poor's 500 Index. The S&P 500 is given the number 1. If your mutual fund has a beta of higher than 1, then your fund will be more volatile than the benchmark. It might move up more, but it might move down more. Funds with lower betas tend to be safer and less volatile. Conversely, the alpha measures how well a mutual fund has performed against the market. The higher the alpha, the better the return of the mutual fund, independent of the market. The higher the alpha the better.

Standard deviation is also a measure of volatility. Stocks and mutual funds usually trade in an accepted trading range. If the stock or mutual fund continues to move outside the trading range, it will have a higher deviation. The higher the deviation, the more risk.

6. *What are the fees and expenses of the mutual fund?* An investor must weigh the fees and expenses of a mutual fund to the return. Obviously, an investor would prefer lower fees and expenses, but don't rule out a fund if the expenses are high when the fund and its performance are superior.

Pay attention to the expense ratio, the ongoing expenses of the fund. These expenses are netted out of the fund and your return is reduced by the amount of the expenses. Furthermore, many funds, usually funds sold through brokers, have additional fees to buy the fund or if you pull your money early. These are called loads. Be aware of the loads prior to investing.

7. *Did you choose a mutual fund that is going to hand you a bill?* You need to consider taxes on your mutual funds three times: before you buy the fund, every year when you get your 1099 form, and when you sell. I consider the 1099 form a bill, since you'll have to pay taxes if you receive one.

What if your mutual fund has bought and sold many

stocks throughout the year? You see the fund is doing well, so you invest in the fund late in the year (say, November). All of the sudden in the middle of December the fund pays a long- and short-term capital gain of $2 per share. You get whacked! For tax purposes, timing when you buy a mutual fund is critical. Before investing, call the company and find out if there will be a long- and short-term capital gain and the amount. There could be a chance that the fund had losses from a previous year to help offset the gains of a current year.

8. *Are you buying a closet index fund?* Many mutual funds buy almost identical stocks that are in a certain index such as the S&P 500. Often they weight the stock holdings similar to the index as well. These are known as closet index funds. Many of these closet index funds have higher fees than the index and don't have as good a return.

9. *Should you get excited about big mutual funds?* Sometimes people only invest in big mutual funds. Big funds often get too big; fund managers have too much money to invest prudently. Further, when they want to sell one of their stock holdings, the big funds usually have so many shares they can't sell a big chunk all at one time. This position could affect the return of the fund.

Mutual funds have become the investment of choice for many individuals. They are easy to invest in, to track, and to sell. Quite simply, they are easy, and that is actually one of the possible problems with this method of investing. Because it is easy, people are not doing the proper amount of homework. They aren't researching the fund, the fund's holdings, expenses, and risk. People know more about popular sports figures than they do about who is managing their money, the mutual fund manager.

Because mutual funds are easy, mistakes are made. Statistics show people aren't owning their mutual funds very long, with evidence showing that investors are selling their funds when the market starts to go down. Shouldn't you be buying more when the market goes down? Follow me on this scenario:

Mrs. Stern decides to buy XYZ Mutual Fund. She invests $10,000. One year later the stock market starts to drop. She gets nervous. So do many other individuals. The mutual fund is 100% invested, meaning there is no money in cash to buy more stock. The mutual fund manager desperately wants to buy more stocks at these great low prices. Darn it, it's a blue-light special, and the manager has no money to take advantage of it! Usually people invest more money in this mutual fund every day. But because they are so nervous about the market, nobody is investing. Thus, no new money to invest.

But wait, it gets worse. The market goes down further. Now Mrs. Stern really gets scared. She decided to sell her mutual fund. Well, so do a hundred other investors in the mutual funds. Now the mutual fund manager is really in a panic. In order to cash these investors out, the fund manager will need to sell stocks to raise cash. But this is the wrong time to sell stocks. All of the stocks are down. If you sell now you would be taking a loss. The manager screams at these investors that they should be buying more. But to no avail.

Now that the investors are pulling money out, the mutual fund manager sells the stocks. The mutual fund now is reporting a loss, all of the investors panic and sell. And all sold at the wrong time. I repeat: One of the problems with the ease of investing in mutual funds is the ease in investing in mutual funds. By selling at the wrong time, you aren't allowing the fund manager to do his or her job. Any person investing in mutual funds must do as much, if not more, research than if investing in a stock.

Background

Almost everyone who has ever invested in a mutual fund has heard of Morningstar in some way, shape, or form. Morningstar is considered the premier source for unbiased, insightful mutual-fund information. Either its "star" rating has been part of the advertising a mutual fund used, you have read its research through *Morningstar Reports,* or you have seen it on the Internet. But are you, and are the fund companies, using Morningstar correctly? Morningstar has been much debated among mutual fund companies, investors, and even regulatory bodies such as the National Association of Securities Dealers (NASD) and the Securities and Exchange Commission (SEC).

This candid interview provides unique and first-hand insight as to the helmsman of Morningstar, Don Phillips. You will learn about the mutual fund industry, running a dynamic company, and the future of the mutual fund industry. I am sure you will enjoy it as much as I did.

The interview is followed by an explanation of how to read a Morningstar report.

Preinterview Info

As you have been reading, I have been on a quest for my image of Wall Street: people in pinstripe suits, starched shirts, and polished wing-tip shoes. I wasn't going to find it in the Morningstar offices. Located in the business district of Chicago, Morningstar's offices are comfortable (not plush) and large. The male receptionist was dressed in "casual Friday" attire. As a matter of fact, I didn't meet one employee in a suit. And as I toured the offices I found there were none, offices that is. Officials at Morningstar decided offices were unnecessary, a waste of space, and counterproductive. I couldn't wait to ask Don Phillips how he gets away with no offices and casual day. I heard from the employees that Don doesn't even have an office.

The feel you get in the Morningstar office is not one of a Wall Street firm, but more like a technology firm located in

Silicon Valley. In fact, Morningstar employs as many web-designers and programmers as it does mutual fund analysts.

What I enjoyed most about getting to know Don Phillips was his strong conviction and philosophy regarding the mutual fund industry. He talks of a long-term debate between the academic world of investing and the practical. Don Phillips believes that certain mutual funds are truly all-star performers and that certain funds can consistently beat the index.

The Interview

KS: *Don, please enlighten us about your background and how you came to be here today.*

DP: I am from Texas and went to the University of Texas to study economics. About the time I was getting ready to graduate, Texas was in a major recession, everything was slumping. This was not very appealing to me as I was graduating as an economics major. I didn't think I would get a job in economics, so I went to the University of Chicago to study American literature. My thinking was that I would become a professor and teach literature. I would be an active investor for my hobby.

The reality was that I didn't love graduate school. Books and literature all became secondary. It was very political. I spent all my time reading criticism of literature. Everything you think you are escaping from in academia you end up exactly with that. It was political and unrewarding.

So I decided to switch things around. My new goal was to see if I could get job investing and writing about investing. Then I would read books as my hobby.

KS: *I can't wait to ask you what you recommend us to read.*

DP: Actually we have a reading list here at Morningstar
        that is updated regularly. However, it deals mostly
        with stuff on how to understand this business. Under-
        stand, many of our employees are web designers and
        computer specialists.

        However, my view on literature is that you should
        read deeply and broadly while you are very young to
        gain the advantage of different viewpoints. And then
        read very deeply later in life so you can reflect back
        upon what you have gone through bringing in all of
        your experiences. Somewhere in the middle you have
        to live your life. In Chicago people used to be drawn
        around a phrase "the unexamined life was not worth
        living." I thought the inverse of that is even more true:
        "The unlived life isn't worth examining."

        I wanted to make decisions and help people, and
        I wasn't sure I could accomplish that in literature.
        Teaching people about and how to understand invest-
        ing could do that. But my background of literature
        helped me invest. In literature you are inundated with
        all these different facts through a book. You need to
        sort through all the overload of information, all the
        noise. You need to know what to throw away, what
        salient group of points makes a cohesive argument.
        This ability, this analytical thinking, is helpful as an
        investor.

KS: *So what reading do you recommend?*

DP: When we started Morningstar we developed a recom-
        mend reading list. My advice is to get a broad sam-
        pling. In the investment realm, the following are a few
        good books to get started with: Andrew Tobias's *The
        Only Investment Guide You'll Ever Need* has a very
        common sense approach; *A Random Walk Down Wall
        Street* by Burton Gordon Malkiel; and John Bogle's
        Bogle on Mutual Funds.

KS: *What about magazines and periodicals?*

DP: Again read broadly. My dad used to tell me to read both papers in town; read the blue collar and white collar.

      Definitely read all the major business magazines and papers. What a wonderful bargain! To get all that insight, all these different views! I mean, what they put together at the *Wall Street Journal* on a daily basis is phenomenal. All for just 75 cents!

      I read *Fortune, Forbes, Business Week,* and *Newsweek.* Even bucking the Wall Street establishment, I believe you can get good information from magazines such as *Money.*

KS: *But aren't some of their* (Money Magazine) *ideas overly simplistic?*

☆ ☆ ☆ ☆ ☆ ☆ ☆ ☆ ☆ ☆ ☆ ☆ ☆ ☆ ☆

A great idea can't be the enemy of good.

☆ ☆ ☆ ☆ ☆ ☆ ☆ ☆ ☆ ☆ ☆ ☆ ☆ ☆ ☆

DP: *Money* might be overly simplistic, but think of how this magazine has elevated financial understanding in this country. A great idea can't be the enemy of good. You simply can't disagree that *Money* isn't for anything but good.

KS: *Great point. It's refreshing to talk to a practical person that does not have his nose pointed skyward. [Pause] When you did get into the investment community, what were your thoughts?*

DP: Coming from the outside I was a little more skeptical. It seemed like a group of insiders. People who work in investments (Wall Streeters) have this lingo and special jargon. And if you didn't know all the latest jargon, the Wall Street insiders would think less of you. That is plain crazy. I remember a line someone once told me: Warren Buffett wasn't the brightest person he knew, just the brightest person that went into finance. Just because people on Wall Street get so much attention and get paid so much money doesn't necessarily mean they are the cream of the crop—the best there is to offer. To some extent you hope that isn't the case.

KS: *Who would you consider your role models?*

DP: I think that will change over time. On average I would say my dad; Jo Vinsweto, the founder of Morningstar; John Templeton; and Louis Rukeyser.

My dad is a typical hard-working American. He saved money every month. He taught me the value of saving and investing. Like other kids, I received many gifts growing up. However, the only gift I remember growing up with was the money he put into a mutual fund for me. That fund was the Templeton Growth Fund. I learned a lot about Mr. (Sir) Templeton, I read his books and watched my money grow.

☆ ☆ ☆ ☆ ☆ ☆ ☆ ☆ ☆ ☆ ☆ ☆ ☆ ☆ ☆ ☆

The only gift I remember growing up with was the money my dad put into a mutual fund for me.

☆ ☆ ☆ ☆ ☆ ☆ ☆ ☆ ☆ ☆ ☆ ☆ ☆ ☆ ☆ ☆

KS: *Why Louis Rukeyser?*

DP: As you know, he is host of the extremely popular *Wall Street Week*. He has hosted that show for decades. Louis Rukeyser is the consummate professional. Even after all these years, he has complete quality control. He writes his own material and cares passionately about the quality. I believe that's how people, and how he, can stay on top as he has after all these years. After the show you would think he rushes back to his home (which is hours away). But that is not the case. Even after all these years, after the show he sits and watches (while munching on carrots) the entire replay of the show. That is truly sweating the details.

KS: *So how did you get to Morningstar?*

DP: I wanted to be a mutual fund analyst. All of the advertisements I saw were for salesmen. Morningstar was started by Jo Vinsweto in 1984, I answered an ad in the paper and I started in 1986.

I started working at Morningstar when they had three employees. They were publishing a quarterly source book at the time. Jo wanted to make a publication that was more timely (as opposed to quarterly) and included written analysis. The problem was Jo wanted to create this and begin shipping immediately. (Jo is a true entrepreneur.) So he gave me the project. I started in October and by December we came out with the Morningstar mutual fund report. One of Jo's favorite lines is "A violently executed plan today is better than a perfectly executed plan tomorrow."

KS: *You talked about Louis Rukeyser sweating the details. Do you sweat details?*

DP: At Morningstar we have over 360 employees. I hired people to do a job and believe they will do it. What I do sweat is the details in my writing. I still do all my writing and don't believe that anyone should ever delegate that.

KS: *I must confess, I don't feel like I am sitting in a Wall Street investment firm.*

DP: Well that's good. When we developed the firm we looked toward Apple Computer as opposed to, say, Goldman Sachs for our role model on how we want our company to run. As you look around you will not see any offices. I don't even have an office. The only office we have is for our human resources director. We have no corporate hierarchy. Our working environment has an energy, a vitality that is often lost in investment firms and we don't want to lose it.

KS: *I noticed that everyone is dressed casual.*

DP: We actually started out wearing suits. The reason we decided to go to casual dress is as a result of the computer programmers. As we hired more computer programmers, Web designers, etc., we couldn't hire the best—they wouldn't dress up.

KS: *You are perhaps as close to the mutual fund industry as anyone. Share with us your perspectives on the industry in general.*

DP: Mutual funds have been woven into the fabric of financial planning in America. This has been codified with 401K. Part of the reason mutual funds have become popular is that they are the perfect investment for baby boomers. Baby boomers were not good at savings and investing. So investing was shaped and repackaged into something baby boomers are very familiar with: spending and consuming. With mutual funds you have brand names, you buy in even dollar amounts, and even have sales. If you take investing and shape it as consuming, that is what mutual-fund investing is like.

I do believe as people continue to learn and familiarize themselves with investing, they might "graduate" from mutual funds to stocks as they become more astute.

The growth in 401(K) plans has been great to get people to take an active role in investing. People are now being introduced to investing a little earlier in life and recognizing they have a stake at providing for their own retirement. I believe after we achieve success in 401, many of us will move beyond and perhaps "graduate" to closed-end funds and then possibly individual stocks.

KS: *How will the new tax code affect mutual funds?*

DP: People will begin to pay more attention to taxes inside of funds. This has become a major issue for two reasons. One reason is the tax law change. The second reason is the average everyday investor that has been investing in mutual funds has probably seen his or her accounts grow to the point that the taxes are beginning to affect them.

   The fund industry has ignored taxes and this can't continue. If you and I ignored taxes we would go to jail.

KS: *But what about fund managers becoming tax planners and affecting the returns?*

DP: The question is how to best solve it. Who should be responsible: the financial planner, the investor, or the fund manager? Taxes are an investor, not an investment, issue, meaning that investors need to know how to allocate their money, in which funds and investment choices, to handle the taxes the fund will produce. With that said, if there are things the fund manager can do to make the fund more tax efficient, they need to be mindful of this, or to communicate if they will be paying attention to the tax situation or not.

   One question that should be asked, and fund managers should tell you, is: Is the manager's compensation linked to pretax or posttax compensation?

   [Note that when you read Bogle's interview, he was critical on this subject.]

KS: *Are there other strategies for lowering taxes on a mutual fund?*

DP: This may sound odd, but an investor might consider investing in a fund that has large losses. An investor can get into a fund *after* the losses have occurred and when the fund starts making money, the capital gains will be offset by the losses of the previous years. For example, take some of the funds that have lost so much money in Asia. Some of these funds might have losses that will be offset by future gains.

KS: *What about tax-deferred variable annuities?*

DP: Holding mutual funds inside of variable annuities could be great. What an investor needs to do is weigh the cost of the annuity versus the benefit. Obviously there is a trade-off. Oftentimes one focuses too much on one side of debate.

KS: *What are your thoughts regarding mutual fund managers and the future of the industry?*

DP: There's an interesting phenomena in the investment world. Wall Street is missing a generation. People who were not entering the market in 1970s didn't enter during a bear market. You now have a seasoned veterans, in the twilight of their careers, turning over big funds to people in their early 30s. Sir John, who is in his 70s has turned over the reins to Mark Holowesko, in his 30s. Understand, I believe Mr. Holowesko to be every bit up to the task and extremely confident. But you see that a generation is missing.

KS: *So much information is available for investors today, how do you feel about that?*

DP: It's great in the fact that many of the artificial barriers are down. Wall Street always thought individuals were dumb. Now we have access to same information as they do. This information has created a "power shift." This shift poses a different challenge on how to get through overload of information. Although there is no doubt it is better to have information than not.

    Now we need to learn how to bridge the gap between data and knowledge. Now the investor has to learn how to make sense of the information. Now everyone has access to the same stuff. Investing isn't just understanding the investment, rather it's deciding what information is important.

In my experience, certain managers exist that sit around and try to analyze the direction of the market, other's don't. So if the big question is where the market is going to be, and you try to find information to answer that, I think it is a dumb question and a waste of time. The guy that wins turns over more rocks. Why do you think Mario Gabelli is so popular?

It's the same with a financial planner. A financial planner's worth isn't trying to forecast the market five years from now. No one can answer that—not even your financial planner.

KS: *Talk about the financial planner.*

DP: With all the available information out there, the financial planner's role has shifted. Financial planners' expertise is not that they have information the public doesn't. Financial advisers should know how to make sense of it, should know how to match the right investment with the right investor. Financial advisers should be able to get clients to answer questions about themselves more honestly than you would on your own.

A financial adviser should be able to get investors to stick with a program.

KS: *Can't people do that on their own?*

DP: Sure, and sometimes they should. However, to have an impartial third party is helpful for many reasons, including as a sounding board for a second opinion or new ideas.

In the past, financial advisers used to represent a product. That may still go on to an extent today. However, I believe this has shifted so that financial advisers are now representing clients.

Investors want two services that have value: security selection and portfolio construction. Both have value. But an investor can't pay 2% in mutual fund fees and 2% to the financial advisor. Both services are available, but a happy medium needs to be found.

Unfortunately, the price of mutual funds (the expense ratio) has been creeping up, which does not leave a great deal on the table for the financial adviser. That's unfortunate, especially because I believe the service that the investor needs more is portfolio construction and portfolio assembly, not the security selection.

KS: *Index (passive investing) has become extremely popular. What are your thoughts on passive versus active investing?*

DP: Active versus index funds has been misportrayed as being an either-or situation. Think of a horseshoe. On one hand you have low-cost passive strategies such as indexing. On the one hand you have great managers at moderate cost. Either option is a solution for prudent investing. Probably some combination of both is the solution. The enemy is the middle of the horseshoe. The funds that have higher cost and do not particularly manage the funds well are the lion's share of the industry. The key is for the investor to find one of the ends.

         I think it is wrong to compare funds to the index (Standard & Poor's 500). I look for funds that do something different than the market. I don't want a closet index fund. If I am willing to pay for active management, I want them to do something different.

KS: *But many academics state that you can't beat the index. That is the whole theory behind efficient markets. And the index has beat most funds.*

DP: To say that an investor can't beat the market assumes that there is no talent on Wall Street. That is what academia wants you to believe. But you can't say that about people in art, science, or medicine. Academics can't put individuals in a database.

KS: *Why is Morningstar important?*

DP: It is a great tool to help investors screen funds. It provides baseline facts and distills information I need to know before investing. It is partially objective and partially subjective. It provides investors with critical insight as to the fund manager, the risk associated with the fund, historical returns, etc. With all information available to an investor, Morningstar should be able to take the raw data and make sense of it.

      However, I do want to remind you that investing is not just understanding the investment; it's matching the investment with the investor.

KS: *What did you mean by "partially objective" and "partially subjective"?*

DP: We have trained analysts who meet with fund managers and get a feel for the actual manager. Our thoughts will be relayed in the commentary section of our report. That part is subjective. If we think the manager is well suited for the task of managing the fund, or if we think that the manager will aggressively look for good stocks, we will talk about it. The returns, risk, and investment style are much more objective. A mutual fund manager cannot "talk us into" receiving a five-star rating. It's totally based on what the manager has done. That is totally based on the risk-adjusted, cost-adjusted, return-adjusted numbers. It is purely objective.

KS: *Certainly many people use Morningstar for their "star rating." Do you think too much reliance is placed on the star?*

DP: Star is an achievement test, not an aptitude test. These funds have made certain achievements. They have had better returns relative to the risk that they have taken. They have had lower cost and have done well relative to their peers. But investors must continue asking, "Are the people and practices that helped earn this star still in place?" And, "Is the market environment representative of one we will encounter in future?" Funds and markets are not static.

The star is an intelligent first-stage screen. There are 8,000-plus mutual funds. You can't look at each one individually. This will help you begin the process.

But the star, or anything for that matter, cannot be used as a surrogate for exercising judgement. Investing is about exercising judgement. No mechanical screen can tell you if this investment is right for you or if it will continue to perform as it has. However, it can be helpful in screening.

KS: *Many planners say don't buy a five-star fund. The thought is that a five-star fund has already seen a great deal of growth. Perhaps the sector or types of stocks that managers invested in were the hot stocks over the last few years, but an investor might be better suited to buy a three- or four-star fund on its way to a five-star fund.*

DP: I have heard this rationale and there is some merit to it. However, five-star funds have become five-star for a reason. For those astute investors who can look at a three- or four-star fund and see its possible growth pattern, this concept might make sense. This strategy will also depend on the market conditions as well.

KS: *You talk about risk. How do you measure it?*

DP: Actually it's one of the most difficult things we do. And it is very limiting. Whenever you talk about risk measures such as standard deviation, alpha, and beta, these are great measures but they measure *what has already happened—it's in the past.*

Morningstar deals with results, risk, and cost; what is the historical change? When we measure risk, we focus on downside risk. To do this we will look at what the fund has historically demonstrated in performance. When we measure risk, we focus on downside risk. To do this, we will look at what the fund has historically demonstrated in performance. Instead of defining loss as zero, we raise the standard a little higher. We figure out what the Treasury Bill rate is and consider that rate to be the break-even point. This is because a Treasury Bill is still considered a minimum risk investment. We then look at the return of the fund month by month. We look at the last three years, and isolate all months the fund did not hit the Treasury Bill rate. Add up all the months that are negative and divide it by the number of months in the sample (usually three years). This number will give us the average loss. By doing it this way, it takes into account frequency and the severity of the loss. We then take this average loss number and compare it to the average loss of all funds in the same asset class. We compare it on a loss scale with 1.00 being the average loss. So if the fund had a Morningstar risk of 1.25, it would have an average loss 25% greater than the average loss in the peer group.

KS: *How important is it that the mutual fund managers time the market or determine the direction of the market?*

DP: "Are interest rates rising?" "Which way is the market headed?" These questions are often the least important to ask because no one could answer them with any degree of certainty or consistency. Questions such as, "Where will the market be six months from now?"

At Morningstar we look for good mutual funds. One of the trends we have found is that the fund man-

agers that tend to perform the best over time are the
ones that tend to spend the least amount of time debating which way the market is heading.

KS: *What other, more specific trends have you witnessed?*

DP: Probably the most important variable regarding a
good mutual fund is the manager. What is the manager's expertise? Will the fund allow this manager's talent to be used to his or her highest and best ability? I
value the managers and want them to be used.

☆ ☆ ☆ ☆ ☆ ☆ ☆ ☆ ☆ ☆ ☆ ☆ ☆ ☆ ☆ ☆

**Probably the most important variable regarding a good
mutual fund is the manager.**

☆ ☆ ☆ ☆ ☆ ☆ ☆ ☆ ☆ ☆ ☆ ☆ ☆ ☆ ☆ ☆

I have found the trend is that managers that have
been at a fund for a long time tend to have better performance. Funds with lower manager turnover tend to
perform better over time as well.

Of course, cost is a major factor in what the net
performance of a fund is. The lower-cost funds tend
to do better. I also like funds that are not overly diversified. If the fund has too many holdings, it is a closet
index fund.

But keep in mind there are no set rules or disciplines. Just when I think I find a magical key, the theory is blown. There is no definitive trend and no norm.
It works differently for everyone.

KS: *How often do you suggest looking at your asset allocation and portfolio structure?*

DP: I try and keep my investments on autopilot. I review
my fund selections annually. However, I rarely sell
funds in my own portfolio.

Try to look at the trees instead of the forest. If
each of your funds all have the same blue-chip stocks,
you don't really have as much diversification as you

thought. Consider rebalancing your funds to get the proper amount of diversification for your portfolio. Or as you invest new money, chose a different asset class.

KS: *Do you sell your mutual funds often?*

DP: Very rarely. I sell, or may sell, if the fund changes its focus or charter. I may sell if the fund manager changes and I don't like the new manager. But I don't often sell.

KS: *In the asset allocation section I included a chart showing that asset allocation is the most important thing. How do you feel about that?*

DP: Investors have had an ongoing major debate with security selection versus asset allocation. Academia says that in a perfect world, 90% of investment returns is based on asset allocation. But this is not a perfect world. In a perfect world, there would be black and white. A perfect world would have no ambiguity.

KS: *Any last parting shots?*

DP: Investing is great. Over the last several years, investment returns have been well above the historical norms. Investments have in the past, still can, and probably will lose potentially significant sums of money. Before investing you must ask yourself what you would do if you lost 20% or 30% of your money. How would it affect your standard of living?

If you are going to invest in mutual funds, I recommend diversifying among funds—perhaps four or five funds. I also believe that before people invest, they should pay down their mortgage and any other significant amounts of debt.

A Morningstar Case Study

The following is an actual example of the Morningstar report on one of the funds discussed in this book, Brandywine, managed by Foster Friess. Figure 11-1 shows the actual report, while Figure 11-2 shows the key to its various components. The following information supplied by Morningstar explains those components.

1. *Total Return.* Total return is calculated by dividing the change in a fund's net asset value, assuming reinvestment of income and capital-gains distributions, by the initial net asset value. Total returns are adjusted for management, administrative, and 12b-1 fees, and other costs automatically deducted from fund assets. Total returns indicated here are not adjusted for sales load. Total returns for periods longer than one year are compounded average annual returns.

2. *Yield.* Yield represents a fund's income return on capital investment. There are two yield measures on the page: distributed yield and SEC yield. Morningstar computes distributed yield by summing all income distributions for the past 12 months and dividing by the previous month's NAV (net asset value adjusted for capital gains distributions). SEC yield is a standardized figure that the Securities and Exchange Commission requires funds to use when mentioning yield in advertisements. An annualized calculation based on a trailing 30-day period, SEC yield can differ significantly from distributed yield.

3. *Performance Graph.* The top line of this graph expresses the growth of a $10,000 investment as of the more recent date: the fund's inception or the earliest date indicated on the graph. The horizontal dotted line shows the fund's performance relative to a benchmark (the S&P Index for equity funds and the Lehman Brothers Aggregate Bond Index for fixed-income funds). When the dotted line slopes upward, the fund has outperformed its index; when it slopes downward, it has underperformed its index.

4. *Morningstar Return.* Morningstar Return rates a fund's performance relative to other funds within the same class. Morningstar calculates a fund's total return as the excess of the 90-day Treasury bill return, adjusted for fees, and com-

Figure 11-1. The Morningstar report on the Brandywine Fund.

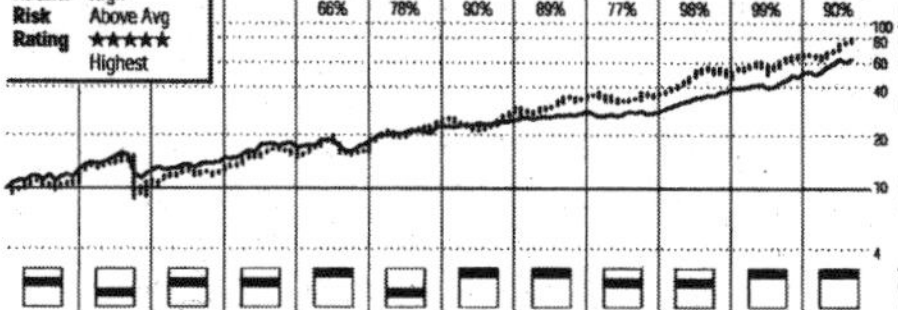

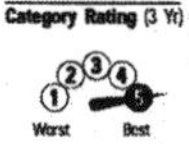

Source: *Morningstar Mutual Funds.* Reprinted with permission of Morningstar.

Figure 11-2. Key for the sample Morningstar report shown in Figure 11-1.

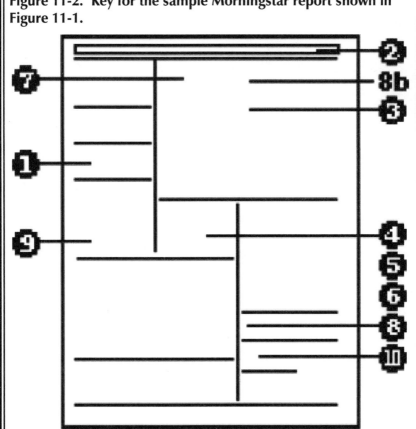

Source: *Morningstar Mutual Funds.* Reprinted with permission from Morningstar.

pares this figure to the average excess return of the fund's class or the 90-day T-bill, whichever is higher. The average figure for any investment class is set at 1.00.

5. *Morningstar Risk.* Morningstar Risk evaluates a fund's downside volatility relative to that of other funds in its class. To calculate risk, we add up the amounts by which the fund's returns trail those of the three-month Treasury bill, and divide that sum by the number of months in the rating period. The average Morningstar Risk rating for any class is set equal to 1.00.

6. *Morningstar Risk-Adjusted Ratings.* These star ratings represent a fund's historical risk-adjusted performance compared with other funds in its class. To determine a fund's rating for a given period, Morningstar subtracts the fund's Risk score from its Return score, then plots the result along a bell curve to determine the fund's rating: If the fund scores in the top 10% of its class, it receives five stars; the next 22.5%, four stars; the middle 35%, three stars; the next 22.5%, two stars; and the bottom 10%, one star. Ratings are recalculated monthly.

7. *Historical Profile.* This provides an overall assessment of a fund's historical returns and risk, and its overall risk-adjusted star rating. The three time periods (3-, 5-, and 10-year) are combined as a weighted average, with more weight given to the longer periods. The same bell curve used in the calculation of the risk-adjusted rating is used for a fund's historical risk and return profiles.

8. *Style Box.* This proprietary tool reveals a fund's true investment strategy, which may or may not match its stated objective. For equity funds, the vertical axis categorizes funds by size: Funds with median market capitalizations of less than $1 billion are small cap; $1 billion to $5 billion, medium cap; and more than $5 billion, large cap. The horizontal axis denotes investment styles: value-oriented, growth-oriented, or a blend of the two. A stock-fund portfolio's average price/earnings (P/E) and price/book (P/B) ratios are computed relative to the combined averages of the S&P 500 Index (set at 2.00). Funds with a combined relative P/E and P/B figure of less than 1.75 are considered value funds; 1.75 to 2.25, blend funds; and more than 2.25, growth funds. Along the vertical axis of fixed-income style boxes lies the average quality rating of a bond portfolio. Funds with an average credit rating of AA or higher are categorized as high quality; between BBB and AA−, medium quality; and BBB− or below, low quality. The horizontal axis focuses on interest-rate sensitivity; it shows the bond portfolio's average effective maturity (average weighted maturity-

for municipal-bond funds). Funds with an average effective maturity of less than 4 years qualify as short-term; 4 to 10 years, intermediate; and more than 10 years, long-term.

The style box located in the lower right (8a) of the page represents the fund's investment style as of the most recent month-end. The style boxes located above the performance graph (8b) represent the fund's investment style at the beginning of each calendar year.

9. *Tax Analysis.* Tax-adjusted historical returns show the fund's average annualized after-tax total return for 3-, 5-, and 10-year periods. It is computed by diminishing each income and capital-gain distribution by the maximum tax rate in effect at the time of the distribution. Percentage pretax return is derived by dividing after-tax returns by pretax returns. The highest possible score is 100% for funds with no taxable distributions. Potential capital-gain exposure gives an idea of an investment's potential tax bite. This figure shows what percentage of a fund's total assets represent capital appreciation, either unrealized or realized. If unrealized, the fund's holdings have increased in value, but the fund has not sold these holdings; taxes are not due until the fund does so. Realized gains represent actual gains achieved by the sale of holdings, on which taxes must be paid. Unrealized appreciation may turn into realized gains at any time if the fund's management decides to sell profitable holdings.

10. *Special Securities %.* Here we show whether a fund can and does hold a variety of complex or illiquid securities, including derivatives. A solid black circle indicates that a fund holds the securities; an empty circle indicates that the fund may but doesn't currently hold them; a dash means that the fund cannot own the securities. Percentages held in each category also appear.

Commentary

Just 20 years ago, mutual funds were obscure investment vehicles. Now they are all the rage and enjoy virtually the same awareness as stocks. Companies like Morningstar have helped increase this public awareness. Furthermore, Morningstar has not only helped public awareness regarding mutual funds, but it has been instrumental at educating the public regarding mutual funds, specifically in how to research and properly analyze funds.

Don Phillips has been the visionary behind Morningstar and their mission of educating the public. The fact that Don Phillips was not trained in the Wall Street community is an advantage for us individual investors who are not Wall Street insiders either. Don is a practical thinker. His pragmatic organized thought process relates well with the common person. It gives us a platform on which to explore our investment thoughts and ideas to the fullest.

12

The 20-Point Checklist: A Summary of How to Use the Best of the Best

How to Put Your New-Found Knowledge to Use

Congratulations! You have accessed the wisdom of the world's best investors. As a result you now know more than most investors (a better word is gamblers) will ever know. Just think about what you learned:

* How the stock market works
* How to find and interpret important research information
* How to use fundamental and technical analysis to evaluate a stock
* The stock-picking strategies and life-lessons of the world's best investors

Take a step back and assimilate what you have learned. Put it in perspective. With all this new knowledge it would be easy to overload. Prioritize. Create your own personal strategy. Then dive in!

The Investment Process

Even prior to the investment process, you must create a plan. The plan should be to decide what your investment goals are, how long you plan on investing for, and how much you want and need to make on the investment. The plan should also be created in conjunction with your tax- and estate-planning goals and objectives.

Once you know what you are investing for, you should know how much of a return to expect on your investments. It is at this point you can begin the actual investment process. The process encompasses everything from the model you will create to how to obtain the information you will need to make an informed investment decision. I caution you not to skip or short any steps in the process. Remember: Being a successful investor takes work.

The pyramid depicted in Figure 12-1 clearly illustrates, not so much the model, but the levels of investing. From conservative to aggressive, remember that most investors' models in-

Figure 12-1. The all-stars' investing overview: Plan, prepare, invest.

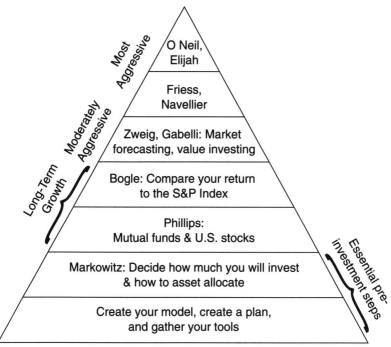

clude a little of everything. How much of each is up to the individual. As you continue reading, the six-step process is explained in further detail.

One of your probable reasons for reading this book is to learn how to become a better investor. Imagine that you wanted to bake a cake. If I gave 10 people the same recipe to create my mother's "Almost-Better-Than-Sex Chocolate Cake," the cakes all would turn out a little differently. None, of course, would be as good as my mother's cake. Relate this to investing. After reading this book, you now have several recipes for stock picking. Experiment to find which recipe works for you. Sometimes you can take the best of each of the recipes and create a superrecipe. You can only do this, however, if you follow the one most important rule. I have stated this, all the all-stars have stated it, yet it is worth stating again: You must follow your discipline—whatever it may be. If you change course midstream, you will be an unhappy investor.

So as not to become overwhelmed, take the investment process step by step.

Step One: Choose a Model

Decide what model you will be using to find good stocks. Will you be a bottom-up or a top-down investor? Remember, bottom-up investors look for stocks that fit their model. Any stocks that match their criteria would be a buy candidate. Although William O'Neil, Foster Friess, Louis Navellier, and Mario Gabelli are all different investors, they all take a bottom-up approach. They have a system and find the stocks that match their criteria. This is opposed to a top-down management style that first looks for an area to invest in and then researches potential stocks to buy in that area.

Some bottom-up systems are more subjective than others. Gabelli needs to get a feel for the company and management.

He has guidelines for a model, but while he uses his model to guide him, it is not the sole secret to his investment success. Conversely, through a quantitative analysis program, Navellier has a model. If you recall, he starts by finding the stocks with the highest risk versus reward and the highest alpha with the lowest standard deviation. That is his first screen. Once a stock goes through the entire model, he buys and sells specifically based on what the model dictates. Navellier never talks to companies and there is little thought when a stock is actually purchased. Thought goes into the model, not the stocks purchased.

Perhaps the easiest method of bottom-up analysis is O'Neil's (Chapter 7). His system allows an investor to use *Investor's Business Daily* (*IBD*) and perhaps a chart book to find stocks. Using only two sources to obtain information streamlines the entire stock-picking process, and, according to O'Neil, this model is still extremely thorough. One of the advantages of using a bottom-up tool such as *IBD* is that it offers an excellent first screen to give you a handful of stock ideas. After you determine this handful, you can follow the rest of O'Neil's CAN SLIM approach, or, for that matter, whatever criteria are in your model. For example, after this first screen you might want to do further research on the industry to see if it is either growing (or turning around from a recessionary period). You might want to find out more about a company's particular product or service. You might weed out the ones you think are expensive. And, of course, you will compare it to the company's competition.

Creating a bottom-up stock screening model is fairly easy. Wonderful tools exist for you to gather the information in your model. Use your computer to go to investors' research Web sites and to the Web sites of companies you are interested in. Go to brokers for analysts' research reports. Use the library for reports such as *Value Line*, Standard & Poor's reports, and *Daily Graphs*. Use the newspapers such as *Barron's* and *Inves-*

tor's Business Daily as tools. The problem is not finding research, it's having too much. If you create the model prior to reading these papers, you will now look at these papers as a specific tool and know precisely where to look.

As we discussed in Ron Elijah's chapter, looking at the market from the top down has many wonderful advantages. Top-down enables the prospective investor to look at the sectors of the economy and the business world that have the most potential for growth. Looking at a demographic trend could show the growth of the health care sector. Now one just needs to whittle it down to find the best stock in that sector. This approach is especially beneficial to the individual investor who, through their own experiences, work, or hobbies, may be in a unique position to spot and capitalize on certain trends.

Can you be both a top-down and a bottom-up investor? Yes. You can combine the systems. The fact is, as long as you know why you are buying a stock, who cares how you became familiar with the company? If I am enjoying a cup of Starbucks coffee, I might go the library or look on the Internet for information about the company. If I find the company is public and the stock is traded, I will then compare the company to my criteria to see if I want to own it or not. The bottom line is that the best stock pickers are the ones that analyze the most companies to decide on the handful they will choose to buy.

And although it sounds basic, like drinking a cup of Starbucks, *do whatever it takes to find stocks.* For example, at one point I was analyzing restaurant stocks. Of my two favorites, restaurant number 1 had slightly better "numbers" than restaurant number 2. But when I went to each of the restaurants, restaurant number 2 was far cleaner, friendlier, and had a better overall feel. I figured that if I get this impression, so will other people. I ended up buying stock in restaurant number 2 even thought its numbers weren't as high as number 1's. A year later the stock of restaurant number 2 dramatically outperformed the stock of its competitor, restaurant number 1.

Step Two: Get Your Tools

Chapters 1 and 2 are your tool chapters. They tell you where to find information, how to search the library or annual reports, what information you want the company to give you.

But tools aren't just what information you will need and where to find it. Tools also give you the ability to make sense of the information you gather. Some of our all-stars use charts and graphs. Others talk to management. My suggestion is to use as many indicators in your model as possible. If the stock still passes your tough test, then it's probably a pretty good candidate.

Step Three: Determine Your Asset Allocation

Throughout your life you will have different goals with your investments. Sometimes you will be saving for a new home a few years out. Other times you may be looking long-term to pay for a college education or the ultimate goal of retirement. Regardless of your goal, chances are you probably would never want to put 100% of your money in stocks. This approach would probably be too aggressive for anyone. You'll need some cash ready to buy more stocks. You should have money in a short-term reserve type of an account. The rule of thumb is that the older you get, the less you should have in equities. However, of course, the actual amount is really up to you.

Harry Markowitz reminds investors of our ultimate goal: "To make the most amount of money given our risk tolerance." It is essential before you start investing to decide what your risk tolerance is, how much you need to make, how long you plan to invest, and how much you can afford to lose. Once these questions are answered you will decide how much of your money should go into stocks, bonds, or cash.

Proper diversification is more than just deciding how much money you will have in equities, bonds, or cash. You must also decide if you will be using active management through mutual funds (Don Phillips of Morningstar), passive management through an index (John Bogle, Vanguard Group) or individual stocks. My experience suggests that a combination of all three is prudent. It shouldn't be an all-or-none situation. Some of the all-stars profiled in this book are managers of mutual funds. They are excellent money managers. Perhaps they will always be better investors than you or I can be individually. Paying these advisors to manage a portion of our money through mutual funds could hardly be a bad decision.

The amount of stocks you should own in your portfolio is another decision. If you only buy one or two stocks, you are gambling much more than if you buy ten stocks. As a student of the market, I have found that your risk would be greatly reduced and your return usually would not suffer by owning more stocks as opposed to just a few. In that regard, shoot for a stock portfolio of at least 20 stocks. Although this may sound like a great deal of stocks, the average mutual fund represented in this book has well over 100 stocks.

Step Four: Compare Your Return to the Index

Throughout this book I have discussed "the stock market." Often I referred to an index, the two most popular being the Dow Jones Industrial Average and the Standard & Poor's 500 Index (S&P 500). The S&P 500 index, being the broader, is more widely used by investors for choosing stocks.

During the interview with John Bogle, he presented a compelling case for simply buying the market; in other words, buying a fund that mirrors the S&P 500. Although our all-stars proved it is possible to beat an index, the fact is the S&P 500 is a very efficient way of investing. It is extremely difficult to beat the index with the same level of risk. In that regard, I look at the S&P 500 as a "core holding." It's something any investor should have as part of his or her portfolio.

Use the index as a benchmark for your portfolio. If the index consistently outperforms your other stock or mutual fund holdings, consider investing a heavier amount in the index. My research suggests that in excellent economic times, when companies are by and large doing well, earnings are great. In a bull market, the index performs spectacularly. When times get tough, you may want more control in what you own. You may want to actually buy a Coca-Cola. So when times are tough, consider lightening up on the index.

Step Five: Evaluate Your Mutual Funds

So why not just put all your money in mutual fund? Mutual funds are an integral part of any investor's portfolio. They offer an individual investor the ability to broadly diversify and obtain professional management, thus making investing much easier. However, as great as mutual funds are, they do have negative points:

⋆ *Limited Control.* Say your mutual fund buys Intel. You are happy because you think Intel is a great company. The markets start to go down and many investors of your mutual fund begin to sell their shares. The mutual fund manager needs to sell stock to pay off the investors who are liquidated. As a result, Intel is sold. Even though the company may still be a fundamentally sound investment, it gets moved out of your portfolio for reasons that have little to do with following a sound investment model—yours or the fund manager's.

⋆ *Taxes.* Mutual funds regularly buy and sell their investments. On average, a stock mutual fund manager doesn't hold a stock for a long period of time. If a mutual fund manager sells stock for a gain, the tax is passed on to you, the shareholder. Worse, if the stock was not held for at least 18 months (which is often the case) you would be subject to a short-term capital gains tax, which is based on a higher tax rate compared to long-term capital gains. The worst part is that a mutual fund might be down for a whole year, meaning that your investment is down, but you still owe a tax because the mutual fund sold certain stocks at a gain.

⋆ *Fees.* It's sometimes hard to determine exactly what the fees are in your mutual fund. All mutual funds charge an ongoing fee. This fee would be in addition to any commission or load you might pay to invest in a particular fund. Often these fees are excessive. Excessive fees can cause your investment to not make as much money as you should have based on the risk you were taking. As a result you are not maximizing your return for the level of risk incurred.

Step Six: Model Your Approach After One of the All-Star Managers

As you have learned, each one of these managers are unique in their investment style and level of risk, and how they deal with and enjoy life. Yet all are successful, and all have a wonderful model that one would be so lucky to emulate.

> *Bogle:* Mr. Bogle has created the second largest mutual fund institution in the world based on sound investment principles. His simplistic approach to investing has made him and other investors billions. He has championed the rights for the individual investor. While many Wall Street insiders would like him to go away, his views are here to stay.

> *Elijah:* Ron Elijah is our top-down all-star. He finds a theme and goes for it. To him, finding the right pockets of growth and the right themes are more important than current multiples. If you are wrong, sell the stock quickly; if not, let the stock keep going. This approach produces excellent returns but is not for the faint of heart.

> *Friess:* Foster Friess seems to be at the middle in terms of risk and stock-picking criteria. He searches for stocks

that have very strong growth prospects but, based on valuations, he doesn't want to pay a premium for these stocks. So although he misses some great growth stories, his casualties are fewer as well. He will also increase cash positions if he feels the market is headed for a downturn.

Gabelli: Mario Gabelli searches for companies that are unloved and undervalued. He seeks stocks having private market value worth more than what the company is currently trading for. Once found, he narrows his search by looking for a catalyst—a reason why the stock will be forced higher.

Value investing tends to be more conservative because value managers are looking for an undervalued asset. As a result the downside is usually limited. Conversely, typical value managers don't find (or look for) stocks that might double your money in a year.

Markowitz: Remember the key goal of almost all investors is to find the highest return possible for the level of risk you are willing to take. To do so, diversifying (asset allocation) is essential (maximize your return). Markowitz literally invented the math to do this. For his work, he won a Nobel Prize. His theory, which is the standard for diversification, is called Modern Portfolio Theory.

Navellier: Louis Navellier has created a strict model for picking stocks. He has entered into his search system every reason why stocks have gone up in the past. His method is completely unemotional as to what stocks are bought or sold—the model is everything. He has attempted to reduce risk by using his own reward versus risk measuring system. He finds the stocks with the highest alpha and divides it by the standard deviation. He will only take the stocks with the lowest ratio, thereby reducing his risk. However, since he does look for high-growth stocks, this model tends to be fairly volatile.

O'Neil: Of the fact that "Stocks hitting new highs tend to go higher," William O'Neil uses *Investor's Business Daily* and his CAN SLIM method to find stocks reaching new highs. Unlike many of the other all-stars, traditional valuations such as price to earnings or price to sales are not as important to O'Neil as are indicators such as increasing earnings, high relative strength, and accumulation.

CAN SLIM can offer the investor a terrific turnkey system for finding high-growth stocks. However, unlike as it is for Gabelli, the private market value of the company is not as important to O'Neil as how he thinks the stock should go. In that regard, be ready because these stocks can fall faster than they shoot up.

Phillips: Mutual funds are an essential part of investing. Morningstar is an incredible source for research and information regarding mutual funds. Don Phillips's insight and views regarding mutual funds (and more) should be mandatory for any investor, potential or experienced.

Zweig: First and foremost, Marty Zweig follows his model for forecasting the market. His bullishness or bearishness dictates the amount of stock or cash he owns. His stocks are bought using a quantitative model.

Checklist for Picking a Stock

When discussing asset allocation strategies in order to maximize return while minimizing risk, it is suggested that an investor maintain three major stock categories: a value stock, a core holding, and a growth stock. Based on the best strategies from each of the all-stars' chapters, I have made a list of all of the factors I would want to analyze or consider before investing in a stock and created a model or checklist for picking a stock (Figure 12-2). Understand that many of the criteria might apply to one style of management, but not to another. A stock that is paying and continually increases its dividend may be important when finding value, but not for a growth stock. In that regard, you will need to determine how much of this model is applicable to the stocks you will buy.

Sample Evaluation of a Growth Stock

As I read the paper I see editorials referring to a possible recession. As a result, many stocks have been beaten way down; some perhaps too much. I've also read an economic report that stated many travel and leisure stocks actually do well through a recession. One of the fastest growing aspects of travel and leisure is cruising. This interests me. So I went to one of the Web sites listed in Chapter 1. I did a search for all stocks that have had earnings and sales growth of at least 25% for the last quarter, and 25% annual earnings increases. I further looked for a profit margin above 8%.

To lower my risk, I included in the screen to only select stocks that aren't trading at more than a 5% growth premium to their current price to earnings (P/E) ratio. By that I mean if the stock has historically grown 20% per year, the stock can only be trading at a P/E ratio of no more than 20 times earnings.

One of the stocks that came up (on my short list) was Carnival Cruises. I decided to do further research. Using the 20-point checklist, I attempted to determine if this is a worthy growth stock.

Again using the information on the Internet, I went to Microsoft Investor (www.msn.com) to find more data on Carnival. I first wanted to look at their earnings and revenue growth. Both Figures 12-3 and 12-4 gave me the information I needed to look at sales, earnings, and revenue growth.

I used Figure 12-3 to view a broad amount of data on CCL. I noticed the profit margin was high, ROE was strong, and the

Figure 12-2. A 20-point checklist combining the best of the best stock-picking models.

Question	Impor-tance to Value	Impor-tance to Growth	Research Comments (use this space for your own notes)
1. Why does this world need the product, how do we benefit?	✓✓	✓	
2. 20–25% current quarterly earnings growth		✓✓	
3. Consistent annual earnings gains	✓	✓✓	
4. Both quarterly and annual sales growth	✓	✓✓	
5. Strong increasing profit margin pretax over 15%	✓	✓✓	
6. Positive cash flow	✓✓		
7. Low multiples compared to the competition and compared to the stock's growth a. price to cash flow b. price to earnings c. price to sales	✓✓	✓	
8. Increasing dividend	✓✓		
9. What is the stock's book value? (Try to avoid paying over three times book value for most companies)	✓✓		
10. Return on equity between 15% and 20% and growing.	✓	✓	
11. Compare company to the competition— is the stock in question doing better, trading cheaper or growing faster than the competition? multiples, growth, management, efficiencies	✓✓	✓✓	
12. Does the company have a great deal of debt? (Stay away from companies that have more than twice the amount of debt compared to equity.)	✓✓		
13. Is the industry strong and can it expand or turn around?	✓✓	✓✓	
14. How can the company grow in the future?	✓✓	✓✓	
15. Is there a catalyst that will help to increase the stock?	✓✓	✓✓	
16. Is the current news favorable?		✓✓	
17. Is the stock being accumulated?		✓	
18. What is the downside risk?	✓✓	✓	
19. What are the unbiased analysts saying?	✓	✓	
20. Graph stock look for following: increasing volume a breakout of its moving average (either 50 or 200 day)		✓	

Key: ✓✓ = Very important; ✓ = could be important depending on your investment model; no check mark = not important.

Figure 12-3. Broad data on CCL.

Carnival Corporation

Financial Highlights (All data for latest 12 months)

Sales	$2,805 Mil	Revenue/Share	$4.71
Income	$771 Mil	Earnings/Share	$1.30
Net Profit Margin	28%	Book Value/Share	$6.89
Return on Equity	19%	fyi Dividend Rate	$0.36
Debt/Equity Ratio	0.33	Payout Ratio	23%

Revenue - Quarterly Results ($ Millions)

	FY (11/98)	FY (11/97)	FY (11/96)
1st Qtr	557.8	521.1	448.8
2nd Qtr	661.4	596.6	516.8
3rd Qtr	1,061.5	805.4	772.0
4th Qtr	NA	524.4	475.0
Total	**2,280.7**	**2,447.5**	**2,212.6**

Earnings Per Share - Quarterly Results

	FY (11/98)	FY (11/97)	FY (11/96)
1st Qtr	$0.19	$0.15	$0.14
2nd Qtr	$0.27	$0.22	$0.19
3rd Qtr	$0.58	$0.50	$0.46
4th Qtr	NA	$0.26	$0.20
Total	**$1.04**	**$1.13**	**$0.99**

Courtesy *Microsoft Investor*

debt to equity was low. I also noticed that both revenue and sales were increasing every quarter and every year. This information warranted me to further research the stock. In that regard, I looked specifically at the income, sales, and earnings numbers. This is done in Figure 12-4.

Figure 12-4. Comparative data on CCL.

Carnival Corporation

- ▶ Growth Rates
- Price Ratios
- Profit Margins
- Financial Condition
- Investment Returns
- Management Efficiency
- Ten Year Summary

Growth Rates %	Company	Industry	S&P 500
Sales (Qtr vs year ago qtr)	18.60	81.10	7.90
Income (Qtr vs year ago qtr)	20.50	-5.60	14.40
EPS (Qtr vs year ago qtr)	19.80	-34.30	7.60
Sales (5-Year Avg.)	11.50	12.46	7.12
EPS (5-Year Avg.)	17.43	-14.89	1.11
Dividends (5-Year Avg.)	13.92	11.30	-7.28

Media General Industry: General Entertainment
Computed ratios are based on latest 12 months' results.

MEDIA GENERAL FINANCIAL SERVICES Stock data provided by Media General Financial Services.

Courtesy *Microsoft Investor*

1. The Carnival Corporation (CCL) is the world's largest operator of overnight cruises. It currently owns 40% of the United States market. CCL owns three cruise lines and travel tour companies. Statistics show that the demand for cruising is growing in the high double digits. Of the people who take

vacations, a small number of those willing and capable to cruise have yet to do so.

2. The company's sales, income, and earnings have all increased in the last quarter between 1% and 20%. All of these are increases over the historic five-year norm.

3. Look at the Value Line chart shown in Figure 12-5. CCL has consistently increased its sales, cash flow, and earnings since 1988. Over the last few years it appears that those annual earnings have been increasing at a faster rate. This occurrence is usually very bullish for a stock.

Figure 12-5. CCL investor information available from Value Line.

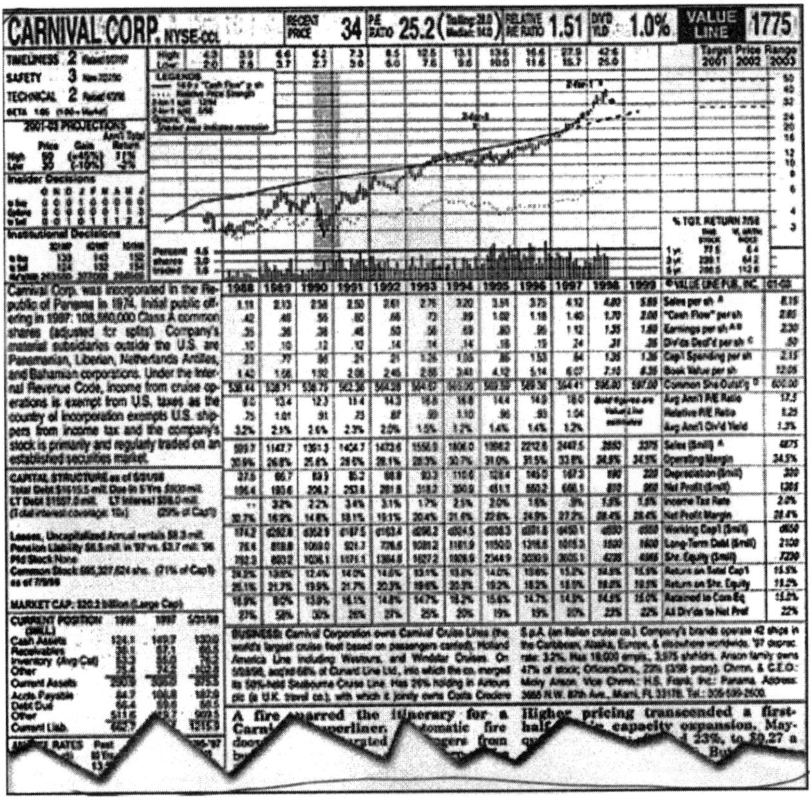
CARNIVAL CORP. NYSE-CCL RECENT PRICE 34 P/E RATIO 25.2 RELATIVE P/E RATIO 1.51 DIV'D YLD 1.0% VALUE LINE 1775

Courtesy Value Line

4. Figure 12-5 also shows that, like earnings, sales have been growing at an exceedingly rapid pace.

5. The profit margin is extremely high; pretax it is over 27%. This is above its five-year trend of roughly 23%, clearly illustrating the all-important fact that its margins are growing. According to the Microsoft Investor chart shown in Figure 12-6 (provided by Medial General) this is above both the industry and the S&P 500 average.

Figure 12-6. CCL's profits.

Carnival Corporation

Growth Rates
Price Ratios
▶ Profit Margins
Financial Condition
Investment Returns
Management Efficiency
Ten Year Summary

Profit Margins %	Company	Industry	S&P 500
Gross Margin	46.2	38.3	46.7
Pre-Tax Margin	27.6	11.1	9.8
Net Profit Margin	27.5	9.3	7.0
5Yr Gross Margin (5-Year Avg.)	43.8	32.3	45.4
5Yr PreTax Margin (5-Year Avg.)	24.2	15.4	9.5
5Yr Net Profit Margin (5-Year Avg.)	23.8	12.7	6.1

Media General Industry: General Entertainment
Computed ratios are based on latest 12 months' results.

Courtesy *Microsoft Investor*

6. The *Value Line* report (Figure 12-5) also shows that cash flow is strong and increasing. This cash is good if CCL wants to buy smaller companies or needs to weather an economic slowdown.

7. Knowing how many times a stock is trading in relation to its earnings, sales, book value, and cash flow can be important. Compare this information to the stock's growth, its competition, and the industry as a whole. According to Figure 12-7, CCL has a current P/E of roughly 25 times its earnings and while that is high, CCL has been growing its earnings by roughly 20% per year. To have growth that high without an even higher P/E ratio is unusual. Recall from Chapter 2 the example where Coca-Cola had been growing earnings at roughly 15% per year, yet the P/E ratio was roughly 50 times earnings!

The tricky question is, will CCL be able to continue growing its earnings, even if the economy slows down? That is the gamble and perhaps the reason why the stock is not trading higher. Figure 12-7 compares CCL multiples to that of the industry and that of the S&P 500 Index. It is a plus that the P/E ratio is below that of the industry. The stock is expensive. However, since CCL's P/E is lower, their growth and profits are much higher than that of the industry. Therefore, the stock is justified to trade at higher sales and cash flow multiples.

I don't believe Mario Gabelli would consider CCL a value. However, let's assume that Ron Elijah, from a top-down approach, thought travel and leisure should be "themes" that investors should include in a portfolio. CCL is the best of the bunch. Finally, William O'Neil would go back in time and cite what, throughout history, has made stocks go up. He might suggest that history illustrates that if CCL increases earnings and sales more every quarter, and every year, then current multiples are not important.

8. Again referring to Figure 12-3, I notice that CCL recently increased its dividend (late 1998). To increase a stock's

Figure 12-7. Comparing price ratios to the industry and the market.

Carnival Corporation   Glossary How Do I...

Growth Rates
▶ Price Ratios
Profit Margins
Financial Condition
Investment Returns
Management Efficiency
Ten Year Summary

fyi Price Ratios	Company	Industry	S&P 500
Current P/E Ratio	24.5	53.0	27.2
P/E Ratio 5-Year High	24.9	39.8	30.4
P/E Ratio 5-Year Low	12.0	8.8	14.7
Price/Sales Ratio	6.75	2.76	1.78
Price/Book Value	4.62	3.04	4.41
Price/Cash Flow Ratio	19.80	16.10	14.60

Media General Industry: General Entertainment
Computed ratios are based on latest 12 months' results.

Top

MEDIA GENERAL FINANCIAL SERVICES Stock data provided by Media General Financial Services.

Courtesy *Microsoft Investor*

dividend after the stock market drops (as it did during 1998) and when recession fears are rampant is a bold move. It tells me that management is confident that CCL can continue to grow and earn money. If they didn't think so, they wouldn't increase their dividend.

For a growth stock to have a dividend at all is a positive. Stocks that pay dividends are historically more conservative and offer more value as you are being paid a certain percentage every year, over and above what the stock may grow at. CCL is currently paying a dividend of $0.36 per share. To figure the percentage yield, divide this by the current stock price. At a price of $32 per share, the dividend as reflected in a yield is just over 1%.

9. The book value is basically the assets of the company minus the liabilities. Every dollar you pay over book value is premium over and above the company's worth on paper. It is justified to pay over book value for stock in a company if you see an excellent future. But how much? Value investors try not to pay over and above what they see as book value. It would be a stretch for a value investor to pay two times book value.

Other companies that don't have a great deal of hard assets (property and inventory) usually have stocks trading well above their book value. A technology stock would be a good example. Growth investors pay less attention to book value, but you should always watch how many times you are paying over book value. For CCL at $32 per, and assuming the book value is $6.89, an investor would be paying just over 4.5 times book value.

10. The return on equity (ROE) for CCL is currently 19%. Not only is this much higher than my low-end criteria (15%), it has steadily been growing for CCL.

11. For item 8 on the checklist, CCL's ratios were compared to the competition's. I also went on the Internet and compared the stock's growth in earnings and sales to the competition. I found that CCL was growing faster, and had lower debt. I asked a broker for analysts' reports on both CCL and its

competition. These reports covered management. I felt that CCL hired excellent management in addition to the family that controls the majority of the shares.

12. Again viewing the CCL financial summary from Figure 12-3, the debt to equity ratio is .33. This is extremely low debt for a growth company. This low debt increases the safety of the investment, especially during slow economic periods.

13. Searching Carnival's Web site and various financial Web sites, and reading the analysts' thoughts, I find the industry can grow. When reading up on the industry, I found that the vast majority of travelers have never cruised. Over the last five years, cruise ships have been 100% occupied for virtually all the larger cruise companies. That tells me that, although the cruising business may be competitive, the industry is large enough to support each of the main competitors.

14. Cruise prices range from budget to high-end. Economically it's a very efficient and exciting way to travel. CCL is currently ordering new ships, furthering its dominance. It should be able to increase its gross revenue, sales, and net earnings. See above.

15. Reading more about CCL uncovers many potential catalysts. For example, the founders of CCL own an extremely large percentage of the stock. This could be a catalyst if they ever want to sell out. It could also be a catalyst if they offer some of their shares to the public. Institutions might be hungry for these shares. In addition, the simple fact that the cruise industry is so new and growing so rapidly is a catalyst.

16. Click on current news in one of the financial Web sites. Read the articles. If you see a positive tone for the articles, it could be a good sign. Articles entitled "Carnival Earnings Better Than Expected," "Carnival Increases Its Dividend," or "Carnival Buys Another Ship" are the types of articles that would provide favorable news.

17. *Investor's Business Daily* stock reports provide much of the research concerning a stock's being accumulated. Notice in Figure 12-8 that CCL earnings are better than 80% of all other companies, that the price strength of CCL compared to all other companies is 85% better, and that the industry group has not been doing that well (it's rated C). Actually I like that. Everyone thinks that a recession will come and CCL will per-

Figure 12-8. *Investor's Business Daily*'s stock report.

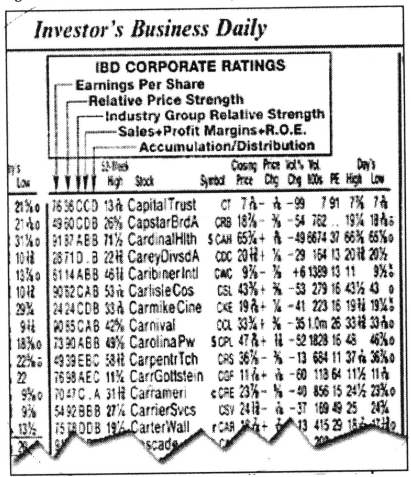

Courtesy *Investor's Business Daily*

form horribly. As a result, travel and leisure stocks, including Carnival, have not been doing well. I look at this as a buying opportunity.

Finally, the stock is being accumulated as evidenced by its "B" rating.

18. Although many positives exist, CCL has a downside. Unless CCL has paid for ships that are currently not showing as an asset on its financial statements, I doubt anyone would consider this a value stock.

If we do go into a recession, there is a high potential for the cruising industry to slow down. Remember that although the earnings and revenue growth has been exemplary, this is past news. As a growth investor you must predict the future.

Many of the cruising companies have been building more ships. This could lead to oversupply.

Finally, a common method for determining a stock's downside is to compare what the analysts think the stock will earn next year. If you take the current price-to-earnings multiple and assume that this multiple remains current based on the future earnings, what would the price of the stock be next year? As you can see in Figure 12-9, if you take the average earnings estimate for 1999 at $1.61 and multiply it by CCL's current P/E of 25.00, you'll see a product of $40.25. So if CCL hits its earnings numbers and still trades at the same earnings multiple, the stock should fetch $40.00 per share. However, if CCL has dismal earnings, you can see how the stock could fall just as dramatically.

Conversely, if you value CCL based on the industry's current P/E rate, it is a much different story. Many stocks in the General Entertainment Group are trading at excessively high prices compared to their earnings. Thus, the P/E ratio is much higher than average. As per Figure 12-10, the average P/E for the General Entertainment group is 53. If you try to determine what a CCL stock share should be trading at if it fetched a P/E of the industry group's average (53), the stock price is much

Figure 12-9. Earnings comparisons.

Valuation using Carnival's current multiple (P/E):

Fiscal Year	Est Low/High Price Range	Avg. Est. Price	% Change for Average
11/1998	$32.83-$33.81	$33.32	4.74%
11/1999	$37.73-$41.41	$39.45	23.99%

Carnival current price:	$31.81
Carnival current multiple (P/E):	24.50
Carnival average 11/1998 estimate:	$1.36
Carnival low 11/1998 estimate:	$1.34
Carnival high 11/1998 estimate:	$1.38
Carnival average 11/1999 estimate:	$1.61
Carnival low 11/1999 estimate:	$1.54
Carnival high 11/1999 estimate:	$1.69

Courtesy *Microsoft Investor*

higher. However, I don't believe CCL should be trading at 53 times earnings.

19. Go to the library (or your computer) and read what reputable companies like Value Line or Standard & Poor's Stock Report are saying about CCL. Ask your broker for analysts' reports. Read!

20. When graphing the stock (Figure 12-11), I like to see more people getting interested in buying the stock (increasing volume); preferably more people buying on the days it goes up, and fewer people buying on the down days. I also want to see some pattern that the stock is breaking out of a certain price or trading range.

Figure 12-10. Valuation using current P/E.

Fiscal Year	Est. Price	% Change
11/1998	$72.08	126.58%
11/1999	$85.33	168.23%

Carnival current price:	$31.81
General Entertainment group current multiple (P/E):	53.00

Carnival average 11/1998 analyst estimate:	$1.36
Carnival average 11/1999 analyst estimate:	$1.61

How certain is the price estimate?
Investors estimate the level of unanimity about a stock's prospects among analysts by calculating the range between the most optimistic and most pessimistic estimates.

- Average number of analysts covering Carnival: 20
- Carnival analysts' high/low spread: 6%
- Carnival analysts' confidence: **High**

Courtesy *Microsoft Investor*

Conclusion

Based on Carnival's earnings growth rate, possible future growth, and potential catalysts, the stock is attractive as a growth stock. According to the multiples (P/E, P/S) and the graph that shows that CCL is trading below its norm (less than a 200-day moving average), the stock is priced right. This stock would be sensible to consider as a buy at current levels.

Figure 12-11. Graphing a stock.

Courtesy *Microsoft Investor*

13

Summary Chapter

As a money manager and a student of people and of life, I learned a great deal writing this book. The question is, what should we do with this information and how can we use it to become a successful investor, or perhaps even a better person? I think back to something John Bogle said: "There is a great deal of information, but will it lead to practical knowledge?" I hope that the journey of completing this book will allow you to answer yes to that question. And although the journey is personal, I want to share with you what I learned from *Secrets of the Investment All-Stars*.

The Vision

As I previously stated, before writing this book I thought I was a better than average stock analyst and researcher, but I was confused as to why I couldn't get even better. By getting to know the all-stars, I learned that successful investing involves much more than researching a stock. To be a successful investor, you must possess several traits. Some of these traits are specific to researching stocks. Others are about how you and your personality will undoubtedly affect how well you manage money.

Each of these all-stars possess a true vision. They have a clear and definitive goal, and rarely deviate from that goal. In addition, they are constantly seeking improvement. Each of the all-stars possess something I have come to know as *kaizen*, and without it, you will never become an all-star. *Kaizen* was originally Chinese and later adopted by the Japanese into one meaning: constant improvement. These individuals listen to people. Both Mario Gabelli and Jack Bogle talked about how they listened to their clients and investors, how they read the notes their shareholders send.

All the all-stars have endured serious adversity. They strive to constantly improve. Losing investors' money, almost going bankrupt, bear markets—all pretty serious examples of enduring adversity. They don't quit when they fail. They learn from their failures, and keep climbing higher.

Foster Friess comes to mind. In the beginning of 1998 he followed his gut instinct that the markets were high, possibly too high. He feared that we (Americans) were downplaying the seriousness of the overseas economic crises. As a result he went overseas and confirmed that things were bad over there. He talked to anyone and everyone, from bellboys in the hotels to CEOs of companies. When he returned to America he sold a great majority of his stocks and raised significant amounts of cash. Yet the market kept climbing higher and higher. For a myriad of reasons—mainly pressure from investors who wanted their money in the market, not cash—he began buying stocks again. Shortly thereafter, the market began to crash. This move caused him to lose investors' money (hopefully temporarily), and his decision caused serious heartache and stress. Faced with a similar situation, some of his peers would have retired, become alcoholics, or even committed suicide.

But as Foster said himself, he is a recovering perfectionist. Foster asked himself and his staff where he erred, what had gone wrong, and how they could avoid the mistake in the future. He learned from his mistake, and he moved on with a renewed sense of wisdom and insight. That ability to learn and move on is what contributes to all-star status.

These individuals are so incredibly unique. They are no longer motivated simply by money. They all have a clear vision and very rarely get emotional about investing. Most of all, they relentlessly continue to improve. They get better every time a mistake is made. They learn and never make that mistake again.

These are traits I was never taught when learning how to analyze stocks. I am hopeful that with this knowledge, I have improved and that you will too.

The Analyzing

As much as these individuals taught me about life and how it applies to being a better investor, they did teach me about stock research as well. Most importantly, I learned that there is more than one way to make millions of dollars investing. But the key is to follow your discipline and not to get discouraged. Think about how Marty Zweig, Foster Friess, and William O'Neil said that they might have 30% or 40% of their stocks down at any given time. When this used to happen to me, I thought I was in the wrong career and it was time to open that restaurant. They confirmed that I was not alone. They had the same thoughts. But don't give up the ghost. This is normal and you must stick to your discipline.

Which leads me to my next point. You need a discipline and you need to understand what you are doing and start practicing and getting in shape for it. It will take blood, sweat, and tears. Think of it like this: You want to run a marathon, so you read every book you can about marathon runners. You buy the best shoes and equipment. But if you never ran before the day of the marathon, chances are you won't do very well in race—if you can finish at all. You must go through your conditioning. Practice. Get in shape. Understand your task. Start slow and work up.

Conclusion

This book taught me so many great tidbits, you should go through this text again and again to get every last crumb. I now know it's okay to buy a stock high (as long as I sell it higher). I know to get out of a stock if it starts to turn against me—even if I still like the stock—because there is no sense in fighting the market. I learned about what forces drive the market, how to allocate a portfolio, the important steps to picking a mutual fund, and so much more.

This book will put a quantum leap in your research process. Borrow the wisdom generously given by these all-stars. Use it and reap the reward that awaits you.

Would You Like to Know More About Ken Stern's All-Star Money Management Program?

FREE NEWSLETTER

- No Commission
- A Registered Investment Adviser
- Employing the Best Money Management Techniques of the All-Stars
- Risk Averse
- Tax Efficient
- Low Fees

After years of research and study, Ken Stern has developed "The All-Star Approach to Investing." The goal is to maximize return while minimizing risk.

The key to our success is digging deep to find the "diamonds in the rough." The Asset Planning Solutions' stock selection process begins where other investors' search stops. Through exhaustive research, we seek to find stocks that have hidden value. This value should ultimately be realized by Wall Street, thereby increasing the value of the stock price.

Ken Stern is the top-selling author of **Senior Savvy** and **50 Fabulous Places to Retire in America**. He is a correspondent for the nationally syndicated **Today Show** and founder of Asset Planning Solutions.

Call 1-800-529-2884 for more information
on Ken Stern's nationally syndicated radio series
and
Asset Planning Solutions Resource Centers in your area.

Receive a free subscription to our newsletter!

Index